PETER SHILTON'S NEARLY MEN

A PLYMOUTH ARGYLE STORY

PAUL ROBERTS

The History Press

First published 2009

The History Press
The Mill, Brimscombe Port
Stroud, Gloucestershire, GL5 2QG
www.thehistorypress.co.uk

British Library Cataloguing in Publication Data.
A catalogue record for this book is available from the British Library.

ISBN 978 0 7524 4878 7

Typesetting and origination by The History Press
Printed in Great Britain

For my Dad

3 p.m., 22 August 1987

CONTENTS

ACKNOWLEDGMENTS

In no order whatsoever, sincere gratitude in spades to the following kind souls who helped with the production of this book: Lostwithiel's finest, Paul Sweet, for the programmes and incredibly comprehensive scrapbook collection (the latter saved me immeasurable toil stuck in a library); Steve Nicholson, who entrusted Royal Mail and myself with an exceedingly rare collection of *Rub of the Greens* fanzines; Rick Cowdery for the many contacts, advice and proofreading help; Celia and Alan Nicholls for talking so openly about your son; Andy Rolle for your exceptional proofing services and almost daily book-related email exchanges; Chris Butson and Nick Ellis for the video loans; Tony Chowell for your invaluable assistance in finding Dwight; John Lloyd for the proof-reading and for banging the *Nearly Men*'s drum for me so resoundingly!; Michelle Tilling and Richard Leatherdale at The History Press for all your help; Robby Bullen for permission to reprint your superb cartoons and for drawing me a brand new one!; Steve and Trev for permission to use the magnificent Greens On Screen resource; Dave Rowntree for his photographs; other photographs reproduced with kind permission from the *Plymouth Evening Herald*; much thanks also to all the former Argyle players, directors and journalists who were so willing to reminisce; and last, but absolutely not least, much love and thanks to my wife, Nicki, who – despite juggling a pregnancy and a high-powered job – still found the time and patience to endure my constant Shilton-related witterings. And you didn't think I'd forgotten you, Noah, did you? I never thought dirty nappies and baby sick could be so inspiring…

AUTHOR'S NOTE

'Why a book about sporting failure?', I can well imagine you asking. It's a perfectly reasonable question, for Peter Shilton's Home Park era was an unequivocal failure; arguably the most spectacular buggering-up of managing Plymouth Argyle in the club's long history of managerial bugger-ups.

But Argyle fans – for anyone unacquainted with their unique ways – are paradoxically at their most gleeful when the chips are down; 'Janners' thrive on a sort of inverted schadenfreude, and Shilton's reign offered them an almost endless excuse to wallow in a mudbath of misery and frustration.

However, it also offered them some of the finest attacking football Home Park has ever hosted, conjured up by such hallowed names as Steve Castle, Paul Dalton and Steve McCall – outstanding talents who routinely appear in all-time Argyle XIs to this day. Together with their team-mates and the most famous manager in the club's history, not to mention the wealthiest chairman, they had greatness in their sights. They shot for the stars but missed by a mere twinkle, before plummeting back down to Earth, a rampaging comet on a collision course with disaster.

I hope the less-than-rosy ending to this humble tome doesn't make it any less enjoyable. *Titanic* remains one of the highest grossing films of all-time, you know...

For his part, Peter Shilton was gracious in his acknowledgement of this book, but politely declined to be interviewed – stating that his version of events has already been covered in detail in his autobiography.

Now for a gentle warning. The language of the football changing room is an industrial one, and if this book was a pre-watershed TV programme, certain sections of it would beep like a metal detector in a scrapyard. Parents: please be aware of this if any young Pilgrims are likely to want a read.

Don't blame me, though, blame Peter Swan.

FOREWORD

To paraphrase an opening line from a writer considerably more adept than I am, Peter Shilton's Home Park era saw the best of times and the worst of times.

Many people remember the rare quality of football from names that will forever be held in esteem by the Green Army. Steve McCall, Paul Dalton, Steve Castle, Kevin Nugent, Mark Patterson – to name but five – were brought to Argyle by England's greatest ever goalkeeper. They were good players, good enough to play at least a division above the third tier that the Pilgrims occupied, and good enough to overcome the coaching and tactical shortcomings of a figurehead as naïve in the dark arts of management as he was well-practiced in keeping goal. I firmly believe that, under Paul Sturrock, Neil Warnock or Tony Pulis, Argyle would have won the 1992/93 Barclays Second Division by a huge margin, and gone on to rip up the First Division, too. The talent was certainly there, largely bought in thanks to chairman Dan McCauley's generosity, but there was not enough discipline or organisation to shape that talent into the truly efficient unit that it should have been.

Off the field, the beautiful game turned ugly rather quickly after Peter Shilton's appointment as manager. For reasons that Paul Roberts explores in depth in the story that follows, Dan McCauley and Peter Shilton did not enjoy the sort of relationship that is needed to build a lasting, successful club. Again, I am convinced that if they had been as united as, say, Paul Stapleton and Paul Sturrock later were, they would have jointly laid the foundations of something very special. Sometimes they seemed as far apart as it is possible for two people who are working for the same cause to be. I will leave you to decide where the blame lies. Suffice to say that Dan McCauley fell out with more than a few people during the time I knew him, myself included. To his credit, he also fell back in with a lot of them, although sometimes as a precursor to falling out with them again.

I am pleased that this story has been chronicled, and delighted that Paul Roberts is the chronicler. I first met Paul after he was somewhat publicly scathing of my first book, *Tommy: A Life at the Soccer Factory*, the first of now two biographies of living Pilgrims' legend Tommy Tynan, written when I was working for the *Western Morning News*. From that inauspicious start, Paul somehow managed to become an occasional Argyle reporter for the paper and thus started out on the rocky road of journalism – the latest fruits of which you now hold.

I am happy to be more charitable to his debut tome than he was to mine. It tells the tale very well of an age that needs to be remembered, for the good times and the bad.

Rick Cowdery
Head of Communications,
Plymouth Argyle Football Club

Chapter One

KEMPY

David Kemp strode into Home Park's humble executive box no.8, a dark cloud above his head. His struggling Plymouth Argyle side had just succumbed to a 1–0 home defeat to Cambridge United on a bleak February night in the winter of 1992, and the hyenas were beginning to smell blood.

Barely 4,000 frost-bitten souls had witnessed Kemp's journeymen pass John Beck's industrial visitors off the park, but a third consecutive defeat and tailspinning attendances made the sword of Damocles a pervasive presence as Kemp prepared to meet the assembled pressmen in the executive box affectionately known as 'Hodgie' – after the club's long-serving no.8, Kevin Hodges.

Gordon Sparks, then a reporter for Plymouth Sound radio station, joined his colleagues in dissecting the not-so-fine details of the evening's fare with Kemp, before delivering the loaded question that had been waiting impatiently on everyone's lips since the final whistle. 'As a journalist, if you've got the money question you always leave it till last, so if they don't like it at least you've already got some quotes,' remembers Sparks of that pivotal evening. 'With the bad run we'd had, I asked him if he was in fear of his position after not getting the result that night.'

In fear he might well have been, but Kemp was not about to admit it to the press. 'He started to answer the question, but then something took over in his mind and he said, "I'm not answering a question like that." He ordered me to give him the cassette out of my machine and told me to get out. I had to go back to my editor to explain that I had no audio.'

The normally amiable Kemp may have lost his rag, but later that week he was to lose a whole lot more.

The Plymouth Argyle of the late 1980s had been breathlessly treading water in the second tier of the Football League – then simply known as the Second Division – for several seasons. The warm glow of promotion under 'Ciderman'

Dave Smith in 1986 had been replaced by the cool chill of an annual struggle for survival. Crowd favourites had departed and the impassive Plymouth public had returned to Saturday afternoon shelf-shopping in their thousands.

With local hero Smith lost to Dundee, and former Norwich City boss Ken Brown given just eighteen months to attempt a repeat of the success he had enjoyed in Norfolk, the Argyle Board turned to a former Home Park favourite in a bid to halt an abysmal sequence of results and an alarming and costly slide in attendances during the season of 1989/90.

David Kemp was the natural choice for chairman Peter Bloom and his directors in the late spring of 1990. His fine Home Park goalscoring record during the '70s and '80s notwithstanding, Kemp was also a member of the coaching staff at the original Wimbledon FC – a club at that time vastly experienced when it came to punching and scrapping above its weight.

The Board had got their man, and their man was about to take punching and scrapping to a whole new level. 'People look at that period as not being successful, but we had the lowest wage bill in that league by a country mile,' Kemp remembers. 'I don't think they'd won in fifteen games when I turned up, and I had to try and turn that around. If you can go out and get the best players then brilliant, that's easy, but I had to do it with my hands tied.'

Under Kemp's stewardship, the rot that had set in under Brown was successfully treated and a creditable sixteenth place was secured by season's end. But if the fans had deserted a poor team playing good football under Ken Brown, they certainly weren't going to give up their Saturday afternoons to watch a poor team playing poor football under David Kemp.

Goalkeeper Rhys Wilmot had joined the club from Arsenal in 1989, and from between his posts was in a better position than most to survey the stark change in style, as he explains:

> The Ken Brown team that I joined had your Kevin Summerfields and your John Matthews, players who knocked the ball around a lot. I remember one game we played at Leeds on a Tuesday night and we got beat 2–1, Howard Wilkinson said we were the best footballing team that had been at Leeds all season. We were a cracking little side but we just couldn't grind the results out, so that did for Ken. We went from one extreme to the other when Kempy joined, but we started to get results with a different style of play, a more direct approach to the game. Unfortunately, the style that David wanted to play wasn't really accepted by the crowd.

It wasn't just the crowd who were unimpressed by the agricultural long-ball fare. Adrian Burrows was an honest lower-league centre-back with an incongruous desire to keep the ball on the deck. 'Not all the players liked Kempy's style that much,' he remembers. 'But it was a case of trying to adapt to what the manager wanted. I didn't particularly like the long-ball, but I could see why he was doing it and the reason behind it. I must admit I didn't enjoy it at all.'

It was a view shared by ball-playing midfielder Martin Barlow, then a teenage hopeful on the fringes of the first team. 'When you're just coming through and you're trying to make the grade as a pro you don't really care about the style of play, you just want to be out on the park. You'd do anything to get out there,' says Barlow. 'I was on the wing back in those days, I started off there. But it was just chase basically, hit the ball and chase. It wasn't the football I liked to play. Kempy had some good ideas but he was limited to what he had and what he could spend. I think long-ball was the only way he could do it because of the lack of money.'

Rick Cowdery, then sports editor at the Plymouth-based *Western Morning News*, concurs, 'I suppose he did have a reputation for playing long-ball football, but there was a reason for that – he couldn't afford not to. He had to limit the mistakes. He always said that it's best to make mistakes in their third of the field and not your two-thirds of the field, so you get it up there as soon as possible.'

Kemp's brief was pressure-cooker simple: to keep Argyle in the Second Division. With gates averaging around 6,000 and gradually heading further south, relegation could have sounded the death knell for a club already teetering on the financial brink.

'I was never really in a position to build a team because I was always firefighting,' reflects Kemp.

> I was always trying to get results with the least number of players possible. I even had a player who actually played for nothing . . . in the first team, and played for nothing, just win bonuses – unbelievable really. That's where we were at. You've got to win games and you're playing the likes of Newcastle, Wolves, Portsmouth, Leicester, Sunderland, Middlesbrough . . . they were big clubs in that league and had much bigger budgets than we did, and we were trying to compete with these people. I was trying to keep our heads above water. I do understand the fans criticising the style of football, I don't have a problem with that, but you have to realise the position I was in.

In the summer of 1990, with the nation gripped by Italia 90 fever and Gazza-mania, Kemp set about revamping his squad under the terms of his modest budget. Out went Kevin Summerfield, Tommy Tynan, Leigh Cooper, Julian Broddle, Sean McCarthy, Mark Stuart and Greg Campbell; in came Robbie Turner, Steve Morgan, Andy Clement, Adam King and Dave Walter to galvanise a squad that Kemp had already added to shortly after his appointment with the signings of Mark Fiore, Danis Salman and Paul Robinson. The names Tynan, Summerfield and Cooper tripped off the tongue on the Home Park terraces. The rustic figures of Turner, Salman, Clement and Morgan, on the other hand, didn't so much trip off the tongue as elbow you in the tonsils before hoofing a molar into orbit.

Despite the heavy and rapid dilution in on-pitch finesse, the 1990/91 season began reasonably well – with an opening-day 2–0 reverse at Newcastle being the solitary defeat in the first six games. However, four draws and just one win in that spell underlines Kemp's 'we had to make ourselves hard to beat' mandate.

The surprising find of the season – the beginning of it at least – was Andy Thomas, an attacking midfielder signed from Bradford City the season before who was pushed up front by Kemp with some aplomb. Eight goals in the first sixteen games of the season pointed to a bright future for club and player, but a frustratingly troublesome back injury put Thomas in the treatment room and Argyle's hopes of a decent season in the can. The loss was desperately disappointing for Kemp, but even more so for Thomas; after the 4–1 win at home to Hull City on 27 October 1990, he would make just one more appearance in the Football League before being forced into retirement.

Kemp's best-laid plans were in tatters. 'That was probably the best team I put together at the club,' he laments.

> We had Robbie Turner up front with Andy Thomas playing off him, Andy was knocking in the goals and we were going well. We were in the top half of the division and we knocked Wimbledon out of the League Cup – they were in the First Division back then. Unfortunately, Andy got a back injury and never played again. It was such a small squad that there was no way of replacing him. I had to use a youth-team player, Paul Adcock, who I tried out but who couldn't get the job done. As a manager you're trying to build a team and then you lose your best player.

Shorn of the prolific Thomas, Argyle won just nine of their remaining thirty-two games to finish eighteenth – a discomforting five points off relegation.

Kemp is keen to emphasise that his long-term goal at Home Park was always to mould a passing side at youth-team level capable of making the step up to Second Division football – at which point he would have dispensed with the much-maligned long-ball game. 'It was important to try and stay in that division. And so we had to play a style of football that would keep us up,' he says.

> But while I was doing that, I was bringing through all these younger players: Martin Barlow, Marc Edworthy, Mickey Evans and so on. Over a period of time it would have evolved into a much better style of play – a more attractive style of play. I just felt we had to stay as high in the league as we possibly could, bring these young players through and then we would have been up and running. But I never had the time because I constantly had my back up against the wall trying to get results with what was the bare minimum of a squad.

Former Argyle defender and then youth-team coach Gordon Nisbet supports Kemp's assertion. 'David spoke to me when he took me there as youth coach, he was totally up front with me and said he didn't want the youth and reserve teams to play like the first team,' recalls Nisbet. 'He was under mega-pressure to get results, but he wanted us to teach our teams how to play football. Alan Gillett [Kemp's assistant manager] worked with me and he was all about playing football. But obviously the first team had to get results and they [Kemp and

Gillett] had both been successful with the long-ball style of play at Wimbledon. David wasn't happy with it though.'

With another season of poor results and even poorer gates behind them, the Board clammed up and the bottom fell out of Kemp's already rickety budget.

The close-season of 1991 was arguably the most uninspiring in the club's history. The humble talents of Morrys Scott, Mark Quamina, Mark Damarell, Steve Morris and Tony Spearing were drafted in on free transfers, more to make up the numbers in a threadbare squad than anything else, and traditional pre-season optimism flatlined.

With the season fast approaching and the bookmakers unanimously pinning their relegation flags to Argyle's mast, Kemp took a gamble on a young blue-collar Jamaican who worked in a north London office block and played non-league football for Grays Athletic in his spare time.

'I'd heard good things about a young lad called Dwight Marshall, so I took him down to Cornwall on a pre-season tour,' recalls Kemp. 'He'd come out of non-league – that's where I had to do my shopping. I paid £35,000 for him and I had to beg for that. It sounds ridiculous by today's standards. He was the first player I'd signed for money in fourteen months, and it wasn't as if I hadn't brought money in. I'd sold the likes of Sean McCarthy and Kenny Brown [both for six-figure sums], so I'd brought a lot of money into the club.'

Cowdery, a self-confessed Kemp 'loyalist', felt considerable sympathy for the manager. 'He had no resources, absolutely none whatsoever,' he says, 'With Dwight Marshall, he had to go to the Board and chisel the money out of their hands – £35,000! He was really limited to getting what players he could – loans, cast-offs, freebies – and trying to mix and match. Dwight was a decent buy, so it wasn't that Kemp didn't have an eye for a player. But his mission was to find players that he could get something out of on the cheap, and I think he did a difficult job very well.'

The 6,352 faithful few who turned up at Home Park for the opening day of the 1991/92 season wouldn't have been expecting much from Kemp's ragtag outfit. The subsequent 2–1 victory against visitors Barnsley would have raised their sagging spirits, but it was a moment of magic from the summer's 'big-money' signing that really got Janner tongues wagging, Marshall's overhead kick from about 12in off the ground preceding Robbie Turner's rather more rustic winner.

The collective grins that greeted the Jamaican's debut strike could have stretched from Milehouse to Montego Bay, but any calypso cheer under the early-season summer skies was to prove ephemeral. Just two wins in the next fifteen games followed, a dire run that usually would have seen the manager led to the gallows. The Argyle directors, however, were far too busy staring wide-eyed at the club's rapidly escalating overdraft to contemplate taking another costly ride on the managerial merry-go-round.

'It was a difficult period we were going through,' recalls chairman Peter Bloom. 'You've got to put a lot of money into a football club if you want success, and I think the directors at that time thought they'd put enough in. If we could have got 20,000 gates we would have been on a winner. But you've only got to get a small downturn on the pitch and all of a sudden the spectators don't turn up. To get 5–6,000 is just not good enough. They've just got this Westcountry feel about things, unless you're successful they just don't turn up.'

Bloom and his directors – David Forshaw, Graham Jasper, Ralph Burroughs and Cliff Hartley – embarked on a desperate bid to raise the necessary capital that would prevent the club spiralling into receivership. Local businessman Steve Tiller was the first to throw his hat into the takeover ring, running a very public campaign through the local media in a bid to force the club to accept his mysterious £2 million 'rescue' package. Tiller's approach split the Board, with Burroughs and Hartley deciding to throw their lot in with the devil they didn't know rather than the devil they did.

The very day before the full Argyle Board was due to meet Tiller for the first time to discuss his proposal, a certain Tiverton-based millionaire was heading north on the A38 when he learned of the club's quandary. 'I was going up to Gloucester that day. I had the radio on and they were saying it was D-Day for the Board at Argyle,' recalls Dan McCauley. 'They were being criticised for not raising any funds. By the time I got to Gloucester I'd made my mind up to find out what was going on, so I called Peter Bloom straight away.'

'Dan McCauley came out of the blue,' says Bloom. 'I didn't even know him at that time, I'd never met him. But he phoned me at work and said he would like to arrange a meeting. That was on the Tuesday and on the Wednesday we were going to meet with Tiller.'

With the Tiller consortium turning the screw on the front and back pages of the local press, Bloom arranged to meet McCauley at the inauspicious surroundings of the motorway services at Exeter. 'David Forshaw and myself went up because I couldn't get hold of anyone else to go,' says Bloom. 'We met up and talked him through our situation, and he was more than happy to come down and put up a lump sum of money to join the club.'

McCauley's recollections of the deal are typically forthright, 'Tiller was the number one choice, I was in the background and no-one knew about my interest. But at that meeting, the Board told me how much debt they were in and that they wanted a £400,000 injection. I didn't look at the books because I knew they'd be lousy. If you do due diligence when you buy a football club you'd never buy it because you know you'll just open up a can of worms.'

With the Tiller offer still very much on the table, McCauley made a crucial addition to his offer that turned the tide decisively in his favour. Says Bloom:

> We were delighted that Dan was going to put money into the club, but he also told us he was more than happy to keep the existing directors on the Board. It wasn't a condition that we made, he just said he'd be happy to keep it that way. He said he wanted everyone to stay on because he'd never run a football club

and wanted to know the ins and outs of everything. So we met up at a solicitor's office, went through the fine details and agreed to meet up at Home Park to introduce Dan to the media. He made a cheque out and paid it into the club. That was it – simple as that.

Or, in McCauley's rather more succinct terms, 'I paid up the £400k and bought the club in three days.'

Rick Cowdery believes Tiller's front-foot approach backfired, and played straight into the hands of McCauley. 'Tiller mounted a very public campaign to try and get hold of the club,' he says.

> I think his tactic paid off, except that it wasn't Tiller who benefited from it, it was McCauley. Tiller wanted to take over lock, stock and barrel with his own directors, whereas Dan came along on the blind side and said, 'Right, if you sell to me you can stay on the Board.' I can remember seeing Peter Bloom at the time and he looked an ill man – this was after weeks of Tiller putting the pressure on. I think Dan just gave them the get-out that seemed to serve them well at the time. He was the Board's white knight if you like, because he offered them a way of staying involved in the club but effectively selling it at the same time.

So why Plymouth Argyle? After short-lived and undistinguished stints on the Boards of Exeter City and Torquay United, why a return to football with a club haemorrhaging money hand over fist? 'I'd only been to Argyle once,' says McCauley, 'and to me Plymouth was a long way away from Tiverton, but I had to have roots. I used to watch Portsmouth in their heyday when they won everything; they were a great side. Brighton I used to support, Chelsea I used to support, I lived in London so I used to support Tottenham as well. I lived in America but they don't play much football out there. I've been a football fan all my life, and it was always a good way to put down roots.'

By the time the nomadic McCauley had been given the go-ahead to sprout his roots in Plymouth, the city's football club had itself become firmly rooted in the lower reaches of the Second Division.

By 8 November 1991, Argyle were bottom of the table with just three wins under their belts – the protracted off-field events providing an unwelcome distraction. 'There was that period before McCauley came in when there was a dreadful atmosphere around the place,' says Kemp. 'We had a very poor run because morale was low, I couldn't get any players in and I had to put patchwork teams out. I wasn't allowed to sign anyone because there was a takeover going on and it was just very, very awkward. That was when I most needed some support really.'

Takeover duly completed, McCauley wasted little time in dipping his hand into his pocket to provide that support. Striker Dave Regis arrived from Notts County for a club record £200,000, while winger David Smith quickly followed from Bristol City for £185,000. The pedigree troops Kemp had craved for so long had finally arrived. Says Regis of his decision to sign, 'I had a bit of time with Notts County in the top flight, but I wasn't getting a game as such. I was out of favour and it was a choice between Plymouth or Fulham. Fulham were in the Third Division at the time, so I went for Plymouth – even though it was miles away!'

With a wealthy chairman and a pair of expensive new signings freshly installed, mid-table consolidation was a realistic target. Robbie Turner – having lost his target-man role up front to the newly-arrived Regis after a spell out injured – was successfully converted into a centre-back and a run of four wins in five games followed. But by the turn of the year, Argyle were still in the bottom three and Regis – having scored just once in his first eight games – had become the crowd's scapegoat of choice. 'I had problems settling in at the club,' he explains. 'My family stayed in Nottingham, so I was down there on my own and that didn't help. But saying that, the team as a whole didn't perform at all and, unfortunately for me, scoring goals didn't come easy. That's what Kempy bought me for. The season before that I scored seventeen goals for Notts County in thirty-odd games, but I just couldn't pick my form up at Plymouth. As much as I tried, it didn't work out for me and the fans started getting on my back.'

But any melancholy in the dressing room started and ended with Regis. Forced to build his squad from an almost empty warchest, Kemp knew all too well that team spirit was a priceless resource if he was to keep the club in the Second Division.

Andy 'Jock' Morrison, a salt-of-the-earth centre-back quarried in Scotland and forged in Plymouth, was a huge fan of Kemp's gregarious approach. 'Dave Kemp was fantastic, I had a lot of time for him,' says Morrison. 'He tried to bring the Crazy Gang mentality down with him from Wimbledon. There were people there like me and Robbie Turner who were definitely in that mould. Don't forget, he kept the team in that division for three years all but, and every other manager always said how well he'd done with the team that he had.'

Rhys Wilmot agrees, 'Life was superb under David Kemp, he was a great man-manager and a lovely fella,' he says. 'Team spirit was absolutely brilliant. The training sessions were really good and he kept a good social. I don't think anybody would say they didn't enjoy their time under him.'

It's a view shared by midfielder Nicky Marker. 'We had a good team spirit,' says the former Exeter City man. 'He was a Wimbledon sort of person – team spirit counted for everything. He took us away a lot, not on expensive holidays because they couldn't afford that, but things like army camps in pre-season just to get the togetherness going among the team.'

Marker was also Kemp's captain, a role that the manager believed involved more than just calling the coin toss. 'On a number of occasions he would call me into his office and we'd chat about things,' Marker reflects. 'He had my greatest respect for doing things like that because most other managers would go it alone. He wanted his captain to get the team together and that's how we fought and how we kept our heads above water.'

Kemp's men were more than just keeping their heads above water as 1991 made way for '92. A fine 3–2 New Year's Day win over dockyard rivals Portsmouth was followed by a creditable 2–2 draw at home to Leicester City and a magnificent 3–1 win over Barnsley at Oakwell – in an era when Argyle away wins were as rare as hens' teeth. Dwight Marshall's superb hat-trick in that game took his debut season's tally to twelve – four of which had come against the Tykes – and in Kemp's words, Argyle were 'off and running'.

However, with optimism higher than at any other time during the Kemp era, the manager's good fortune hit the buffers. As dull a 0–0 as you're likely to see at home to Bristol Rovers on 1 February was followed by a 4–1 massacre at Portsmouth and a 1–0 reverse at Watford – leaving the Greens in twenty-first place and feeling the sinister draught from the creaky relegation trapdoor once more.

With Cambridge United coming to town on the Tuesday following the Watford defeat, Argyle had the perfect chance to edge three points closer to safety. The Us were riding the crest of a wave that had taken them from the lower reaches of the Fourth Division to the brink of the top flight, but had warmed up for their trip to Home Park with just two points and zero goals from their previous four games.

In driving rain, the Pilgrims produced one of their most aesthetically pleasing performances of the season – but Lady Luck was steadfast in her refusal to give the Pilgrims a break. Michael Cheetham's fourteenth-minute effort proved decisive for the visitors, and the Us somehow protected their 1–0 advantage despite an incessant attacking onslaught from Kemp's men – who twice hit the woodwork and had a shot cleared off the line.

Cambridge manager John Beck described his vanquished opponents as 'absolutely magnificent, they gave us a lesson in the game,' while Kemp – sent to the stands late on for questioning the parentage of a linesman – tried to remain positive. 'We're playing well enough to win games,' he said. 'And we've got to keep playing well until things turn.'

The morning after the depressing night before, a fearful Kemp resisted the temptation to board up his windows and leave his phone off the hook. 'I just carried on working,' he says.

I'm not stupid, I knew what was going on, but until you're told otherwise you carry on doing your job to the best of your ability. The day after the Cambridge game, I was up at 6 a.m. to drive to Leicester to organise a kit deal for the club. Starting early like that wasn't unusual. I don't want to blow my own trumpet, but I worked all the hours under the sun when I was in that job because I had to. You can't just stay in Plymouth; you have to be out on the road. It's a bit easier nowadays, with DVDs and how much football there is on the TV, but in those days the only way you'd be able to sign anybody was to be out on the road, so I was used to very early starts and lots of travelling about. No-one appreciates what you have to do at a club like that.

The following morning, Thursday 13 February, Kemp returned to Home Park to face what he suspected would be particularly unpleasant music. 'One of the secretaries said the chairman wanted to see me, and of course I knew what it was about,' he recalls. 'So I went in to see Dan and he told me he was giving me my notice. You could see he wasn't comfortable with it, that was pretty obvious. But it's not easy to sack someone, is it?'

In fact, McCauley took his onerous duty surprisingly to heart. 'When I gave David Kemp his notice, I cried,' he says. 'He didn't though, but I had tears in my eyes because I liked David; I thought he was tremendous. But it was a rainy old night against Cambridge that did it, when we had all the game but lost 1–0. The Board were pushing me all the time to sack him, but I didn't want to do it.'

Kemp took the news like a man and insists he didn't place the blame squarely at McCauley's feet, 'I had respect for Dan McCauley when he was my boss and I did even after he sacked me,' he says.

I didn't have a problem with him. I knew the problem wasn't him. He was an experienced businessman but he was inexperienced when it came to the workings of football. I think he was pushed down a path he probably didn't want to go down and I believe he regretted it. I think if he had his time again he wouldn't have done it, but we can always be wise after the event. Unfortunately, Cambridge was the sort of defeat they were waiting for and it cost me my job. We actually played very well that night, even in the games leading up to that we'd played really well but not had any luck. I can remember Peter Bloom, the chairman who appointed me, coming in to see me after I'd been sacked and I asked him why they had chosen that route. He said, 'Well, we're frightened of getting relegated.' I said, 'You weren't going to get relegated, but you might now!' I'd kept them up the previous two years and would have done so again. To say we were going to get relegated was nonsense. I would have kept them up, I don't think there's any question about that. They went down because they only won four of the last seventeen games after me. Well, I could virtually have guaranteed more than four wins in the last seventeen games because my record says that. Of my last nine home games, we won six, drew two and lost one. And the one we lost was the game they sacked me after. Even if they'd said, 'We don't really fancy you as a manager, we want to give it to someone else,' what they should have done was let it go until the end of the season, stayed in the division and then they could have made the change in the summer. That would have been the sensible thing to do. But to make a change when they did eventually set that club back ten years at least.

If most Argyle fans were happy to see the back of the manager and his widely despised style of football, Kemp's players certainly weren't. 'I got my first pro contract under Dave Smith, but Kemp was really the one who put me in the team and looked after me,' reflects Morrison. 'I had a lot of respect for the man because he was just very good at what he did. I was very fond of him and I was gutted when he got the sack. If he'd been given a decent budget and had been able to bring in the players he wanted, with how organised and disciplined he had his teams, he would have been very successful.'

Captain Marker agrees. 'Results count for everything, and in the end the results didn't quite go his way. I think if he hadn't left we would have stayed up. It was unfair sacking him considering the budget he had.'

For young winger Barlow, Kemp had been something of a mentor. 'I was gutted because Kemp was the manager who got me in the first team,' he says. 'If it wasn't for him I don't think I would have made it so far in my career.'

Wilmot suggests the players knew Kemp's days were numbered, but admits he was saddened by his sacking. 'Cambridge was a disappointing night, and we knew then that the writing was on the wall for the manager. But I was really disappointed to see him go, he was a cracking bloke and a very good coach.'

For the local media, on the other hand, Kemp's sacking came as something of a surprise. 'Initially, McCauley gave Kemp a bit of money to spend – he bought Regis and Smith for quite a bit of money between them,' says Graham Hambly, then Argyle correspondent for Plymouth's *Evening Herald* newspaper. 'In terms of the stage of the season and the money spent, they may as well have stuck with what they had and sacked him in the summer.'

'The timing was very strange,' agrees Cowdery. 'The Cambridge defeat was obviously disappointing, but they played well and there was no indication that it was coming. There was also no Plan B – there was nobody lined up straight away.'

There may not have been a long-term Plan B in place, but the Board's immediate response was to task assistant manager Alan Gillett and youth-team coach Gordon Nisbet with overseeing first-team affairs until further notice. With the fledgling partnership busy planning for the visit of Brighton, the Board – recently bolstered by the additions of Ivor Jones and Dennis Angilley – turned its attentions to finding Kemp's successor. 'I joined the Board when David Kemp had just been sacked,' remembers Jones.

The first job we had to do was interview for the new manager! As I understand it, the process isn't normally that well organised. The old manager goes and you've got to put an advert in the press for a new one, but then the old boys' network begins working and you get phone calls coming in from everywhere. Before you know it you've got a list of thirty or forty people that you have to whittle down and then you start interviewing. I think we interviewed ten to fifteen people in the first week or so after David left.

Nisbet was one such interviewee. 'I thought I had a good interview and felt I had a decent chance. Alan and I had some good ideas for tactics, players coming in and out and so on. We put all that across and I was led to believe that I was still a frontrunner going into the Ipswich game a week later.'

But there was a major obstacle standing in Nisbet's way that, no matter how well he interviewed, he could do very little about: he wasn't a big name. With Kenny Dalglish being lured by Jack Walker's millions at Blackburn the previous October, and Kevin Keegan's messianic return to struggling Newcastle the week before Kemp's sacking, high-profile Second Division managers were very much in vogue.

McCauley's top two targets were Ossie Ardiles – the man who made way for Keegan on Tyneside – and Ray Wilkins, Queens Park Rangers' former England midfielder. McCauley publicly courted Ardiles through the press, until – when McCauley finally tracked him down – the invitation to apply was turned down by the 1978 World Cup winner, who offered a raft of excuses as to why he was neither available nor suitable for the post.

'There was a lot of adverse publicity about Ardiles being Argentinian. A lot of rubbish came out in the press about that, which may have put him off,' says McCauley. 'I also called Ray Wilkins to talk to him about the job. He did think about it for a few days, but eventually came back to me saying he didn't want it because he was keen to carry on playing at the top level.'

In the midst of the managerial hunt, the caretaking duo of Gillett and Nisbet had led the first team to a 1–1 draw against a desperately poor Brighton side – who were themselves eventually relegated. Tellingly, the loudest cheer of the afternoon came after just two minutes when Rhys Wilmot rolled the ball out to a full-back rather than booting it up-field. The old regime had been kicked into touch.

Three days after that latest on-pitch setback, McCauley and most of his directors met in the Plymouth Novotel to interview the final candidate on their list and to make a decision on the identity of the new manager. Missing was Peter Bloom, who was busy taking what turned out to be a significant phone call from an old friend.

'Lionel Smart was an FA man from Swindon who I had known for many years, and he phoned me up about a week after Kemp was sacked,' recalls Bloom. 'We were discussing the managerial vacancy and he asked if we had thought about Peter Shilton. Right away my ears pricked up and I thought, 'Well, there's a name that's well known to the public, he'd be a top character to bring to the club.' So I told him we hadn't thought about Shilton because we didn't know he was available.'

Ivor Jones takes up the story:

We were in the Novotel and had just finished an interview, when Peter Bloom came in and said that he'd been contacted by someone at the FA and would we be interested in talking to Peter Shilton? We'd actually finished everything and we were into making the decision when suddenly the name Peter Shilton was on

the table. At the time we weren't thinking about a high-profile manager. Gordon
Nisbet was fairly high in our thoughts, all the Board members had a lot of respect
for Gordon, so possibly it would have been him. But there were one or two very
experienced people that had applied and so we were looking at that and trying to
make a balanced judgement.

With Smart as intermediary, an interview was arranged to coincide with the
club's trip to Ipswich Town on the weekend of 7 December. On the eve of
the match, the directors of Plymouth Argyle left their hotel and set off to
meet the most capped player in England's history, in what would turn out to
be a fateful rendezvous for club and player.

'It was my first away match as a Board member,' remembers Jones. 'We had
agreed to meet Peter Shilton at a hotel just outside of Ipswich. We didn't
want the press to know anything about it, we wanted to try and keep it very
quiet – it was all very exciting. We discreetly left the hotel we were staying at
with the players and a few of the press guys, and then a car pulls up outside
with "Plymouth Argyle FC" written across it in big letters! Anyone who saw
us would have known exactly what we were up to.'

If the directors had been excited about the prospect of installing Shilton as
Argyle manager before his interview, they were positively gushing afterwards.
'I thought he was very impressive,' reflects Dennis Angilley. 'Not just because of
his experience and the fact that he was a star, but he talked a lot of sense about
football and at that stage he would have been a rookie manager going for his
first job, so he was enthused and excited as well.'

Jones was even more impressed:

> He was a truly impressive man with a wonderful knowledge of football. During the
> interview he was very composed, very confident. I can remember asking him how
> he had prepared himself for management, and he said he'd obviously worked under
> managers like Brian Clough and Bobby Robson, some of the top people in the
> game. And bear in mind he was going to come as a player-manager, so you're getting
> one of the best goalkeepers in England as well. That was a tremendous bonus. All in
> all, he seemed to be a candidate that could just maybe put Plymouth on the map.

The directors were unanimous in their appraisal of Shilton's candidacy.
'Everybody liked him,' says Peter Bloom. 'You couldn't say a bad word about
him. It was really exciting, and when the interview was over we had a chat for
about twenty minutes and then pretty much said: "This is the man".'

But with terms yet to be discussed, the Board were still keen to keep their
primary target under wraps. Their covert approach to the interview, however,
was somewhat in vain. 'On the way to Ipswich, I rang a former colleague of
mine, Ross Reid, from a motorway service station on the Friday lunchtime,'
says Cowdery. 'We knocked heads, put bits of info gathered from various sources

together and I came away 90 per cent convinced it was Shilton. I was staying in the same hotel as the directors. They thought they'd been very clever and that nobody knew about the interview, but when they returned to the hotel that evening, I said: "Evening gentlemen – so how was Mr Shilton?" To be fair, their faces didn't give anything away, though on the Monday morning he was appointed we ran this piece saying he was in the frame, so we had it before anyone else.'

A thrilling development for a news-hungry reporter, perhaps, but not so for a man who had his hopes dashed by the developments in Ipswich. 'All five directors went out in one car, and when they came back they couldn't look at us,' says Gordon Nisbet. 'Me and Alan looked at each other and said "We haven't got the job, whoever they've just interviewed has got it." It was a kick in the teeth to be honest.'

Argyle lost 2–0 at Portman Road, with Robbie Turner breaking his leg in an accidental collision with Rhys Wilmot, but the directors' minds would have been very much on the second clandestine meeting they had arranged with Shilton for the following day. 'We met him again on the Sunday up at Exeter,' recalls Jones of a meeting that went on into the early hours of Monday morning. 'The deal provisionally took an hour, but then we had to go through all the negotiations with the solicitors, which was very protracted. That meeting went on forever, hammering out all the terms and conditions.'

As the reality of the financial gamble they were about to take to secure one of the biggest names in world football hit home, several members of the Board admitted they did have reservations regarding Shilton's lack of managerial experience. 'Absolutely, that's all we were worried about,' says McCauley. 'And they say goalkeepers never make good managers either. All I know is, when we came to an agreement with the wages I was holding my heart, I think I was laying under the table actually. I just thought "my God." My heart was pumping, we were taking a big gamble.'

Dennis Angilley shared McCauley's concerns, but took comfort from the fact that Shilton's high standing in the game could only benefit the club. 'I took the view that it was an opportunity to put Plymouth Argyle on the map,' he says. 'Peter Shilton could ring up anyone in the country, or anyone in Europe or perhaps even the world, and they'd know who it was. It may have been regarded by some as a fairly high-risk strategy, but it was an absolute coup for Plymouth in my opinion.'

On Monday 2 March 1992, the *Western Morning News* printed Cowdery's story tentatively linking Shilton with the manager's job at Home Park, accompanied by an emphatic denial from McCauley.

But as shoppers and office workers made their way around Plymouth city centre during the busy lunchtime hours later that day, the billboards advertising the *Evening Herald* newspaper stated simply: 'IT'S SHILTON'.

Chapter Two

THE GREEK GOD

The news of Peter Shilton's appointment as Argyle manager rocked the city and reverberated across the country. If the club's directors wanted a reaction from their big-name managerial appointment, they got one in spades.

The grand unveiling took place at the Forte Post House hotel on Plymouth's seafront at 11.15am on Monday 2 March 1992, though by then Rick Cowdery's detective work had spread throughout the gathered pressmen and Shilton's grand entrance wasn't perhaps as emphatic as the Board had hoped. 'We introduced him to the media at the Forte,' remembers Peter Bloom. 'He came into the room from behind a screen on the side and there was an immediate buzz around the place, though by then the news had got out somehow. A lot of the media seemed to know, word had leaked out as it usually does at Argyle.'

'It was terribly exciting,' says Ivor Jones. 'When he walked in it was a really special moment. It was on the national news all that day – it brought the club into the limelight like never before really. No-one could believe that we'd got a manager like Peter Shilton – nor could we really.'

The unveiling nearly got off to an embarrassing start. An hour before the scheduled start time, the local media were sat twiddling their thumbs at Home Park, before an eleventh-hour phone call saw them racing over to the Hoe in readiness for the big announcement. When they finally got there, most had to admit they were impressed by the Board's ambition – if a little reticent about Shilton's lack of managerial experience.

'I found it quite incredible when Shilton was appointed because he was someone who had achieved so much in football on a world stage,' says Gordon Sparks. 'There were severe doubts in my mind, though, because he'd never been a manager or even an assistant. But he'd worked under some of the greatest coaches in the English game and some of that must have rubbed off. Every manager has to have a first club somewhere, so I thought, okay, let's go with it.'

As for Shilton himself, the interest generated by his appointment seemed to take him by surprise. 'I'd not seen him in the flesh in close quarters before, and he seemed a very reserved guy,' recalls Sparks. 'I don't know if he suffered from nerves or what. I suppose it was a different role for him and, although he obviously wanted the job, maybe it was somewhere outside his comfort zone. He just seemed a little apprehensive. He didn't seem too comfortable talking in public – maybe it was the sight of so many journalists in front of him. But the coverage was nationwide, a big-name appointment like that was always going to attract attention.'

Argyle fans, glued to their radios in the days before the internet and Sky Sports News, were in fantasy land, but would have recoiled at Shilton's principal reason for choosing to kick off his managerial career in the south west. 'Potential,' the then forty-two-year-old asserted, instantly joining a group that included just about every Argyle manager in the club's history. Cowdery later summed up the inevitable eye-rolling reaction of the fans to Shilton's use of a word that had seduced, but ultimately tortured, most of his predecessors. 'Okay, the next contestant is Peter Shilton,' wrote Cowdery in the *Western Morning News* the day after Shilton's appointment. 'Peter, your task is to talk for a minute about managing Plymouth Argyle without mentioning the word 'potential'. Ready? Go…' "It's a First Division club with very good poten…." Beeeeeep! You can hardly blame him, though, Plymouth Argyle is a club with very good potential. Fans, though, are weary of being reminded of it.'

The holiday cottage in parochial Bigbury, just a few miles east of Plymouth, was another added attraction for Shilton, a man who had spent his entire career with some of the English game's more unfashionable clubs. 'I really love the area and it's an ideal place to start my managerial career,' he said. 'I like the image of the club and it's a tremendous challenge to be at a club with such huge crowd potential.' That word again.

The picture of Shilton posing with a green and white football was a ubiquitous presence on the back pages of the national media on Tuesday 3 March. The *Sun* even devoted a double-page spread to the news, under the headline 'I wanna be the next Cloughie'. 'I have thought about becoming a manager for some time,' Shilton told the *Sun*'s Brian Woolnough. 'The time is right now and I'm ready.'

England's record caps holder may have been kicking off his managerial career in sleepy Devonshire, but his sights were set stratospherically high. 'I aim to prove that Peter Shilton can be a good, no great, manager,' he said. 'My targets are high. One day I want to manage England.'

Inevitably, much of the focus was on the financial gamble Argyle's Board had taken in attracting one of the highest-paid sportsmen in the country. Shilton was thought to have been earning £3,000 a week at Derby, a £156,000 annual salary that a club with a four-figure average gate simply couldn't justify. The former England keeper signed a three-year contract with Argyle worth £2,000 a week (£104,000 a year), though the shortfall was compensated in other ways. A £125,000 signing-on fee was paid gross, and a 'PR payment' of £75,000 was to be spread over the course of the contract in lump sums of £25,000 each.

With Argyle's modest pedigree and deserted terraces, eyebrows were raised at the reported size of the financial package. Wrote Russell Thomas on the front page of the *Guardian*, 'Plymouth, it was thought, would not have the financial muscle to attract a major name in the game, yet have managed to find enough money to pay – as manager and player – a man who has been earning a reported £3,000 a week with Derby County.'

But for now, any talk of financial risks was to poop the party. Michael Foot, the club's most famous fan, spoke for them all when he said, 'This appointment will give the club a wonderful lift. He is a wonderful footballer and has given tremendous things to football already. Getting Argyle into the First Division [as it still was then] would be the greatest feat of all.'

Some of Shilton's peers and former team-mates were quick to pass on the benefit of their experience in management. The *Sun* described the clutch of former England players entering management as 'the magic circle', insisting the career transitions of Glenn Hoddle, Kevin Keegan, Gerry Francis, Trevor Francis, Peter Reid and Steve Coppell were a 'soccer revolution'. 'I find it exciting that a lot of new ideas are being pumped into the game,' said Hoddle, the future England boss then cutting his managerial teeth at Swindon Town. 'My advice to Peter is never listen to anyone who tries to tell you how to play the game or pick the team. They can sack you, but they can't tell you how to play the game. You have to be your own man, even when things go horribly wrong.'

Terry Butcher, recently handed the second of his four sackings in management, by Coventry City, believed Shilton's international record would stand him in good stead for a career in the dugout. 'Peter was probably the most professional player I ever met,' he said. 'And anyone who wins 125 caps for his country is bound to command respect.'

Lawrie McMenemy, the manager who signed Shilton for Southampton in 1982, emphasised Shilton's professional credentials. 'I have never been involved with a more dedicated professional,' said McMenemy, then Graham Taylor's assistant in the England set-up. 'He has always had his ideas on how things should work. Now he'll have the chance to put them into practice.'

Back at Home Park, Shilton's new squad were digesting the news with excitement and apprehension in equal measure. 'We had absolutely no clue it was Shilton until it actually happened,' says Martin Barlow. 'Your first reaction is one of excitement, but obviously a bit worried as well because he's going to come in, with the reputation he had, and want to bring in new players. You're wondering if you're going to fit in with the plans he had. It was mixed feelings really, I think everyone was thinking that.'

For one player in particular, Shilton's appointment had added significance. Rhys Wilmot's days as the club's number one goalkeeper were now numbered and, as a high-earner and saleable asset, his exit was inevitable. The news did not go down well with the Welshman. 'It was totally out of the blue,' says Wilmot of Shilton's arrival.

Even more so for me because obviously it was my position he was brought in to fill. The game at Ipswich on the Saturday had been quite emotional for me. We got beat 2–0, but the result wasn't really important because I broke Robbie Turner's leg in a collision. We didn't know at that stage that we were about to get a new manager, so I asked the club if I could go and see Robbie in hospital on the Monday – Robbie was a good mate of mine. I went to see him and I was obviously apologetic about what happened, but he said, 'Don't apologise, Rhys, have you seen Teletext?' I hadn't, and so he said, 'I might have a broken leg, but you're out of a job!' He turned the telly on and said, 'There you go, Peter Shilton's the new player-manager.' Typical football gallows humour, but I wasn't laughing.

For Adrian Burrows, a player who had spent his entire career under humble lower-league managers, it was new and exhilarating territory. 'When we heard the news, you could sense a real buzz around the club,' he says. 'Appointing such a big name was exciting for everybody – the fans and players. He brought an aura that you don't usually get outside the top flight, everybody looked up to him and respected his reputation before we even met him.'

The news wasn't so well received by everyone, however. Jock Morrison was still lamenting the loss of David Kemp, and Shilton's appointment brought mixed feelings for the big defender. 'Obviously he's a big name so there was excitement from that point of view,' he reflects. 'But it was tarnished a lot for me by the fact that Dave Kemp had left. I liked the bloke personally and as a manager too, and the feeling that you've let him down doesn't go away overnight.'

Snubbed managerial candidate Gordon Nisbet had worked with Shilton before and found the news difficult to take in. 'I was gobsmacked,' he says. 'Shilton had never managed before, he was a goalkeeper and he had no coaching badges. I had known him since I was fifteen or sixteen years old, when I was a schoolboy at Leicester City, and from what I had seen he took no interest in outfield players at all. As a person he was a smashing fella, but I just didn't see how it was going to work.'

The overall reaction, though, was overwhelmingly positive. For club captain Nicky Marker, the prospect of developing his talents under one of the most famous names in world football was a salivating one. 'I thought "great", there was a man who has achieved so much, who was the best goalkeeper in the world, no question about it. He'd played for England, played under Cloughie, won the European Cup twice, and he'd come down to Plymouth. I thought it was marvellous news. I thought I could really learn from him, that's all I wanted to do. I was looking forward to a new chapter for Plymouth Argyle and for my football career.'

Shilton had already made his first signing before the news of his arrival had even been made public – appointing his former Nottingham Forest team-mate John McGovern as his assistant manager. 'Peter had rung me up before telling me he was in the running for a job and would I be interested in being his number two,' McGovern recalls. 'I can't remember what club it was, but he didn't get it. When he got the Plymouth job he rang me up again and said, "Look, I've got the job. You said that you were interested before, how about it?" I was working for an aircraft services company at the time in Manchester. I had a fantastic boss and didn't really want to leave. But I went and discussed it with Peter anyway and eventually agreed to go down as his assistant. It was as simple as that. My good lady said I must have been crackers going back into football, because everyone knows how dangerous a manager's job is.'

With McGovern on board, the two double-European Cup winners arrived at the humble surroundings of Home Park and set up shop amid the crumbling paint and rusty stands. The juxtaposition wasn't lost on one Argyle director. 'Once all the razzmatazz and excitement of the appointment was over, we went out to the club,' says Ivor Jones. 'Peter wanted to see everyone, all the staff; from the players, the chief executive right down to the cleaners – he wanted everyone there. He walked round this little room talking to everyone about his plans... this charismatic character, he was quite something – he was like a Greek God. Even the way he spoke, the way he held himself, the way he conducted himself. It was quite outstanding how he was with people.'

Shilton may have made a favourable impression on the club's non-playing staff, but his first venture into the Home Park dressing room the following day was an ominous portent of things to come. Recalls Marker: 'We first met him properly the day after he was appointed. He came into the dressing room and he ... well, whether it was a Brian Clough tactic I don't know, but it was, "I'm Peter Shilton, you do what I say." Boom, just like that.'

'He said a few things that opened people's eyes a bit,' elaborates Morrison.

It seemed as though he thought he was coming to a backwater, country-bumpkin club. He was very much 'This is what I've done and what John McGovern has done, and you lot will never reach that.' I was sat there thinking, 'Hang on a second here, this bloke wants us to play for him but he's saying all the wrong things.' That was a bit of naïvety on his part. It was his first job and he was a bit headstrong coming in saying things like that. I'm sure he probably would have regretted it later on. He'd obviously wanted to make his mark but he did it in the wrong way. He probably wanted to take out parts of the managers that he had played for in his career, but a lot of the players thought he went about it the wrong way and he lost a lot of the dressing room before he even started.

For Wilmot, the experience was a particularly unsavoury one. 'I went into the dressing room, all the lads were there, and we were obviously getting ready to meet our new manager,' he remembers.

I sat in my normal place underneath the no. 1 peg, the first peg as you go in the door to your left. So we're all sat there and Shilton comes in and he stood in the middle of the dressing room, and I just knew he was looking for me. He was searching along the faces and eventually he came across me, he just pointed at me and said, 'Oh, don't worry Rhys, got a bit of a dodgy shoulder, you'll be okay for a few weeks.' I just didn't know where to look, nor did anybody else in that dressing room, it was so embarrassing. He then went on to talk about European Cup wins and stuff like that. He's talking to a bunch of lads who are struggling in the Second Division. We're scrapping to stay afloat and we need to stick together – we lose our manager and he comes in and talks about winning the European Cup. It wasn't relevant, and a lot of the lads just turned around and said, 'Shit, if he thinks we're players who are capable of winning the European Cup or are as good as the players he's played with then he's not looking at the right bunch of lads.' We were really struggling, so it didn't go down too well. After about five minutes of him telling his little story, John McGovern had to step in to explain to us what Shilton was trying to say.

If Shilton's introductory speech affronted the squad, his first act as manager exposed a surprisingly ruthless streak. 'We used to change at the ground for training,' says left-back Tony Spearing. 'All the first-team players changed in the home dressing room and all the kids changed in the away dressing room. So Shilton comes in and I'm put in the bottom end, the away dressing room. I was a really happy go lucky sort of bloke, so all that meant to me was that I was encouraged to show my worth. So I just got on with it.'

Not all of the ousted players were so accepting, however. 'When he came in he put quite a few of the pros in the away changing room,' says Barlow.

Basically we were like the leper squad, that was it – 'You lot down there, you ain't gonna play for me, that's it for you.' It was me, Robbie Turner, Steve Morgan, Paul Adcock, Tony Spearing and a few others. He probably hadn't even seen us play, but I think he just decided that we weren't going to fit into his style so he put us in with the apprentices. There was no explanation, nothing at all. So we all sort of looked at each other and said, 'We're on our way out then.' We respected him a lot, but a little bit of respect goes out the window when a legend like Shilton comes in, doesn't even talk to you and puts you straight in the away changing room. Basically we could do what we wanted in there.

Shilton's brutal dichotomy created widespread discontent, but Wilmot had the greatest cause to resent the arrival of the new commander-in-chief. 'The first thought that went through my mind when I heard about the new manager was that I was so annoyed with the chairman and the Board,' he says.

Just the month before, I had been talking to the chairman about a new contract to prolong my stay at Plymouth for another three years, because I was happy down there. I was one of the senior players and I was keeping my fingers crossed that one day I might even captain the team. But lo and behold it was all going on behind the scenes and I didn't know about it – and when I found out I was really, really upset. McCauley came right out with it though, just blurted it out: 'Whatever we get for you, we're going to pay Peter Shilton's wages with.' How callous can you be? How could they turn around and say whatever they sell me for, that's going to pay the first year's wages for the guy who's replacing me? And of course it got worse and worse as the weeks went on, because I put a transfer request in and they said they wouldn't let me go for peanuts.'

Wilmot's contract was due to expire that summer, and in the days before the Bosman Ruling, a club could retain a player on a rolling contract until a suitable bid was forthcoming. With transfer tribunals a common occurrence when two clubs failed to agree on a fee, Argyle set their stall out and slapped a value on Wilmot's head that was four times the amount they bought him for three years earlier. 'They were asking absolutely silly money for me,' Wilmot continues.

Even considering it was 1992 –£400,000 was a lot to ask for. But the contract offer they had made me was equivalent to the package I had signed to go to Plymouth in the first place. So I just laughed at them and told them they wouldn't get anything for me if a club decided to go to tribunal because the offer they made me was derisory. I told them, 'If a club decides to go to a tribunal for me, you're snookered.' They laughed at me, 'No, no, no, we'll sell you, Rhys. We'll get good money for you and we'll pay Peter Shilton's wages with it.' I had nothing in writing to say how much they valued me in terms of wages, only the same terms as I was on already, so they were going to have a hard time convincing a tribunal that I was worth four times what they paid for me.

One man who was expecting to join Wilmot in being jettisoned by the new regime was Gordon Nisbet. With rumours circulating of a former Nottingham Forest coaching 'dream team' being established at Home Park, many expected Shilton to clear the decks of all remnants of the Kemp era. They were wrong. 'John McGovern was brought in to work with the first team alongside Peter, but they decided to keep me and Alan [Gillett] around because they needed somebody to work with the youth team and the reserves,' says Nisbet. 'I more or less did a ball boy's job, though. I had no input whatsoever from that point on. Very little with the reserves either – even though I put match reports in, I had no input at all in terms of team selection.'

Unaware of their new big-name manager's slippery start behind closed doors, many of the club's stay-away fans were keen to witness the inception of the new regime in person, and the Home Park box office experienced a significant spike in ticket sales ahead of Shilton's debut match in charge, ironically against the club he left to join the Pilgrims – Derby County.

If the caretaker reign of Nisbet and Gillett had yielded an immediate change in playing style, Shilton was to take it a step further by enforcing his fantasy formation on his new charges. The rookie manager had told anyone who would listen in the days after his appointment that he had learned from the best in the business, and rapidly went about illustrating just that by deploying a system for his first match in charge that he had studied first-hand under several of his managers. Lawrie McMenemy had favoured a sweeper while at Southampton in the '80s, and Arthur Cox had occasionally deployed England international Mark Wright as sweeper in front of Shilton at Derby. But it was during Italia 90, when Bobby Robson reverted to five at the back against Holland, that Shilton became convinced. As he told *All Played Out* author Pete Davies while sitting beside a pool the day after the 0–0 draw against the Dutch, 'As far as I'm concerned, I think all First Division teams in England should play that way [the sweeper system] because it encourages players to think about the game, to make their own decisions,' he said. 'In England, this pushing up and playing in the middle third of the pitch – that's got to stop. It's not football. It's just tactical warfare, really – managers in England have got to open their eyes. The game is there to be played – it's not just picking up three points any old how, it's got to be played as entertainment. There's one or two managers in England who've got to get their blinkers off and realise their little world isn't the be-all and end-all of football.'

Shilton's bold new vision for English football got off to a respectable start in front of almost 9,000 star-struck Argyle fans eager to say 'I was there' when the Shilton revolution began on Saturday 7 March. Derby briefly threatened to rain on their former goalkeeper's parade when Paul Simpson gave them a seventeenth-minute lead, but stirred on by a performance of assiduous effervescence by transfer-listed midfielder Steve Morgan, the home side levelled through Jock Morrison eight minutes later and held on for a point against their high-flying visitors. The Home Park press box was creaking at the seams for Shilton's dugout debut, and goal-scorer Morrison believes the media circus actually gave the squad some much-needed breathing space. 'I just remember all the hype,' says Morrison.

> There was a lot of press there, loads of them. But with it being Shilts, it was all about him, which was a good thing as it took the pressure away from us lot. I scored the equaliser in that game with the outside of my right foot, I bent it into the right corner. It was brilliant for me. I just remember feeling afterwards that on the day I had made the right impression with the new manager.

The new director's opening matinee went down reasonably well with the paying public and attracted generally positive reviews, but any curtain calls would have to wait until the final act was over. Argyle remained deep in the relegation mire and still had to play four of the top six and the two sides immediately above and below them in the bottom three.

Despite Argyle scrapping for their lives, Shilton was adamant they wouldn't be resorting to desperate measures in the name of self-preservation. 'There is no way that I would ever, under any circumstances, revert to playing 'kick and rush' football because I simply don't believe in it,' said the manager ahead of the visit of Bristol City the Tuesday following the Derby match. 'I don't think it's the way to approach any situation, be it promotion or relegation, and it's certainly not the way to approach a short-term situation. At the end of the day, football is about passing the ball around and whether you're struggling or not, you'll get better results by passing the ball than you will by simply hoofing it around.'

With a bunch of players indoctrinated into the long-ball methods of David Kemp, it was perhaps no surprise that results didn't improve dramatically under their new purist scholar. Hot on the heels of the Derby draw came three 1–0 scorelines – with Argyle on the right end of two of them at home to Bristol City and Tranmere Rovers. But the third, to a distinctly ordinary Wolves side at Molineux, indicated the travel sickness that had plagued Argyle for several seasons required a more potent cure than a change in on-pitch aesthetics.

An acknowledgement that the new methods were not having quite the desired effect came when Shilton ditched the sweeper system after just three games. With the 26 March transfer deadline fast approaching, the management team looked elsewhere for a much-needed shot in the arm.

'I played for Leyton Orient against Torquay on the Saturday, and I got a phone call on the Monday morning to speak to Peter Shilton,' recalls striker Kevin Nugent, the first signing in Shilton's squad transformation. 'So I travelled down there and met with Shilton and John McGovern. They really sold the club to me and the deal was done pretty quickly really. Shilton being there had a big part to play in me signing, but it was a very good move for me anyway.'

Nugent signed for £200,000 on 23 March and walked straight into a dressing room not exactly united under the Shilton banner. 'When I came in, Shilton had to sort out quite a strong dressing room,' he says. 'There were a few players who were quite fond of the previous manager and Shilton had to get a handle on that quite early on.'

Nugent made his debut as a sixty-second-minute substitute in a 2–0 defeat at Derby – Argyle's second horn-locking with the Rams in just seventeen days – and it was abundantly clear that more recruits were desperately needed to halt an abysmal road trip record of five defeats on the trot.

Argyle fans couldn't have known, but the evening before the disappointing reverse at the Baseball Ground, Shilton and McGovern had taken in a reserve match that unearthed arguably the greatest pound-for-pound signing in the club's history.

In March 1992, Steve McCall was winding down an illustrious career at the top in Sheffield Wednesday's reserves. After great success with Ipswich Town, during which time he came up against Peter Shilton many times, McCall endured four injury-ravaged years at Hillsborough, making just thirty-six appearances. By the time Shilton and McGovern began searching for potential transfer targets, McCall was attempting to make yet another comeback from injury in Wednesday's second-string – which is where the Argyle management team found him on the evening of 23 March.

'I had mentioned to Peter that if he wanted a left-back, he should get Steve McCall,' says McGovern. 'I said, "He'll walk into this team." So we went to Sheffield to watch him play and Peter just said to me, "Does he play like that all that time?" He probably could have gone to a number of clubs, but we managed to grab him very quickly.'

'I played in the Wednesday reserves at Bradford on the Tuesday night, and when I got back in the dressing room after the game I was told of Peter Shilton's interest,' remembers McCall.

> So I met him and John McGovern there and then. We had a chat and they left me with a few things to think about. They were playing Derby the next day, on the Tuesday night, so I met them at their hotel for a chat there and agreed to sign that night. We did all the financial stuff and I signed the paperwork in the hotel before their game. I drove down to Plymouth on the Thursday before their away game at Port Vale on the Saturday. I didn't realise how far it was until I started travelling down – after three hours on the road I was thinking, 'Where the heck is this place?'

McCall may have thought he was on the road to nowhere, but he was signing for Argyle on the strength of Shilton's highway to heaven vision. 'I think that was the attraction, that Peter Shilton wanted me,' said the then thirty-one-year-old. 'He had good ideas for the team, he really seemed to know what he wanted... he wanted to bring in some new players who could play football, he wanted to change things, and obviously he wanted to stay up. I think if it hadn't been for Shilton and McGovern, then I probably wouldn't have signed for Plymouth.'

McCall played the vast majority of his Argyle career in a deep-lying midfield role, but believes it was his versatility that convinced the management to sign him. 'When they saw me at Bradford I was playing at left-back, so I just presumed that's what they wanted me for. Although I had played in midfield a lot, so it wasn't really a case of being tied down to left-back or wherever, it was a case of me being able to play in two or three positions. So that made me more attractive to them I suppose.'

Midfielder David Lee also signed on loan from Chelsea to make it three new additions to the Argyle squad inside a week. For McCall, the atmosphere in the dressing room reflected the on- and off-pitch upheavals of the last few months. 'It was a bit strange, because you had two or three of Shilton's new ones in there who had just come in, and there were a few experienced players who were being pushed out. There was a bit of a them-and-us feeling at that time. To be fair though, everyone was pulling together to try and get results.'

But results remained elusive away from Home Park, and it was business as usual when Argyle headed back up the A38, like a lorry-load of battery hens off to meet their maker, on the Saturday following Shilton's triple swoop. If any indication was needed that the manager's methods and his delivery of them were sticking in the throats of some of his players, it came at Vale Park on 28 March.

Rock-bottom Port Vale hadn't won in four months and had lost their last six matches at home – they were the divisional cannon fodder and a gift-wrapped opportunity for Argyle to secure their second away win of the season. As their under-siege manager John Rudge said ahead of Argyle's visit, 'We're getting increasingly desperate. We're running out of games and have to start winning, it's now or never.'

With Nugent making his full debut, and McCall and Lee appearing in Argyle shirts for the first time, a thirty-fourth-minute penalty from Ray Walker was enough to hand Vale their first win in seventeen matches and condemn Argyle to arguably their most depressing result of the season up to that point.

If things had been bad on the pitch, they got worse off it on the sombre journey back south. 'Shilton had given us a bollocking in the dressing room,' recalls Wilmot.

> We got back on the coach and we'd got about an hour into the trip when he comes up to the back. We're playing cards and having a couple of beers and he says, 'What do you think you're doing?' He starts digging into the younger ones. I remember Martin Barlow was laughing, and he said to him, 'What do you think you're laughing at?' He basically slaughtered us for what he saw as us having a good time after being beaten. So I went down to the front of the bus and said, 'What do you think you're doing? We've been beaten 1–0 and we've tried our socks off. If you're going to dig anybody out, dig out the senior players, not the youngsters. We've got a long journey back to Plymouth, what do you expect us to do? Sit there and sulk? Did you ever do that when you got beat?' He said, 'It's not appropriate you guys sitting back there laughing and having fun,' and I replied, 'We're not having fun, we're just trying to get over a defeat. We're having a game of cards, a couple of beers and we're trying to get back to Plymouth in one piece mentally.' But he wouldn't have it.

Wilmot would play just once more for Argyle, and couldn't have wished for a gloomier end to a Home Park career that had promised so much. With just eight matches remaining for Argyle to save their Second Division skins, a 2–1 home defeat to Grimsby Town, in which Wilmot made his final appearance in an Argyle shirt, left Shilton's men in twenty-second place and expensive new signing Nugent crocked for the crucial run-in.

'I broke my foot in the Port Vale game, without even realising,' he says. 'I did my warm-up ahead of the Grimsby match as normal, but as I was walking down the tunnel, down those big steps there, I heard a snap in my foot. That was it breaking. I played the game anyway, and it wasn't till afterwards that the pain really kicked in. I just got through it with all the adrenaline, but I was on crutches the next day.'

With Argyle having scored just twice in their last five matches, losing a striker who had netted seventeen times that season – albeit in the Third Division – was a cruel blow. McGovern issued a rallying cry of sorts to his goal-shy players ahead of the trip to promotion-chasing Charlton Athletic on 4 April. 'The lack of goals has been a major problem,' he said. 'The emphasis is on us. We've got to take the bull by the horns, be positive and say to ourselves that we're going to get forward and score goals.'

McGovern's call to arms failed to have the desired effect at Charlton, where Argyle drew their sixth goal-scoring blank in six successive away games – though they did at least manage a clean sheet for the first match in four. The headlines went to the player-manager, who finally lived up to his full job title by donning the gloves in Argyle's cause for the first time – leaving Wilmot to see out the season in the reserves.

'I played the first seven games of his reign under the umbrella of his injured shoulder,' says the former Arsenal keeper.

> Though I wasn't that keen to play, considering. I can remember playing quite well during that run, even though we were struggling. On the Thursday before the Charlton game, he put his arm around me as we walked back from Harpers Park after training and he said, 'Rhys, you're not playing on Saturday, I'm going to get in there and kick some ass.' I went, 'Fine, ok.' To be fair to him, he did also say, 'Look, you only have to play a couple of reserve games to keep yourself fit between now and the end of the season.' By that he was obviously telling me I wasn't going to play again. He told me to work hard in training, but I would have done that anyway because I had too much respect for my colleagues not to.

The commendable point at Charlton – in which 'Super Shilts' was 'Argyle's inspiration' according to the *Sunday Independent* – preceded a 2–0 home defeat to Southend United that left the Pilgrims propping up the table with five games left. The first of those, a trip to FA Cup finalists Sunderland, yielded an unexpected three points thanks to Dwight Marshall's first goal in five weeks. The club's first ever win at Roker Park was followed by another north-east escapade just two days later – this time to meet third-placed Middlesbrough. The 2–1 defeat – with Marshall again finding the target – was kept respectable by an outstanding display from Argyle's forty-two-year-old goalkeeper.

Shilton's side recovered from their northern sojourn to outclass Oxford United 3–1 in their penultimate home match of the season – a performance and a result that seemed to convince all and sundry that Argyle's relegation battle had just been one big practical joke. The Lyndhurst belted out a rendition of 'The Greens are staying up' after David Lee made the points safe with the third goal after fifty-one minutes, and even the media was getting in on the act. 'Argyle on course for safe waters' was the match report headline in the *Western Morning News* the following Monday morning.

A win at Swindon Town a week after Oxford would have made Argyle's Second Division status a formality going into the final match of the season at home to Blackburn Rovers, but a twenty-sixth-minute header from Plymouth-born Shaun Taylor put paid to any hopes of a relaxing week for the Argyle squad and their manager.

Thus the scenario was painfully clear: beat Blackburn and survive; draw or lose and Argyle's fate would be in the hands of their relegation rivals: Newcastle, Oxford, Brighton and Port Vale.

Assistant manager John McGovern was pinning his hopes on a Hollywood-style happy ending for his side, who would be coming up against a Blackburn squad pumped full of Jack Walker's cash. 'We don't want to get this match out of proportion,' said McGovern. 'Yes, they have got some very good players, but we've got to go out and give it our best shot, just like the *Rocky* films.'

Blackburn, on the back of a terrible run of one win in nine matches, had at one stage so dominated the division that bookmakers had stopped taking bets on them winning the league. But they journeyed to Home Park needing nothing less than a victory to guarantee a play-off place, a scenario that Argyle really could have done without. 'Both Plymouth and ourselves have a big carrot dangling in front of us for very different reasons,' remarked Rovers boss Kenny Dalglish.

A five-year high attendance of 17,459 packed into Home Park on Saturday 2 May 1992, clogging the antiquated turnstiles and delaying kick-off until 3.16 p.m. Three-quarters of an hour later, Argyle looked to be heading into the half-time break a goal to the good thanks to David Smith's twelfth-minute shot that squirmed under Bobby Mimms. But with much of the crowd filtering away from the terraces for their pasties and Bovrils, David Speedie turned the game and the season on its head with two clinical strikes that gave Blackburn an unlikely 2–1 half-time lead.

With Argyle's match kicking off late and further delayed by first-half injuries to visiting players, by the time Speedie made it 3–1 in the sixty-seventh minute, Oxford had beaten Tranmere and Shilton's side needed to score three times in twenty-three minutes to avoid the icy touch of the Grim Reaper: Relegation Branch. They failed, and Plymouth Argyle's days in the Second Division sun were over; it was time to pack up the suitcase and head back into the all-too familiar arms of the Third Division.

Some fans wept, others ran onto the pitch to commiserate with their fallen heroes. But back in the dressing room, captain Nicky Marker was desperately seeking confirmation of his team's fate. 'I went back to the changing room after the game and asked one of the young lads how Oxford had got on,' he says. 'He didn't know so I sent him off to find out the score. Just as the kid was leaving, Shilton came in and said, "We don't care about other results, we've just lost a game of football." I said, "I know, but if Oxford lost then we stay up." It was a complete shock to him. He went, "Oh Christ," and sent the kid off to find out the result.'

New boy Kevin Nugent had made an unexpectedly rapid recovery from his broken foot and had been sent into the fray after an hour against Blackburn.

'I wasn't really fit but I wanted to get out on the pitch,' he says. 'I came on but unfortunately it didn't really work out.'

Nugent felt Shilton's task had been a formidable one – despite the fact that the club were outside the bottom three when David Kemp was sacked. 'They were fighting relegation there anyway before I joined, that's why the previous manager had left the club, but it would have been a difficult job for anyone to have come in and kept the club up with the position they were in. And it did go down to the last game, but it wasn't quite enough.'

Steve McCall lamented the side's inability to score goals, with only Dwight Marshall ending the season in double figures. 'When I arrived at the club, I thought there was a big chance we'd turn it round,' he reflects.

> But we just failed to do so. The Blackburn game summed us up – we played very well in that game, created a few chances and yet were caught three times. We probably outplayed them on the day and yet they scored the goals and we go down and they go up [as they ultimately did through the play-offs]. But you've got to take your chances and, in the seven or eight games I was there, we didn't do that. At times we would play teams off the park, but we didn't get the goals that our play deserved and that's what costs you. It's a fine line between staying up and going down.

But Jock Morrison believes a terminal rot had set in towards season's end. 'It was Shilton's first job and you could tell it was,' says Morrison.

> We had been fighting and scrapping all the way, but the changing room had gone a bit – the players that were there when Shilton came in probably needed a fresh start. It was a lot of Dave Kemp's players – people who felt loyal to him. Whether it was the players, tactics, whatever, it just didn't work. Kemp would definitely have kept us up that season if he'd stayed, without a shadow of a doubt. Where we would have gone after that I don't know, but we would have stayed up and Kemp would have had one of the largest amounts of money ever spent at the club at his disposal.

Thanks to Argyle's meek surrender, Blackburn edged into the Second Division play-offs where they overcame Derby and Leicester to take their seats on the gravy train just as it was leaving for the brand new, all singing, all dancing Premier League.

Shilton and his men, meanwhile, were unceremoniously bundled into the back of a coal truck that was reversing into obscurity.

Chapter Three

THE CAVALRY ARRIVES

The advent of the Premier League in the summer of 1992 meant that Argyle hadn't actually been relegated at all – in name anyway. The Barclays League Division Two that had just cashed in Argyle's chips and sent them on their way was renamed the Endsleigh League Division One – meaning they found themselves immediately back in Division Two again.

But on the basis that a rose by any other name would smell as sweet [or not quite so sweet in Argyle's case], Peter Shilton couldn't get away from the fact that he would be plying his trade in the third tier of English football for the first time in his twenty-six-year career. 'I've never played in the Third Division and I wouldn't like to do it by choice,' said the player-manager in the summer of 1992. 'The incentive is that, as manager, I have extra responsibilities. I'm trying to build a team here.'

Shilton's squad reconstruction project actually began in earnest several days before his side's Home Park D-Day against Blackburn, when he transfer-listed expensive failure Dave Regis and left-back Tony Spearing, and granted free transfers to goalkeeper Steve Morris, defenders Andy Clement, Danis Salman and future physiotherapist Paul Maxwell, midfielder Mark Quamina and striker Morrys Scott. With Dutch defender Eric van Rossum released from his loan arrangement and Rhys Wilmot and Steve Morgan already on the transfer list, Shilton could have fielded an entire side of rejects and cast-offs.

After relegation had been confirmed, home brews Jock Morrison and Martin Barlow were also publicly announced to have been granted transfer requests, though Barlow insists his transfer 'request' was more a transfer 'order'. 'Shilton wanted to get rid of me,' he says. 'Someone actually came in for me, but nothing materialised from that. Dan McCauley was pretty fair with me in those days and he wanted to keep me, so he stuck up for me quite a bit and I ended up staying.'

Another player walking the plank with a cutlass tip in his back was captain Nicky Marker – at that time the Argyle player with the highest appreciable value. 'From the day Shilton came in, me and him never really saw eye to eye,' reflects Marker.

He wanted to get rid of me from day one. He tried to send me on loan to Aston Villa in pre-season, but I told him I wasn't going out on trial for a month in pre-season. I was twenty-seven at the time, and if they didn't know what I was like by then they weren't going to after a month. If a team wanted me they'd come in and buy me. The Monday after we got relegated, I went into his office with a letter, a pay rise from the chairman that had been agreed before Shilton had come in. He thought it was a transfer request and his eyes lit up. But as soon as he saw it was a pay rise letter, he called John McGovern in, 'John, John, John! Look at this!' he said. And McGovern pointed out that it was a pay rise signed by the chairman and that there was nothing they could do about it.

With Shilton trying to prune his squad with one hand, he was busy cultivating it with the other. Warren Joyce became the first signing of the close season when he made the switch from Preston North End just eleven days after the season's end. McGovern had handed the industrious midfielder his professional debut at the age of seventeen during his spell as Bolton manager, and had obviously given Shilton a convincing assessment of the twenty-seven-year-old's qualities. 'He's just the type of player we've been looking for,' said the manager, after posing on the Home Park pitch with his arm around his new signing. 'He has a tremendous work-rate, marks very well, defends very well, puts his foot in and likes to get forward whenever he can.'

With Shilton casting his net far and wide, thanks to the eyes and ears of a Leicester-based scout named David Coates, next through the Home Park revolving door was a player who gave up a potential career with Manchester United due to a hankering for home. 'I left school and wasn't really interested in football, I didn't join any teams after I left,' remembers winger Paul Dalton of his near loss to the game. 'But then one of my mates asked me to play for this non-league club called Brandon United against Hartlepool. I played and did quite well and they asked me to sign on. My career went up and up from there really.'

'Up and up' is something of an understatement when describing the first and, to date, only transfer of a player between the Uniteds of Brandon and Manchester. 'I signed a two-year contract with United in 1986,' he remembers.

I did quite well in my first year. I went on tour with them to Sweden and Norway one summer, and I was in the squad against Middlesbrough for a first-team match. But shortly after that I started getting a bit homesick, this was about thirteen or fourteen months into my time there. So I went to see Alex Ferguson to ask if I could cancel my contract. He wasn't keen on doing that, but he did say he'd put the word out to the north-east clubs to say that I was looking to move back home.'

Hartlepool United welcomed Dalton back into the comforting bosom of his beloved north-east, and the Middlesbrough lad repaid the favour by giving three years' sterling service in the shirt of his third United. In his final year at the Victoria Ground, Dalton reached double figures and caught the eye of David Coates – and subsequently Shilton. 'The Hartlepool chairman came up to me one day after the season ended and said that Plymouth were interested,' recalls Dalton.

My initial reaction was, 'Where's Plymouth?' I knew it was down south, but the first thing I did was to go and look at a map. My initial thought was that I'd left Man United due to being homesick, so how would I be able to settle all the way down there? But the Hartlepool chairman was – I wouldn't quite say forcing my hand – but he strongly felt that I'd be stupid not to speak to them. So we arranged to meet Plymouth's representatives in a hotel in Derby. There was Shilton, Dan McCauley, myself and the chairman and vice-chairman from Hartlepool. I was telling the chairman on the way down that I wasn't going to sign, I just wanted to listen to what they had to say. I wanted to come away from the meeting, have a think about it and take it from there. So we got to the hotel, met Shilton, listened to what he had to say and basically I was just blown away and signed there and then. As a winger, his philosophy of attacking style of football and the players that he had signed and was going to sign sounded ideal to me. The money was substantially better than it was at Hartlepool too.

Dalton officially became an Argyle player on 1 June 1993 for a club record £250,000 – with young full-back Ryan Cross going the opposite way as a make-weight in the deal. Any fears the twenty-five-year-old had about not settling in the Westcountry were quickly dispelled. 'It was just so friendly there,' he reflects. 'Down in Plymouth people are so laid back. They just take things as they come along, so it wasn't such a big shock for me. Everybody at the club was fantastic, they all made me feel so welcome and I found it easy to settle.'

The ink was barely dry on Dalton's eye-catching signature when another brick in Shilton's renovation project was cemented into place. The day after Dalton completed his move south, Steve Castle became the third prominent lower-league talent to take the tasty bait on the end of Shilton's fishing line.

A Leyton Orient stalwart of almost ten years, twenty-six-year-old Castle had reached double figures from central midfield in each of the past three seasons, but had almost given up hope of moving up the league ladder. 'I watched Kevin Nugent leave the season before on deadline day, and I didn't think I'd ever get the chance to move on,' he says.

I was supposed to go to Wimbledon three years previously, but it fell through because I didn't pass the medical – which was just farcical really. So I carried on doing reasonably well for Orient, scoring plenty of goals, and I'd heard on the grapevine that there were a few opportunities... Liverpool, Newcastle and West Ham were supposedly interested, but nothing ever happened. I was on a three-year contract and had just seen that third year out, which I always did, rightly or wrongly. I just had it in my mind that I needed a fresh challenge that summer. It would have been quite easy to stay – it was local and I had lots of friends round there. But moving away was probably the making of me.

Director Dennis Angilley was frequently involved in transfer negotiations with Shilton, and recalls the protracted talks with Orient over the signing of Castle. 'Peter drove up to Leyton Orient to see him and he left at half-time,' he says. 'He rang me on the way back and he said "We've just got to buy him." He said he was going to be the Bryan Robson of the lower leagues. We subsequently made Leyton Orient offers that they rejected and rejected. We ended up having to go to tribunal. Peter was there with me and we were told to pay £195k for him, which was a great result.'

With permission to talk to the player secured, Angilley met Castle and his agent to discuss personal terms. 'We met in the Holiday Inn for the negotiations,' he recalls. 'Castle's agent was making any number of demands that we were not prepared to meet. We started at about seven o'clock and were still there when it was almost midnight. In the end I said, "Tell me Steve, why do you want to come to Plymouth Argyle anyway?" And he replied, "Because I want to play for Mr Shilton." I think otherwise he might have been persuaded that the club was being too tight with him.'

Once again, a new signing was citing the manager as the key reason for his decision to sign. 'Peter Shilton sold me the club,' Castle reflects. 'Mind you, I was impressed anyway... the fanbase, the surroundings, everything about the club was great. It was a league higher than Orient with good players and it looked very good for the future.'

Argyle fans would have shared Castle's optimism for the unusually big-spending Pilgrims, though were given a reminder of the parsimonious days of the Kemp/Bloom era when the next man through the door arrived on a free transfer.

Similarities between Kemp's freebie signings and Shilton's latest acquisition, however, began and ended with the lack of a transfer fee; Barnet full-back Gary Poole was a man very much in demand. Premier League clubs Coventry City and Southampton had both been tracking the former Tottenham right-back, who had made national headlines by being the player at the centre of a row between Barnet's colourful boss Barry Fry and the London club's controversial chairman, Stan Flashman. Poole had bizarrely been granted a free transfer by Flashman after failing to agree an extension to his contract, leaving Fry spluttering to the media in total disbelief. 'It's a ridiculous situation, absolutely idiotic,' he said. 'Normally I would want at least £250,000 for him. I'm absolutely gutted, it's getting beyond a joke.'

Shilton and the club's fans certainly saw the funny side, though, as Poole walked out on Barnet and waltzed straight into Home Park for absolutely nothing – thanks to a tip-off from the ever-alert Coates.

The quartet of new signings was a conveniently timed boon for the Home Park ticket office. The deadline for the club's cut-price season-ticket offer fell just three days after Poole followed Joyce, Dalton and Castle through the door, and unusually brisk sales were reported over the weekend of 6 June. Fans choosing to view their season's football from the Spion Kop terrace could do so for a modest £70 – little more than three quid a game. And despite relegation, sales eventually eclipsed those of the previous season – illustrating the faith fans were placing in their superstar manager and his big-money acquisitions.

However, despite Shilton's useful status as a player magnet, McGovern insists the club probably paid over the odds to assemble their new-look side. 'We found out that to attract players to come down to Plymouth, you've got to pay a little bit over the odds in terms of wages and transfer fees,' he says. 'Being a little bit of an outpost as it is all the way down there in the South-west, you have to do that. You have to entice players and pay them perhaps a little bit more than other clubs would. So that's the difficulty of managing at Plymouth.'

On the day that Poole signed for Argyle, the Football League held its annual meeting – with the future of the seventy clubs [as there were then] in the new era of the Premier League very much on the table. 'Our mood is not one of despair or dismay that the First Division clubs have left to form the Premier League,' said League president Gordon McKeag. 'I would relish the prospect on a Sunday when there may be an unattractive Premier League game televised to a handful of people on satellite – and we can offer an attractive match between two of our bigger clubs.'

At the same meeting, Jimmy Hill's proposal to award five points to a team winning by more than three clear goals and four to a team winning by three clear goals was considered but thrown out. The forthcoming season was to see the introduction of the backpass law and presumably one radical change to the laws was plenty enough for the chairmen of the Football League.

Back at Home Park, Shilton was under pressure to plug the gap in the club's budget by moving out some of the bodies on his lengthy unwanted list – starting with the unfortunate Wilmot.

Watford were the first club linked with the Welsh keeper that summer. The Hornets had recently sold twenty-two-year-old David James to Liverpool, but manager Steve Perryman balked at Argyle's £300,000 valuation – a reduction of some £100,000 on the club's original asking price. 'The two main clubs in the frame were Stoke and Notts County at the time,' remembers Wilmot. 'I spoke to Lou Macari at Stoke and Neil Warnock at Notts County, but nothing came of either of those. But then Grimsby manager Alan Buckley got in touch, so I went up there and he sold me the club and we also talked money. They offered me a great package to go there.'

First Division Grimsby's balance sheet had just been bolstered by the £650,000 sale of club skipper Shaun Cunnington to Sunderland, but Buckley preferred to take his chances with the lottery of a tribunal. 'Grimsby said to me,

"Okay, we'll go to tribunal for you, Rhys, but whatever we need to pay for you we'll pay." And I said, "Well, you won't have to pay a thing – we'll go to tribunal and I'll become a free transfer. Once all the paperwork is presented, they won't get a penny for me." But the Grimsby chairman told me they'd pay £400,000 if it came to it, which was nice to know.'

In the end, the tribunal settled on a figure of £87,500, an amount that infuriated Argyle and provided sweet justice for Wilmot.

> The tribunal told me I should have been a free transfer, but they recognised the fact that the first contract offer a club puts in is almost always the same amount as the old one. They knew Argyle would have improved that offer, but events took over with them appointing the new manager. I told them that wasn't my problem, they hadn't offered me an improved contract and had shown no willingness to keep me even before Shilton came along. They did tear a strip off the administration at Argyle, though. They told them they couldn't do business like that and risk losing players by trying to keep them for next to nothing in contract negotiations.

The rebuke from the Independent Tribunal stung Argyle far less than their valuation. Winger David Smith had been shipped out to Notts County for £150,000, but with a hole in the anticipated budget of more than £200,000, Shilton's spending plans lay in tatters. 'The valuation was pathetic,' said a stunned McCauley. 'It was a paltry, insignificant sum and I thought it was an insult to Rhys Wilmot. We have now got to cover the amount involved ourselves. If we'd got anything like the amount we wanted, we would have been left with some flexibility in the transfer market. It's a disappointing situation to be in because we want to push the club forward.'

Shilton, all too aware of the implications of Wilmot's fee on his team rebuilding plans, was shellshocked. 'I just couldn't believe it when the fee of £87,500 was announced at the end of the hearing. I thought I had misheard it and that they had left a figure 'two' off it.'

The manager's nightmare week continued when the club's most expensive signing to date suffered an irritatingly needless injury in a pre-season practice match just three weeks before the start of the season. 'It was a bit of a freak injury,' says Dalton of his broken leg.

> We'd finished training and we were having a practice match. It was coming towards the end and Peter Shilton said we'd do another ten minutes. It was in those ten minutes that I fractured my left fibula. I just remember trying to flick the ball around Marc Edworthy and I think my studs got stuck into the ground and my weight went onto the leg. When I stood up I was in quite a lot of pain. It was something that could have been avoided, it was only a practice match. It was stupid of me to put myself in that situation when I should have just let it go, I didn't really have to impress anybody. It was probably just over-eagerness.

Shilton was philosophical about losing his most exciting player for a lengthy spell [which turned out to be two months]. 'That's football,' he said. 'It's better for it to happen now than later in the season.'

With the Board's kitty decimated by the Wilmot verdict, Shilton was forced to downgrade his targets and take a chance on a pair of Scousers – a naïve young goalkeeper and a non-league striker with a family history in comedy.

With Wilmot gone and Steve Morris sent on his way, Shilton was the club's only senior goalkeeper. So it was that he contacted another top-flight goalkeeping legend in his search for a cheap but able deputy. 'I was training with Everton at the time but didn't have a contract, and Neville Southall had recommended me to Shilton,' remembers Ray Newland.

So he invited me down on trial and I obviously did enough to get a pro contract. You can imagine how I felt – I was a twenty-year-old kid being signed by the most successful goalkeeper England had ever had. It was surreal, it was a dream; I couldn't have signed for anybody better. I remember driving home after signing and I couldn't wait to tell my dad – but there weren't really any mobile phones back then so I had to wait. I just kept saying to myself, 'I'm a professional footballer.' I must have said it 400 times on the journey back. Anyone driving past must have thought I was a lunatic. I probably got back to Liverpool in about forty-five minutes!

The other freebie arrival was Paul Boardman, son of comedian Stan. Unlike Newland, Boardman had taken a rather more circuitous route into professional football. 'I was in America on a soccer scholarship for four years, and I came back for six months to find myself a club,' he recalls.

I had a trial at Liverpool for a month and did pretty well. I thought I had a good chance of being signed, but they said because they had a couple of young lads coming through, some blokes called Michael Owen and Robbie Fowler, and because I was a bit old at twenty-two, they wouldn't be signing me. They said they'd recommend me to another club, so I went to Wrexham. I stayed there until the end of the season and played a few games for them. I also played for Knowsley United in the Northern Premier League, though I soon had enough of getting kicked from pillar to post and sick of travelling on a bus that wouldn't go more than 40mph. One day, I got a call from a scout in the Manchester area who knew John McGovern. He said he had watched me play and that McGovern wanted me to go down to Plymouth for a trial. I actually said no initially – I wasn't a young lad any more, I'd had a couple of knockbacks and didn't think my heart was in it any more. I was getting flashbacks to how happy I was in America, sitting on the beach in the sun and I was thinking of going back over there. But a few hours after that phone call from the scout, John McGovern himself called me. I obviously knew who John was from his Forest days, so when he called me

I was really flattered. He said, 'Look, just come down and play, you'll enjoy it and you've got nothing to lose.' So I went and played in a reserve game at Hereford and I really, really enjoyed it. Because I'd been playing in the Northern Premier League with no football, suddenly I came to a professional club and everything was played into my feet, I was getting great service on a nice pitch.'

Boardman made his second appearance for Argyle reserves at Cardiff the following week and netted a hat-trick. With a favourable report landing on Shilton's desk, Boardman was invited down to Plymouth for the manager himself to make a judgement.

'I'd never been to Plymouth before, but I always thought it was about 30 miles past Bristol,' says Boardman.

So I set off in my little Rover 1.6 and got to Bristol by about noon. Now kick-off was at 3 p.m., so I was thinking, 'Great, I'll be there in half-an-hour.' So I'm driving and driving and driving, and then I see a sign saying 'Plymouth 58', and I just about made it for kick-off! So I played against Torquay, did well and they signed me on a one-year contract. It was just a dream come true for me. It was amazing. I remember seeing pictures of Shilton on the TV when he got the Plymouth job, and never dreamed for a second that I'd be down there just a few months later playing for him.

With nine players having been jettisoned from the Good Ship Pilgrim and six newly-hired deckhands coming on board, Shilton and McGovern had much work to do if their new-look side was to hit the ground running at Mansfield Town on 15 August.

Taking a leaf out of Brian Clough's considerable management bible, Shilton insisted on keeping his charges away from the critical eyes of the Home Park crowd for his pre-season friendly program – with Kevin Hodges' testimonial at home to Luton Town the only opportunity his new signings would get to taste the Home Park experience before proper business began. 'I just don't think it's a good idea playing in front of our home supporters while we are still getting fit and making mistakes from the start of pre-season,' explained the manager. 'Hopefully we can get our fitness right and any bad results out of the way before we turn out for the first time at home.'

With away games at Tiverton, Bodmin, Bath City, Cheltenham Town, Hereford United and Cardiff City, Shilton's side had ample opportunity to make mistakes and suffer the odd bad result – an opportunity they didn't pass up. A 1–0 victory at Tiverton on 25 July was to be the only win of what turned out to be a nightmare pre-season campaign for Shilton.

An uncomfortable atmosphere in the dressing room – created by Shilton's heavy-handed arrival at the club back in March – came to a head at Bodmin Town on 27 July, when the manager was involved in an embarrassing showdown with one of the players he had 'relegated' to the kids' dressing room at Home Park.

'It was a real us and them situation,' says Spearing. 'He had his players, the ones he had brought in, and the ones from the Kempy days he just pushed to one side. He put me in the reserves and I really wanted to show him that I was okay for the first team,' Spearing continues.

The reserves were playing away at Bodmin, and he played me in centre-midfield. I'd never played there in my life, I was an out-and-out full-back. So I'm playing centre-mid and the first half was a little bit rough, so I decided I was going to show the boss what I was all about. I was a kicker, that's how I earnt my living, so I started booting everything that moved. I was really competing – I wanted the gaffer to look at me and say, 'This boy means it.' The next thing one of our young kids gets hurt, so I went in and had a little bit of revenge on the lad who hurt him. Before I know it, it's all kicking off. Next thing, I hear John McGovern shouting for me to come off, this is twenty minutes into the game. I blanked him completely and just stood there in the middle of the pitch. 'Tony, you're off! Come off, come off!' he was shouting. One of the lads says to me, 'Tone, you're off,' and I said, 'I'm not fucking going off, bollocks to that.' Then I hear Shilton shouting at me, 'Spearo, come off or you're fined,' so I looked over after about two minutes of them shouting at me, and that's a long time to stand your ground, and said, 'What, me?' So I come off and as I went past him he said, 'You're a disgrace,' or something like that.

With spectators watching on in bemusement as England's record caps holder engaged in a war of words with a lower-league slogger, Shilton waited until half-time to really tear a strip off the transfer-listed full-back. 'I'm in the shower when they all come in at half-time,' says Spearing. 'I'm singing at the top of my voice and trying to hide my old boy when he comes in – and we have a blazing row right there in the shower. He said to me, "You'll never play for this club again." I can just remember saying, "That's alright, I don't want to." I went out there to show my true colours, but he was trying to play football in the right manner and I wasn't like that, I was a fighter.'

Just four days later, Shilton was once more involved in a bust-up against the backdrop of another friendly. The narrow victory at Tiverton had been followed by a goalless draw at Bath City, and a hapless display in a 1-0 defeat to Cheltenham – then one league below the GM Vauxhall Conference – lit the chairman's notoriously short fuse. 'Me and the manager fell out as early as the game at Cheltenham, the friendly we lost,' says McCauley. 'Our relationship was ruffled because he spent all that money and we went to Cheltenham and lost. I said to him, "It amazes me that you've spent all this money and you lose at a non-league club." When you're under money pressure you need results. We had many more rows after that, but it started at Cheltenham.'

Shilton suffered another blow a week later when Steve Castle limped out of the 2–2 draw at Hereford with a knee injury that would keep him out for more than two months. 'I did my medial knee ligaments,' says Castle. 'Paul Dalton had recently broken his leg and we both missed the start of the season – so there was a lot of money on the treatment table. It was frustrating for me and equally frustrating for the manager I'd imagine.'

Argyle had been installed as third favourites with the bookies to bounce back to the second tier at the first attempt, but a dozen games into the season it was painfully evident that Shilton and McGovern's revolution was destined to be a slow-burner.

It had all looked so rosy at ten to five on Saturday 22 August. Argyle had followed up a respectable 0–0 draw at Mansfield on the opening day with a 3–0 whitewashing of Bradford City at Home Park, a performance that seemed to justify the bookmakers' confidence in them.

Craig Skinner, a twenty-one-year-old winger signed from Blackburn on a month's loan, made an impressive debut against the Bantams after being told he wasn't going to trouble the first team at Ewood Park. 'Blackburn had offered me a contract,' he remembers. 'But it was looking more and more like I was going to have to move elsewhere for first-team football. So I went to Plymouth initially on a month's loan. People have reservations because Plymouth is so far away, but if footballers are happy somewhere and playing then that's the only thing that matters. The second game of the season we played Bradford – I scored on my debut and we hammered them 3–0, we were just all over them. I think we were near the top of the table and things were looking really good.'

Cocksure Argyle went to Hull City the following Saturday with a spring in their step, but were brought crashing back down to Earth in unexpected circumstances.

Peter Shilton had sailed through 1,335 competitive games over the space of twenty-six years with just two yellow cards against his name (both for illegally marking the pitch), but the new backpass law was to blemish his near-perfect record at Boothferry Park. After twenty-six minutes, and with the game goalless, Shilton was given a dribbler of a backpass by the 'Beast of Bodmin', Tony Spearing, and was forced to bring down Hull's Graeme Atkinson, who had burst clean through.

'I got him sent off. Fantastic that was,' reflects Spearing. 'What a claim to fame that is, the man who got Shilton sent off – that's a pub quiz question. I mis-hit a backpass to him, and the fella's gone around Shilton and he's brought him down, sent straight off. As he's run past me, he's gone, "Thanks very fucking much." And he's absolutely slaughtered me at half-time, caned me completely.'

The sending-off made national news, and left Shilton hankering for the good old days. 'They don't make things any easier for goalkeepers these days,' he said. 'There's the four-step rule, the four-second rule, the professional foul and now the backpass rule. It's a lot harder than when I started out.'

The *Plymouth Evening Herald* touched a nerve with their 'Blunder Boss' headline the day after the Friday night game. 'Shilton actually phoned us up and had a go at us about that one,' remembers *Herald* sports reporter, Mark

'I think it was Peter Shilton's idea to protect his expensive signings ....'

Halliwell. 'He said, "Why have you put Blunder Boss as the headline? I didn't make a blunder, I didn't make a mistake." And Kevin Marriott, my sports editor, explained to him that he did actually make a mistake because he brought Atkinson down and got sent off.'

With Dalton and Castle still out, Shilton thought he had lost another important first-team player for a lengthy period when Jock Morrison took a knock against Bradford that was initially diagnosed as a broken leg. Alan Walker, a thirty-two-year-old centre-back recently released by Gillingham, was drafted in on a one-month contract to cover Morrison's absence. Says Walker, 'I'd literally just got down there and was sat discussing the way the team played, when Jock walks into the manager's office and said he'd had the all-clear from the specialist and his leg wasn't actually broken.'

With Morrison returning far sooner than anticipated, Walker only managed two appearances for the Pilgrims – against Leyton Orient and Stoke – before signing permanently for Mansfield, but left Home Park convinced that Shilton and Argyle were going places. 'I scored the equaliser at home to Stoke, and there was a picture of me in one of the local papers and I'm about ten feet off the ground,' says Walker. 'It meant an awful lot to me. I really wanted it to work at Plymouth. I wanted to be a part of it because I really thought they had a chance of doing something special. I thought Shilton was going to go on to bigger and better things. They paid a lot of money for certain players and it looked very, very strong.'

Meanwhile, the relationship between manager and club captain was at an all-time low, and it was sweet relief for both parties when Nicky Marker was catapulted straight into the Premier League with Blackburn Rovers on 21 September.

'I knew the situation, I knew Shilton wanted to get rid of me to get some money in,' recalls Marker. 'But in one way it was sort of like, "Unlucky, I'm still here." I don't know exactly what it was, but we just didn't see eye-to-eye and he didn't have the guts to drop me. He knew that if he didn't play me, the crowd would be on his back because I was one of the better players at the club. He had to play me and he didn't like that. I always went out and gave 100 per cent, though. I was still Plymouth Argyle through and through.'

When Shilton contacted his Blackburn counterpart Kenny Dalglish to request an extension to the loan period of Craig Skinner, Dalglish upped the ante and negotiations over the transfer of Marker began. 'Shilton told me to stay by my phone for news of a move, but Kevin Hodges had a boat trip for his testimonial and I didn't want to sit at home so I went out and supported his function,' says Marker.

I went into training on Monday and nothing had happened. I was waiting around to hear what was going on; one minute it was happening and the next it wasn't. I didn't agree a deal until near enough midnight on the Monday night. It was my chance to play at the top, that's all I wanted to do. Once the opportunity came for me to go and play in the Premier League I jumped at it, I wasn't going to stay down there. But I had to bide my time, I wasn't going to be driven out of the club by someone like that. Other managers you would give 100 per cent for, but with him I just didn't care. I was pleased to get out in the end. I was very, very disappointed with him.

A £500,000 deal saw Marker leave for Lancashire and Skinner, Rovers defender Keith Hill and £250,000 head in the opposite direction.

For Hill, a twenty-three-year-old centre-back with more than 100 appearances for Rovers, the move came completely out of the blue. 'I spoke to Kenny Dalglish about it on the Monday,' he says. 'Dalglish made it perfectly clear that I was still part of the squad, but that I would find it increasingly difficult to get into the first team because of Nicky Marker coming the other way.'

Despite the bleak outlook, Hill was still reluctant to leave the only club he had ever played for.

Craig Skinner persuaded me to sign for Plymouth, if I'm being honest. I've been a family friend of Craig's since I can remember – our parents were friends through football and we were both apprentices and then professionals together at Blackburn. I didn't really want to leave, I still thought I had an outside chance of getting into the side there. But then I got a call from Craig and he persuaded me to make the journey to Plymouth. Obviously I had a bit of persuasion from Peter Shilton too. So you know, a little bit of deliberation with the family, some persuasive phone calls from Shilton and Craig and I went down on the Tuesday to play against Luton on the Wednesday.

Hill was thrust straight into the action at Kenilworth Road, becoming the sixth Argyle debutant of a hugely transitional season. But it was an old face who made unexpected headlines in the Coca-Cola League Cup double-header against the Hatters.

David Regis had been farmed out to Bournemouth on loan in mid-August in a bid to force him into the shop window, and his two goals in five games suggested the experience had reinvigorated the transfer-listed striker. Back at Home Park, Regis looked a different player and scored three times in the two legs against Luton to see Argyle safely through, 5–4 on aggregate. Two more strikes, against Bolton and Preston in the league, looked to have completed an unlikely Lazarus-style return for the twenty-nine-year-old. But just two weeks after his winner at Deepdale, Regis was gone.

'I didn't really think I had a future at the club even when I was scoring those goals,' says Regis. 'I think Shilton just brought me back from my loan spell to sell me. I wasn't his favourite, I wasn't his choice, it was best for both parties that we parted.'

Stoke City offered Argyle the chance to recoup three-quarters of their initial £200,000 outlay, and Regis was only too willing to move back to the Midlands. 'I seemed to hit it off quite well with Kevin Nugent,' says Regis. 'But Shilton had different plans and a move to Stoke, not too far from my family, was perfect for me. Stoke were a better club in my eyes at the time, I'd looked at the squad and thought it had to be a good career move for me. What happened at Plymouth was unfortunate, but no regrets, you just move on to the next thing.'

Argyle had collected eighteen points from eleven games and were lying just outside the play-off places when they boarded the coach to bogey ground Port Vale on 17 October. However, several hours later they were returning in the opposite direction having been on the receiving end of a 4–0 spanking that ripped the wind right out of their sails.

Paul Dalton had made his full debut for the club at Vale Park, but admits he was nowhere near ready, either physically or mentally. 'It was tough because I was staying in a hotel at the time and was a bit unsettled,' he remembers. 'I had a pot on my leg for about six to eight weeks and I couldn't do anything physical. When I came back I could still feel it, so I don't think I was fit. In fact, I know I wasn't. I was probably a bit overweight too, but I put that down to living in the hotel and having everything on tap. When you come back from such a long time off and then you're playing with new team-mates and trying to gel with them… I found it a bit hard really.'

Steve Castle also returned the following week and scored on his debut in a 2–0 home win against Wigan, but the defeat at Port Vale had set the tone for performances on the road. After Vale Park, Argyle drew only two of their next eight away matches, losing six and scoring just twice. 'We always tried to make Home Park a fortress and teams did tend to struggle down there, but we just couldn't click away,' says Dalton. 'I think it was probably the cavalier football that we played. It was a bit like the Keegan mentality if you like, it doesn't matter if we concede four as long as we score five – it was just attack, attack, attack. That was probably our downfall away from home, when you probably need to be a bit more disciplined in your defensive duties.'

So wretched was Argyle's record on the road that their FA Cup first-round tie at little Dorking was seen as a genuine test. Third Division Scarborough had ended Argyle's Coca-Cola Cup hopes the previous week, and Dorking manager John Rains smelled blood. 'Our ground has seen better days, we've got weeds and grass instead of terraces and our dressing rooms should have been bulldozed years ago,' he said. 'If they don't fancy it or underestimate us, we're definitely in with a chance.'

Adding to the visitors' nerves was the fact that reserve-team goalkeeper Ray Newland would be starting a senior match for the first time in his career. Says the then twenty-one-year-old:

> I remember in the week before the game, the lads were coming up to me and saying, 'Get ready for the weekend, you'll be playing.' I didn't believe them though, I didn't think I'd be playing – not in the FA Cup. But the lads were saying there was no way Shilton would fancy playing on a non-league mudbath against two giant centre-forwards. They kept saying, 'Shilton will have an injury, Shilton will have an injury.' All week the lads were winding me up about it because the cameras were going to be there for *Match Of The Day*. So I travelled up with the team for the first time since I'd signed. They were winding me up all the way, making fart noises at me – saying I was shitting myself – which I was!

Dorking fans were denied the incongruous presence of Shilton at their Meadowbank Ground when the player-manager ruled himself out with a groin injury to validate the squad's hunch, and thus his rookie deputy was thrust into the spotlight at a ramshackle stadium with a pitch that wouldn't have looked out of place in an allotment. But Newland took inspiration from his days spent toiling in the League of Wales. 'I was on non-contract terms at Everton and they used to let me go and play for Newtown in Wales,' he says.

> I had two years of playing at non-league football grounds against monsters, so it was actually better for me to play in those types of conditions than on a bowling green. I knew Dorking were just going to pump the ball into the box because I was making my debut, so they would have been wanting to put pressure on this young kid. They were trying to intimidate me. I can remember the first cross coming over, and their big 6ft 5in centre-forward tearing towards it. I just remember thinking, 'Ray, mate, you've got to go through him, make a statement here.' I came out and battered into the side of him, and I can remember him looking at me as if to say, 'Where did that come from?', and I just winked at him. The next cross that came over, I shouted 'Keeper's!', and he ducked out the way.

'Is that the biggest you supply?'

Newland went on to win man-of-the-match, as a double from Paul Dalton and one from Dwight Marshall saw a relieved Argyle edge through 3–2. 'I can remember John McGovern marching through the mud in his trainers at the end,' says Newland. 'He was slipping everywhere, blanking all the other players and walking straight towards me. I was thinking, "What have I done here?" He walked up to me and, without saying anything, just shook my hand, gave me a look and walked off.'

After seeing off Peterborough United in the second round, Argyle's FA Cup adventure ended at Premier League Ipswich in the third round. The Pilgrims, though, scooped all the plaudits for their classy display in an unfortunate 3–1 defeat.

Alan English had by that stage taken over the Argyle reporting reins from Rick Cowdery at the *Western Morning News*, and came away from Portman Road gushing with praise. 'There were moments when that Argyle team played football that really was high-quality stuff,' says English. 'I know they got turned over in the FA Cup at Ipswich but, Jesus, I remember being blown away by the football they played. They absolutely matched them big time. The trouble was, they didn't produce it enough that season.'

But Shilton's faltering players needn't have worried about attracting too many negative headlines for their erratic displays. Bored of mid-table drudgery, chairman Dan McCauley was in the mood to create some headlines of his own.

Chapter Four

STOP THEIR WAGES

In his rookie season as a reporter, Alan English broke a story that threatened to completely derail Argyle's already stumbling fortunes. In late October, with an immediate return on his considerable investment looking increasingly unlikely, Dan McCauley decided the time was ripe to threaten a Home Park walkout.

'I remember I was in the office quite late one night, when McCauley phoned up looking for Rick Cowdery,' says English. 'Rick wasn't around, so he said, "Who are you?" I told him I was the new guy and he noticed I was Irish. He's from Northern Ireland, so we got chatting and eventually he told me he was ready to quit the club. He said he'd been involved in a big bust-up with the directors.'

English's scoop made public McCauley's supposedly tenuous Home Park future, with directors Peter Bloom and Graham Jasper the root cause of his disillusionment. 'I'm at the end of my tether,' McCauley told English – and in turn the entire Westcountry. 'Rules are being laid down for me which don't apply to the others. I'm still hopeful of resolving the situation but it can't go on like this any longer.'

Having pumped around £1.5 million into the club since his arrival twelve months earlier, McCauley had been forced to dig deep on three occasions since the summer of '92 to ensure the club stayed within its overdraft limit. With only 50 per cent of the holding company in his possession, McCauley found himself putting up most of the cash, despite not being able to exercise overall control. But the chairman's philanthropic commitment to the club was to stop short of outright altruism. 'We were at a Board meeting and the clock was ticking – we were going to be closed down by Barclays,' remembers McCauley. 'I was left holding the baby. I was putting a lot of money in, sometimes £200k at a time. It was getting out of hand but I had to persist, I had to keep going.'

Bloom and Jasper were stunned into action by the chairman's public rebuke, and agreed to make a 'substantial cash injection' into the club at an emergency meeting held just hours after McCauley's concerns hit the streets. A statement issued by the Board read, 'The directors of Plymouth Argyle held an emergency

Board meeting tonight and all of their problems have been resolved. This crisis was brought about because we have invested very heavily in the club with first-class management and top-class players on the field, but we have not had sufficient support through the turnstiles. The Board, which remains intact, is completely united and is now looking forward to a successful season. We are asking our supporters to show their support by turning up in increased numbers.'

Home Park gates were averaging around 7,000 at the time, and eventually settled down to about a thousand less than that – more than 5,000 below the Board's rather ambitious break-even figure of over 11,000. 'Let's get the gate up, because otherwise we'll have more and more problems,' said McCauley after Bloom and Jasper's financial intervention. 'We want the fans there in force and we want to go forward together.'

The off-field distractions showed no signs of abating when Craig Skinner was forced to fly halfway across the world to be at the bedside of a stricken relative. 'My brother had a serious accident in Australia, so I had to go over there with my mum,' he says.

> He had a head-on collision and was on a life support machine – when we got on the plane we weren't sure if he'd be dead or alive when we got off it. It was a terrible experience getting the call in Plymouth, then getting the train up to Manchester and having to organise flights out to Australia not knowing if he was going to be alive when we got there. The club were great – it was a case of get over there and do what you have to do. I was over there for about five weeks in the end, and I did get a call from the club towards the end of my time there, but my brother had just started to come off the life support machine by then. He wasn't talking but he was on the mend.

The bad news continued for Skinner shortly after he returned from his enforced absence. 'When I came back I'd obviously lost a bit of fitness, but I eventually got back in the team and played in the FA Cup game at Ipswich,' he recalls.

> I was on the receiving end of a bad tackle by Jason Dozzell in the first-half, and my ankle was hurting quite a bit. I mentioned it at half-time and they said just see how it goes. But I remember walking out for the second-half and my ankle was giving way as I walked. I knew something wasn't right. I lasted about ten minutes of the second half before coming off. At the time I thought it would just be a few weeks, but the more the doctors looked into it, the more it became apparent that it was quite serious. I think it was called osteochondritis, which is basically a disease that stops the flow of blood to the bone. The medical support at Plymouth was poor, and I ended up seeing a specialist in Bolton and having most of my scans looked at by him. I was out for about a year in the end, it was a total nightmare, it took what seemed like a lifetime to heal.

With the injury list spiralling as the hectic Christmas period approached, Shilton took the bizarre step of offering to pay for a new loan signing out of his own pocket – a suggestion that was rejected out of hand by his chairman. 'It's time to put the brakes on for a while,' McCauley said. 'We just feel it is time to settle down and there should be enough resources with the present squad.'

Those resources were being stretched to the limit, with the treatment room conspicuous by the absence of a full-time physiotherapist. Mark Leather, a physio recruited from Preston at the start of the season, had quit the club after just three weeks – leaving Shilton with a lengthy injury list and no-one to address it. In the first half of 92/93, Dalton, Castle, McCall, Morrison, Marshall, Spearing, Skinner, Hill, Boardman and Shilton himself all had spells on the sidelines of varying duration, and their only chance of treatment came in a two-hour window in the evenings when NHS employee Paul Sumner had finished his day job. 'I came back from America where I was working and thought I'd pop down to the club to see if they needed anyone,' recalls Sumner of his transformation into a football physiotherapist.

> I spoke to John McGovern and he told me Mark Leather had just taken the job, so I went and signed a contract with the NHS instead. Then a few weeks later McGovern phoned me up because Leather had left. At first I would go in and look at the players in the evening after my NHS job and treat some of them in my shirt and tie, which I wore for my day job. It was like that for four weeks while I was serving my notice with the NHS. Two hours a night. For a professional club it wasn't ideal, but being a relatively small city there obviously weren't a lot of people they could call on.

In his autobiography, Shilton laments the lack of a specialist physio, and suggests Sumner's judgement was occasionally wide of the mark. 'Paul was a super lad but he hadn't had a lot to do with sports injuries,' wrote Shilton.

> He had been at the club for just a week or so when one of the players went over on his ankle in training. I was concerned about losing yet another player. 'How long is it going to be? A week? Two weeks?' I asked. 'About eight weeks,' he said. 'Two months for a turned ankle? You must be bloody joking.' That prognosis may have been acceptable in the NHS but in football you want your players back as soon as possible. Eight weeks was ridiculous. I'd known players return quicker from a broken leg. Paul wasn't wise to the ways of football, so I had to put him right. His expertise lay elsewhere in physiotherapy. He did well for us in time, but it must have been a steep learning curve for him.

Sumner admits he was somewhat out of his depth initially, but was taken aback by the expediency with which professional footballers are rushed back into action. 'In the NHS, you advise that someone needs four or five weeks for certain minor injuries,' he says. 'But as time went on I realised that players are pushed back into the team as soon as possible, whether they're hobbling or not. I had arrived all clean cut from the NHS, where you do things by the book. So if a certain injury needs four to six weeks to heal, that's what you tell the manager.'

By the turn of the year, Argyle lay in fourteenth position – firmly entrenched in mid-table thanks to an away record that read: P12 W1 D3 L8. By far the most wounding of those eight away defeats was a painful 2–0 Boxing Day reverse at local rivals Exeter City, in which Shilton's frustration over the club's walking wounded boiled over in a post-match soliloquy dripping in pathos. 'We've got only half of our team out and it showed today,' he said of the absence of Morrison, Poole, McCall, Dalton and Mickey Evans. 'When you have five players missing of their quality, it doesn't help. There was no other team I could have picked, my hands were tied coming up here.'

The derby debacle marked the end of Shilton's honeymoon period in the eyes of the club's fans, who let their celebrity manager know just what they thought of his efforts during the drab 0–0 draw at home to Hull City in late January. Slow handclaps and several choruses of 'What a load of rubbish' from the lowest gate of the season prompted Shilton to turn to the Devonport End of the ground and visibly appeal for a more upbeat attitude from the supporters. Unfortunately for the manager, the chairman also heard the chants from his seat in the directors' box, and made it clear whose side he was taking. 'I feel let down and I am wholeheartedly behind the supporters,' he said after Argyle moved closer to the drop zone than the play-offs. 'We are in relegation form at the moment and we have been since November. Things have got to change.'

Things did indeed change: but not for the better. On 2 February, Shilton's Argyle were dumped out of the Autoglass Trophy by Third Division neighbours Torquay United. To rub considerable salt into the wound, it was club stalwart Kevin Hodges – released by Shilton just weeks earlier after more than 500 appearances in a green shirt – who scored the eighty-first-minute winner. For McCauley, a former Torquay director, defeat to a team that cost next to nothing to assemble was a personal nadir – or in his own parlance, 'An absolute disgrace to the supporters, the club and the city of Plymouth.' John McGovern recalls the chairman's passionate reaction after the final whistle had blown at Plainmoor. 'I went in to see the chairman afterwards. I thought – I'll take it, I'll be the martyr,' he says.

The manager didn't want to join me because he knew what would happen – but I thought I'd go in and take it and then get on with things after that. And he gave me a royal shellacking that one of his directors was astounded at – they said they'd never seen anything like it in their time in football. But somebody had to take some stick for the performance – and he really fucking gave it to me as well. The other directors ran out of the way, embarrassed. He said we were a disgrace… pigs, dogs and all that kind of stuff. But the performance warranted that sort of bollocking. He gave us money, so he had a right to have a go at us.

Shilton himself was almost speechless after being on the end of his second Devon derby defeat in just four weeks. 'It's a terrible day for us,' he said. 'I appreciate how the fans feel about this result, but I can tell you that I feel a lot worse.'

Alan English penned an open letter to Shilton in the *Western Morning News* later that week, in which he summed up the mood of an increasingly malcontent fanbase. 'Your team's latest shambolic performance at Torquay begs several questions,' he wrote.

> The Argyle fans I spoke to want answers. They're angry and hurt. You haven't won for two months, but they could probably accept that – albeit painfully. It's the way you lose that upsets them – no spirit, no pride. There is still time to get yourself out of this mess. You have been a manager for less than a year. Will you not accept that your philosophy has failed you? The supporters, and this newspaper, want you to succeed in the way you did so outstandingly as a player. But it's time for a rethink. If you can't do that, it's time to go.'

Argyle fans may been put through the mill since relegation, but could at least console themselves that – on top of death and taxes – there were two other certainties in life: Argyle were class at home and crass away. But even that comforting constant was turned on its head in the space of seven days in late winter.

On 20 February, Burnley became the first side to leave Home Park with all three points since Blackburn Rovers on the final day of the previous season. John Pender's double in the Clarets' 2–1 win handed Argyle their first home defeat in nineteen matches and left Shilton's men hovering precariously above the relegation zone.

A week later, however, the Pilgrims notched their first League win on the road since 3 October when they travelled to struggling Chester City and snaffled a nervy 2–1 victory. Despite a 4–0 Home Park thrashing of Preston the following Saturday – in which young Tottenham loanee Lee Hodges stood out – Argyle's ability to be consistently inconsistent continued to break new ground, though with a rather topsy-turvy spin on it.

Burnley started a trend with their Home Park victory, and by the end of March, Argyle had lost at home thrice more; while the win at Chester on 27 February was the start of a four-match unbeaten run on the road – which also included a 3–1 win at Bournemouth and draws at Rotherham and Blackpool.

Paul Dalton began to find his feet just as Argyle's season began to peter out, scoring five times in just three games towards the end of March. However, his purple patch yielded just three points from nine, much to the winger's chagrin. 'It's always nice to score goals, don't get me wrong,' he says. 'But if the team doesn't win then it's a bit of an anti-climax. We'd started to get a bit cavalier at that stage of the season. Obviously we had defensive frailties throughout the whole team – because you defend from the front – and it cost us points.'

One player perhaps grateful for the inability of the first team to mount a sustained play-off challenge, was Martin Barlow. Deemed surplus to requirements since his demotion to the reserve team dressing room in Shilton's very own Night of the Long Knives, Barlow had been stuck in the stiffs awaiting an inevitable exit. But fourteen second-string goals since the turn of the year alerted Shilton to his undoubted talent, and Barlow was brought back in from the cold for the run-in. 'When I was transfer-listed, John McGovern said to me, "I don't really see you as a winger, you haven't got the pace to be an out and out winger," and I always knew that,' Barlow reflects.

> My trickery used to get me past defenders, but I always preferred midfield, I'd always played there anyway. McGovern said to me, "I like your attitude, just knuckle down and see what happens." So I thought I'd give it a shot. I started playing midfield for the reserves, scoring lots of goals and playing well, McGovern was telling Shilton that he'd seen me doing well in the reserves, and to give me a chance. At the time, we had very good ball players in midfield but no-one would run around and make tackles and all that stuff. They were just getting a little bit stale and that's why I got a chance.

Despite Barlow's inclusion, Argyle's play-off ambitions were effectively put to bed by a 1–0 home defeat to Swansea City on 20 March. But any lingering hopes of an extended season were blown apart in emphatic style when Exeter crucified Shilton's men in a chastening 3–0 Easter Saturday drubbing at Home Park.

McCauley – for whom the prospect of three Devon derby defeats in one season was unthinkable – cranked up the pressure on his manager by several notches on the eve of the game. 'A win is vital for me, because I'm a fan and we all know how important it is to beat Exeter,' said the chairman. 'Anything less than a victory would be very disappointing.'

'Very disappointing' were two words McCauley definitely wasn't using when the final whistle was drowned out by a vicious chorus of boos and jeers at ten to five the next day. Alan Ball's Exeter, displaying all the guts and guile their manager possessed as a player, saw off their supposedly more illustrious rivals thanks to a first-half strike from Stuart Storer and a devastating second-half double from John Hodge.

Shilton and his players were subjected to a bloodthirsty reception as they left the pitch, with venomous catcalls and unwanted season-ticket books following them down the tunnel. 'I understand their frustration,' said the manager. 'If you lose two derby games they are not going to be very happy. It's as simple as that.'

Paul Dalton refutes suggestions by fans that Argyle were outgunned in the desire stakes by their rivals. 'We didn't go out on the field to show a lack of passion, but these things sometimes happen,' he says. 'I've played in plenty of derbies, not massive ones, just Yorkshire and north-east derbies, but they're strange because the form book goes out the window and there's a lot of passion from the fans and a lot of rivalry. You certainly don't go out on the field as professional sportsmen to play poorly or not perform, but these things happen.'

'They were absolutely horrendous and Exeter were everything that Plymouth should have been,' reflects Alan English. 'They were tight knit, they had a good relationship with their manager, they were smarter, tactically more astute, more urgent ... they were just superior in every way and it was just an absolutely wretched performance by Plymouth.'

Director Ivor Jones witnessed first hand the extent of the supporters' wrath. 'I remember walking out of the stadium after the game. It must have been an hour or so after the final whistle and the supporters gathered around were so angry about the result. Some of them were really quite abusive.'

Shilton somehow maintained a defiant front, and insisted his rebuilding project was proceeding as planned. 'I believe we have the basis here of a decent side, but we still have one or two areas we need to make right. I know what needs to be done and it's just a matter of being allowed to do it.'

Shilton's timing could hardly have been worse, for the chairman was in no mood to listen to pleas for more cash – quite the opposite in fact. 'We were abysmal,' said the chairman. 'Our players should not be paid any wages. None of them have earned their bread. They should suffer like we all suffered. Not only the players, but also the management team. Our management should realise that a result like this will turn our fans away in their droves.'

Dalton provides an insight into how McCauley's missive was received in the dressing room. 'That was the chairman's prerogative,' he says. 'He's the money man and pays the wage but to publicly come out and say that ... well, that's his decision.'

Whether they were in fear of their livelihoods or simply relieved to play some football away from the lion's den that Home Park had become, Argyle visited West Brom on Easter Monday and rediscovered the passion in emphatic style. Steve Castle bagged a hat-trick and Dalton and Barlow grabbed one each as the battered and bruised Pilgrims responded in the best way possible by thrashing Ossie Ardiles' promotion-chasing Baggies 5–2 on their own turf. 'Everything we did that day came off,' remembers Dalton. 'We kept up our cavalier approach and every time we went forward it looked as though we were going to score. On our day we were probably the best team in that division without a shadow of a doubt, it was probably just our defensive frailties that let us down.'

'That was typically us that season,' says Castle – the third Argyle player to hit an April treble at The Hawthorns. 'West Brom were right up there in the promotion hunt. We went 1–0 down and it was "here we go again". But then

'It must be around 4.30 because that's when the big match is on Westcountry today'

we started to fire. People were setting things up at will, Dalton in particular was setting up chance after chance. Martin Barlow came in and was absolutely excellent and we had a block of games when we stayed together and did reasonably well.'

The 92/93 season stayed true to form right to the last kick of the ball. Following the Exeter/West Brom paradox, the final five games produced two wins, two defeats and a final-day draw at home to Reading.

A final Division Two placing of fourteenth – twelve points off the play-offs and thirteen away from relegation – was not what anyone would have expected at the height of Shilton's summer recruitment campaign. But for those occupying the inner sanctum of the dressing room, mid-table was perhaps the best anyone could ever have hoped for. 'A good group of players together is not necessarily going to make for a successful team – not overnight anyway,' reflects Castle.

> Shilton had kept the lads that did well for Dave Kemp, he didn't get rid of everybody. Andy Morrison, Nicky Marker, Steve Morgan, Dave Regis, Tony Spearing… they were all good players and they all played a part. Yes, he brought in a few players, but they were to blend in with other lads who had played at a higher level – which is no mean feat. The old players invariably know the writing is on the wall. We came in after having a fair bit of money paid out on us, so we were expected to play and blend quickly and become successful quickly. But it was all very disjointed, it was a transitional period and we never had a settled team. I came back in late October, Dalton was roughly the same sort of time. I'd come back not having had a pre-season, Dalton the same, so we were adjusting to a new team, new surroundings and new formations without proper preparation. And we just didn't fire on all cylinders. I actually ended up getting thirteen goals, Paul Dalton got himself thirteen goals as well, but we were really inconsistent. At our best we were as good as anything in that league, but we suffered from far too many poor results early on when people were coming into the team without proper match practice. But because they'd paid money out for us they probably put us in before our time.

Goalkeeper Ray Newland picks up on the theme of an awkward sense of transition in the dressing room. 'Peter brought a lot of his own lads in, and I'd say for the first few months of me being there, there was a bit of a clique between the old players and the new ones,' he says. 'You get that at any club though, players who have been together under another manager for two or three years tend to stick together. I can remember being at Everton and players physically fighting each other, though I never saw anything like that at Plymouth.'

Kevin Nugent – who, like Dalton and Castle, also ended up on unlucky thirteen goals for the season – pins much of the blame for the side's inconsistency on injuries. 'It was a nightmare at the start of the season,' he says.

> Paul Dalton broke his leg out on the training ground, he just tripped over a bit of grass or something and snapped a bone. Stevie Castle got injured in a friendly match. All very unfortunate injuries, nothing anyone could do anything about really, no-one's fault. Personally, it took me quite a while to get going I felt. Once I got my first goal [at home to Bolton in late September], I felt things picked up. But it was always going to be tough. There was a totally new set-up, a new regime following on from relegation. So with all that in mind, mid-table wasn't so bad.

Keith Hill was another player who admits he found the move to Plymouth challenging initially. 'My whole experience of professional football had been with Blackburn, so I found it very difficult,' he says. 'The transition was very hard that first season – a new manager, a new environment, new team-mates. But there were some very good players there and that was obvious from the first training session and through the course of that season. Our results were a bit indifferent but there was obviously a lot of potential within that squad so it was just a question of gelling everything together to get the best out of everybody.'

McGovern agrees, suggesting the management team were working on the 'Rome wasn't built in a day' principle. 'When you sign a clutch of new players, the training methods are different and they end up getting strains and pulls and things when it's totally unexpected,' he says.

> It took Steve Castle a while to settle down, a bit longer than we would have liked, Kevin Nugent too. But when you move to a new club you've obviously got to relocate to a new area, and obviously Steve and Kevin were from London and you can't go nipping home to London every day after training. But they were all what I would consider to be very good professionals and even when things weren't going well there was no problem with commitment. It took everybody a little longer than we'd hoped to get to know everybody and settle down and gel as a team and a club.

McGovern also insists that the season's low points actually proved beneficial in the long run. 'Sometimes everything works and sometimes it doesn't, but that is perhaps how you start to make progress,' he says. 'Maybe at times the supporters think it's getting worse and then all of a sudden you get a fantastic result like at West Brom, and you think, "Well at least we know they can do it, we know it's there." All we were thinking that season was that we needed to find the final player or two to make it consistent and then we'd all be happy.'

As for Shilton, a player who kept himself remarkably fit throughout his playing career and hardly suffered so much as a stubbed toe in nearly three decades, the injury situation that plagued his first full season in management was a source of immense irritation. 'I think it was unbelievable,' he said.

> There was hardly a senior player who didn't have an injury that kept him out for more than a month. We had the lot – broken legs, cartilages, everything you can think of. On Christmas Day I came home from training and was just about to sit down for lunch when Paul Dalton rang and said his mother had gone to hospital and could he be released to see her. Then Craig Skinner had to go to Australia because his brother was in a serious road accident. That's how it went on, right through the season. It was just one thing after another and I only hope management isn't going to be like this all the time.

Chapter Five

THE GAFFER

Peter Shilton's first full season in management was everything he hadn't been as a player: maddeningly inconsistent, stifled of high-class performances and plagued by injury.

The Plymouth Argyle that stuttered and stumbled to fourteenth place in the Second Division in 92/93 were the complete antithesis of the obsessively dedicated and physically sublime figure their manager had been as a goalkeeper. But, as many a great player has found to his cost, the visceral ease with which they were able to master a football does not necessarily translate to the successful mastery of football players themselves.

For goalkeepers, the challenge is even greater – and particularly so for such a zealous and fastidious custodian as Shilton. 'The great players rarely make great managers,' says James Lawton of the *Independent*. 'The great managers are generally those who finish playing slightly unfulfilled, and Shilton was certainly a fulfilled individual when he retired from international duty.'

Nevertheless, England's record caps holder was convinced he had the qualities required to make his biggest leap yet – that from the goalmouth to the dugout. 'I had been giving my future some thought and had come to the conclusion that management was the next logical step,' he says of his post-England existence in his autobiography. 'I always felt I could become a good manager. I had played for some of the all-time great managers in English football and had learned a great deal about the game from them. The knowledge I had gleaned from Sir Alf Ramsey, Brian Clough, Bobby Robson, Ron Greenwood, Tony Waddington and Lawrie McMenemy, together with my own experience and ideas, would stand me in good stead.'

Hull City were the first club to approach the then Derby County keeper with a view to cutting his managerial teeth at Boothferry Park, but Shilton 'didn't fancy a move' to the Second Division club. But when managerless Argyle came a-knocking in February 1992, the self-confessed Devonphile jumped at the chance. 'Plymouth appealed to me,' he said. 'I had a holiday home in Devon, knew the area and loved it. I had always thought of Plymouth Argyle as having tremendous potential. The club enjoyed a good bedrock of support, and history showed that when the team had done well, attendances in excess of 20,000 were not uncommon.'

Shilton's appointment as Argyle manager was a major news event, if only because he was such a high-profile figure and a significant thread in the fabric of English football. When he had appeared on *The Wogan Show* following his starring role for the national team at Italia 90, Terry Wogan was forced to cut the interview short such was the fervour emanating from the almost delirious studio audience.

But despite his new-found status as an unlikely symbol of public worship, little was known about a man who dedicated practically his entire life to his art. He was neither a media-savvy object of housewife lust such as Gary Lineker, nor a working man's kind of bloke like Stuart Pearce or Terry Butcher. And forget comparisons with terrace darling Paul Gascoigne.

'Shilton wasn't the most forthcoming character,' says Lawton. 'He was one of those players who you thought of as departmentalised. On the field he was wonderful, off it he was a guy who was not easily accessible. So you just sort of celebrated him as a supreme operator.'

Shilton's contemporaries are generally of the same opinion. 'He kept himself to himself really,' says his former England and Nottingham Forest colleague Viv Anderson. 'He would mingle with us, but he could be quite shy. He would never ring people up and say, "Are you coming out for a meal with us?" or anything like that. It took a while to get to know him, put it that way.'

During his seemingly interminable career at the top, Shilton's many team-mates included a plethora of future managers. But while the likes of Kevin Keegan, Alan Ball, Martin O'Neill and Terry Butcher were either impassioned or cerebral enough to stand out as potential leaders of men, Shilton was so myopically committed to his own brilliance that it was almost impossible to imagine him caring enough about any other footballer than himself. 'In training, Shilton went on and on, long after the other players had left for the day … till he got it right, or till it hurt,' writes former Leyton Orient keeper Peter Chapman in *The Goalkeeper's History of Britain*. 'Clough adopted his haughty "ay young man" tone, ordering him to "get in the bath, Peter." Clough's assistant Peter Taylor, a former goalkeeper, tried gentle persuasion. When this got nowhere, he became frustrated and called Shilton an "obsessive". Shilton didn't disagree, and just carried on.'

Certainly Viv Anderson didn't mark his team-mate's card as a future gaffer. 'I never really thought Shilts would become a manager,' he says. 'He had his opinions, but he was quite quiet in general. Although saying that, you don't have to be as vocal as everybody expects you to be. Sometimes a quiet manner gets the point across just as well.'

Tony Woodcock, another Forest team-mate of Shilton's, agrees. 'In terms of who I thought was manager material,' he says,

> I always looked at the ones who were showing an interest in tactics and how clubs were run and so on. Peter didn't really do that. But we've seen over the years that

there are players who you don't think are going to become managers who turn out to be quite successful. In the Forest dressing room we had a very successful team, you would have thought most of them had a lot to offer the game, but then the situation with Clough was so unique and so crazy that it was always going to be a hard act to follow for any of us.

The reaction at Home Park to Shilton's appointment was one of near exaltation, but not exclusively so. 'I think it's been proven many times that even if you're a great player, it doesn't make you a great manager,' says Gordon Nisbet. 'I think if Peter Shilton had gone to America and started goalkeeping coaching or something like that, he would have been amazing... he's the best goalkeeping coach I've ever seen, he was unbelievable. But there are very few goalkeepers who make good managers, and he was very naïve as a coach. He didn't hold any coaching badges whatsoever, and he took no interest in outfield training in his whole career, and suddenly he's in charge of a squad of players and he's trying to coach them.'

The infamous European Cup speech that Shilton regaled his new players with may have alienated most of them with almost impressive expediency, but Lawton believes the rookie boss was simply trying to replicate the style of his famous gaffer at Forest. 'Brian Clough was a complete martinet, a complete loony,' he says.

> I remember Archie Gemmill saying to me once, 'I would never know why we played for Brian Clough, he scared us, you never knew what he was going to be like from one day to the next. He just had a genius for keeping you on edge, it seemed like the most important thing in the world to play for him and please him. He didn't even have any affection for us some days, but he just had a genius for making us play.' Perhaps Shilton was subliminally trying to reproduce that sort of aura about himself at Plymouth. But Clough was an utterly unique figure.

Striker Dwight Marshall supports Lawton's assertion. 'It looked to me like he wanted to come across as a big character,' he says. 'You know, "I'm the boss now and we're going to do things my way." We all respected him anyway because of who he was, but I just think he wanted to make an impact so we knew where we all stood.'

A couple of incidents that occurred early in Shilton's Home Park reign added further weight to the claims that he was trying to emulate the inimitable style of Old Big 'Ead. 'Shilton wanted a meeting one day after training,' says Nicky Marker.

> I was the captain, so I called the lads into the Far Post Club. I went up to his office and told him we were all waiting for him and he said, 'I'll be down when I'm ready.' He kept us waiting for two hours. That was his prerogative as manager, but

there was no explanation, no nothing. There was football on the telly, so because we'd been waiting so long we put that on. But when he finally came in he had a right go at us about it, saying we should have all just been sat there with the TV off. Just four walls, no telly, no nothing – just sat there for two hours. He treated us like kids.

Defender Tony Spearing recalls another incident in which a few innocent sips of an orange drink became a major club event. 'We'd had an absolutely killer pre-season session, a monster blow-out,' he says.

We walked back into the changing room and all the kit was on the floor. A bottle of orange squash was sticking up out of the bag of one of the YTS lads, so because there's nothing laid out for us, I picked it up and sank some. It goes round the room and I throw it back in the kid's bag. Next thing we know, everything's kicked off. Everybody was hauled out of the offices, all the staff, all the players... Shilton's called a meeting. We're thinking, 'Jesus, what's gone on here? Something big must have happened.' So we all sat down and Shilton comes in, all serious, and he says, 'We have a thief among us.' I thought someone had nicked some money. But he says, 'Somebody has stolen half a bottle of orange squash.' And I just can't believe it. It was thirty degrees out in the middle of July. I straight away said, 'It was me boss – I nicked 5p worth of orange squash,' and we started having a row. He didn't do anything about it, he said it was out of order but that was it. The kid had obviously mentioned his missing orange squash as Shilton walked by, and he's decided it's grand larceny. He called a massive meeting just for that. It was funny looking back, just naïve really.

After the Crazy Gang mentality of the Dave Kemp era, Argyle's players were given a rude awakening upon Shilton's arrival when he immediately instigated a strict disciplinary code around the club. The new rulebook was met with a generally positive reaction, but striker Dave Regis believes it was just another attempt by Shilton to imitate the master. 'I can remember him coming in on his first day and telling us jeans were banned, we always had to be clean shaven and all that sort of thing. He would also keep us behind after training for no reason, which I understand is what Cloughie used to do. But, you know, there's only one Brian Clough.'

Steve McCall spent most of his career in the top flight, and viewed the new measures as necessary if the club was to be successful. 'I was quite happy with the discipline,' he says. 'If you stepped out of line and you got fined, that was part and parcel of being a professional and was part of my upbringing anyway. If you have to be there at 9 a.m. you're there at five to, and that was okay by me.'

The disciplinary measures applied away from Home Park too, and specifically when it came to painting the town red. 'Shilton didn't really like us going out too often,' says Dwight Marshall. 'Under Kempy, the players went out quite a lot, it was just part of that Wimbledon thing. I'm not saying we didn't go out under Shilton, we did, but we were a bit more professional and reserved about it, given what was at stake. Plymouth's a small area, you go down Union Street and get into trouble and everyone knows about it.'

Martin Barlow recalls the tight measures applying even to long coach journeys to and from away games. 'Before Shilton, if we'd had a good away result we'd go and get a few beers to have on the coach, it was always a long way to come back,' he says. 'But Shilton came in and suddenly it was no drink whatsoever. We couldn't play cards either. He told us to learn by his mistakes. To be fair, he was truthful with us, and said he'd lost thousands before games and it's harder to concentrate on the pitch if you're thinking about the cards and the money.'

One player who noticed the discipline more than any other was Dominic Naylor, who came to the club from the Barry Fry fast and loose school of management. 'I came from Barnet, where we were all working class lads just turning up to play football,' he says. 'On Friday nights before games, everyone had to go out – if you didn't go out then Barry Fry would fine you. It was totally different at Plymouth, but I'd gone off track a bit at Barnet so I probably needed it to be honest.'

If Shilton was punctilious when it came to dressing room discipline, he was nothing short of merciless in his dealings with the media. Indeed, it took him just two weeks to freeze out one of the local media's most prominent members. 'Shilton was hopeless with the press, absolutely hopeless,' says Rick Cowdery. 'Instead of meeting the press head on, he would delay and keep us waiting a couple of hours for an interview. Instead of inviting us into his office to sit down, it'd be a quick two minutes standing in the hallway. That went on for a couple of weeks, and I was getting more and more frustrated with his approach.'

Cowdery's frustration turned to outright bemusement one afternoon at Home Park. 'Shilton was down the Far Post having something to eat,' he says. 'I waited for him, and when he was finished I asked him if we could do something for the forthcoming match. But instead of sitting down for a chat, he said, "Yeah okay, come this way," and ushered me into the groundsman's shed and shut the door. So there I was doing a pre-match interview with one of the biggest figures in English football in this tiny, dark shed surrounded by tools.'

Feeling increasingly stonewalled by Shilton's elusive behaviour, Cowdery took matters into his own hands. 'I was getting more and more peed off with the fact that I wasn't getting much good copy out of him,' he reflects. 'One Thursday up at the ground, Danny Salman walked past me looking pretty annoyed, so I asked him what was wrong and he says, "I've just been dropped." For a fair few games Danny had been playing sweeper, so the next day in the paper we had a story about Shilton giving the sweeper system the brush off. I thought to myself, "That'll make him take notice." I just wanted him to know that I wasn't the sort who was going to be easily fobbed off.'

But Cowdery's proactive approach backfired. 'A few days later, I went up to the club to see him,' he continues.

Normally he'd keep me waiting, but I was told to go on through straight away. So I went into his office, John McGovern was there as well, and Shilton pointed to a chair and said, 'Sit down' and brought out the sweeper article. 'Where did you get this information from?' There was no subtlety about it, it was like being interviewed by the cops. Then he said, 'I know your type of journalist, you're all the same. You pump people for information. You go down the Far Post sneaking around my players.' John McGovern chipped in, 'You're the sort who, if you were sitting behind one of the players on the bus and heard something, you'd use it.' But they didn't even know me. Shilton then said, 'I don't want you going down the Far Post any more, I don't want you talking to my players.' By now I was angry, but I didn't lose my cool, I just said, 'Well, with respect, you can't stop me going down the Far Post. It's a private members' club and I'm a member.' Of course, he hit the roof then because I'm answering back. 'I'll have you banned from coming within 100 yards of the club,' he said, and I told him he was welcome to try. And that was it, from then on we had no relationship whatsoever.

Shilton continued to make it clear that Cowdery was persona non grata at Home Park. 'I still went to a couple of press conferences after that,' says Cowdery. 'At a conference after one game, I piped up with a question and Shilton looked around and said, "Did anyone hear that? Did I hear a noise?" You know, something an eleven-year-old would do. It was pathetic.'

Alan English assumed Cowdery's mantle as Argyle correspondent for the *Western Morning News*, though he too eventually ended up on Shilton's black list. 'I went up to Home Park to meet Shilton as a bit of a PR exercise, because him and Rick hadn't got on at all,' he says. 'So I went up there just to introduce myself and told him I didn't have any agendas and I was starting with a clean slate. He appreciated that and was quite pleasant.'

But despite an initial rapport that lasted for several months, English became tired of Shilton's banal post-match excuses and decided to go on the offensive. 'I had supported him on the basis that we got off to a good start on a personal level and I did rate the players he had brought in,' he says.

But there came a time when I felt, enough's enough. I remember writing a piece after the 4–0 defeat at Port Vale, and it was the first hugely negative piece I had written. I phoned him up on the Monday for our usual chat and his mood had changed completely. First of all he suggested to me that I hadn't written the piece at all. And I said, 'If I didn't write it, who did?', and he suggested Rick Cowdery had written it, which I obviously completely rejected. He had this impression that I was the good guy and Rick was the evil puppet master behind me, which was absolutely not the case. I was totally my own man and I had no interference at all from Rick. But it became increasingly tense between us to the point where he just refused to talk to me. That was it as far as our relationship was concerned.

Ian Bowyer, another of Shilton's former Nottingham Forest colleagues who eventually became his youth-team manager at Home Park, insists the ructions would have been like water off a duck's back to the rookie manager. 'It's fair to say that Peter was quite single-minded in his approach to what he needed to do to be a goalkeeper,' he says, 'and that strength of character certainly carried him through in management. Upsetting people or having disagreements with people wouldn't have been an issue for him.'

With elements of the media and a large part of the dressing room estranged before the ink was barely dry on his contract, Shilton carried on regardless, and directed his energies into molding an attractive team out on the training ground. Once again, he was seemingly intent on following the Clough blueprint. 'He was a big fan of Brian Clough and his way of doing things,' says defender Adrian Burrows. 'He didn't just believe in running players for running's sake. He did train players less, physically speaking. He let them do so much and then he'd call a halt to it.'

'To this day, it was the easiest training I've ever done,' adds Martin Barlow. 'We'd do an hour's training and that would be it, Shilton wouldn't let us stay behind and practice. He'd send us home, telling us to look after our legs and they'd do for us on Saturday.'

The minimalist methods were generally positively received by the squad, but some players felt there wasn't enough focus on defensive elements of the game. 'We were always fresh and ready for matches,' says Steve Castle. 'We worked heavily on finishing, and that benefited me and the wingers and strikers. But we didn't do a lot of defensive play in training, so I'm not sure whether the defenders would have found it beneficial.'

Nicky Marker confirms Castle's suspicion. 'I was out there doing extra one day with Adrian Burrows,' he says. 'We were both centre-halves so we were practicing our headers, but the manager just shouted at us, "Get in, training's finished." So we had to wrap it up.'

Shilton's obsessive dedication to improving his goalkeeping skills hadn't diminished by the time he joined Argyle as a forty-two-year-old, and players often found themselves keeping the manager in shape seemingly at the expense of their own development. 'The training was very much centred around himself,' says Craig Skinner. 'It was as if we had to do whatever would benefit him in training rather than the needs of the rest of the team. I remember some mornings in training we'd just be relentlessly shooting at him. At times you didn't feel as though you'd trained, physically speaking, and I think that was a result of him tailoring the training to what he wanted.'

Ray Newland, Shilton's deputy keeper during his first full season at the club, had even greater reason to resent the manager's training routines. 'In some sessions I used to despise working with him,' he says.

When we did shooting practice, all the outfielders would line up and us keepers would switch – we'd have five shots each, say. But Peter would be in there and have fifteen shots, then he'd say, 'Ray, in you go,' and I'd go in and have one, and he'd say, 'Right, Ray, out you go,' and he'd go back in and have another twenty. In the end the lads cottoned on to it and they'd start winding me up. When I'd go in they'd be shouting at me to get out before they'd even taken a shot. So I'd be thinking, 'If I let a silly goal in on Saturday, don't blame me because you haven't given me a chance to prepare.' It wasn't right.

On his arrival at the club, Shilton acknowledged that precious few goalkeepers had made the transition into management, but insisted that his vast experience at the very top and his dealings with some of the best managers in the game would help him to bridge the gap. His players, however, felt differently. 'Training wasn't the best,' says Jock Morrison. 'He was a goalkeeper, and you don't see many of those in management. I think if John McGovern had been left to it I'm sure it would have been much better. But Peter wanted to have an input, and many times he took over sessions that had been going well with John.'

Newland supports Morrison's point. 'In the dressing room Peter used to do most of the talking, but I think the players would have preferred John to have done more on the training pitch,' he says. 'But that might just be down to the fact that players are going to respect an outfield player more than a goalkeeper telling them what to do. That was just the general impression I got from being with the lads and listening to the conversations in the dressing room. If a centre-forward started telling me what to do I wouldn't listen. There's no malice in it, but a goalkeeper is a totally different position to all the others.'

Mark Patterson speaks highly of Shilton's managerial qualities, but reserves his highest praise for McGovern. 'The things John used to say to you were very to the point, but very much common sense, there was no bullshit around it,' he says. 'The little things he'd say to you … you'd think, "Oh yeah, I know what he means, he's right on the money there." There was no going around the houses, he told you what he thought and he didn't mask it.'

McGovern himself admits he tried to play a greater part in coaching sessions, but was overruled by his former Forest team-mate. 'Peter wanted to handle the coaching with the players,' he reflects.

I used to say to him, 'Peter, you're coaching midfield players – don't you think that I could do that? I've got a little bit of experience in that area.' He was telling them things to do and I would say, 'Peter, no, they don't do that.' But he wanted to do all the coaching, so I just let him do it. If you're an outfield player you understand other outfield players. I just thought that he could have utilised my abilities in a far, far more positive way, considering I was stood right next to him at the club. But it was difficult because I'd been a manager myself before, so I knew that your say is the final say. Peter was very, very single-minded, and you do need that as a manager.

But despite his shortcomings as a coach, Shilton did have strong ideas of how he wanted his team to play, as illustrated by director Dennis Angilley. 'I'll never forget seeing one of Peter's training sessions,' he says. 'I went out to Harpers Park to see him for some reason, but he was taking the training session so I had to wait. He was giving the players what-for because his style of football was *football* – pass and move, accuracy of passing and so on. He stopped the game, pulled everyone into the middle and expressed his feelings in strong terms, saying: "It's *football*. I don't want to see the ball up in the air … when it's in the air you've got to go and win it all over again." His philosophy on how the game should be played came over quite stongly.'

Tactically, several players have admitted that some of Shilton's early team-talks were somewhat confusing, and suggest that any success they achieved was mainly due to the manager's eye for a player and his purist values rather than any tactical mastery. 'We used to go to the Holiday Inn for home games and have pre-match there,' recalls Martin Barlow.

> You wouldn't know the side until you left to go up to the game. He'd turn over the sheet of paper and there it'd be – that's the team. Shilton would say a few words, and John would say – 'Just pass the ball, just pass the ball.' That was pretty much it. I think the knack Shilton had was that he brought in good players. It wasn't down to great coaching, because else we would have been out on the training pitch for three or four hours a day. Either that or he knew the players would fit into the system he had in mind. He was either very clever or very lucky.

Keith Hill agrees, but prefers to give Shilton the benefit of the doubt. 'To be honest, good players play good football – we didn't put an awful lot into team shape,' he says. 'But sometimes you can overcook it if you're working too much on shape, discipline and defending and attacking principles. Players want to be able to play football and express themselves in the right manner, and Peter Shilton definitely gave us that opportunity and that's why we scored so many goals from open play.'

Dominic Naylor believes a greater focus on defensive work would have reaped greater rewards in an era when Argyle clean sheets were the exception rather than the rule. 'Shilton didn't bother doing attack vs defence stuff in training,' says the left-back. 'I had coaches like Tony Pulis who did a lot of attack vs defence, and what we should do when we didn't have the ball, but we never really did that at Plymouth. It was more off-the-cuff … if they score four we've got to score five. It was probably entertaining for the fans, but if we'd conceded less, we might have gone up.'

McGovern confirms that the management's philosophy was hinged on the ability of their players rather than a reliance on tactics. 'I don't think systems matter that much,' he says. 'If you've got eleven players giving 100 per cent and you throw in a sprinkling of talent, then you're in business.'

With no great desire for tactical soliloquies, Shilton's team-talks were often low-key affairs, with his players urged to adopt an almost meditative approach to their pre-match routines. Says short-term signing Alan Walker, 'Before a game, the last ten to fifteen minutes would usually build up into a frenzy. You'd want to smash doors down before going out there and beating the hell out of the opposition. But Peter's ideas were totally different, we all had to sit down and not talk – just think about our own game. I'd never experienced that before and found it a bit strange.'

'We tried to work out why he used to make us do that,' says Steve Castle.

He'd never encountered a lower league game where, when you're playing someone like Hartlepool away, you've got to create your own atmosphere to get yourself up for the game. But playing in front of massive crowds like Peter Shilton would have done week in week out during his career, maybe you have to calm yourself down. We'd want to bang our heads together to get up for a game, but he was like, 'No, sit down, calm down.' That didn't work because you had lads in that dressing room who were used to clapping hands and geeing themselves up for that first minute when the first tackle is the most important. That's what we had all our careers until Shilton comes along and wants you to stay calm.

The player-manager may have insisted on a tranquil approach behind the scenes, but his on-pitch demeanour was a contrast in the extreme.

He may have only made forty-three appearances in his three years at Argyle, but that was plenty enough for his players. Terry Butcher and Bryan Robson both wrote in their autobiographies about Shilton's raison d'être for less-than-subtle on-pitch critiques of their performances, and it was a habit he took with him to Home Park. 'When he played in goal, he certainly kept you on your toes,' remembers Adrian Burrows. 'But it got to the point where one or two players thought he was a bit overbearing. Sometimes you thought, "Hang on a minute, I'm not a young kid, I don't need to be told to do this or to do that." But I think it was the born winner in him. I suppose he was finding it hard to catch himself as a new manager.'

Shilton's unremitting quest for perfection from himself and those around him occasionally spilled over into unsavoury rants laced with bucolic slurs. 'You could hear him calling players all the names under the sun,' says Craig Skinner. 'You're trying your arse off, and you're getting called all these words by your boss. You're used to blocking stuff out from the crowd, but it's a bit deflating when your boss is calling you all these names for no apparent reason – and I'd been around long enough to know when a bollocking was justified.'

'There was a young lad at the club when Shilton first came called Ryan Cross,' says Nicky Marker, picking up the theme. 'In one game he let a striker get in front of him at the near post and he scored. He was only eighteen and had played about three times, but Shilton hammered him. If it was myself, a senior pro, I'd have probably had a go back. But as a young kid, Ryan was too scared to say anything back and it just destroyed him.'

Jock Morrison believes Shilton's ageing limbs may also have contributed to his angry bear attitude. 'He was coming towards the end of his career, and it's something I know myself, you're not as agile, you're not as sharp as you once were,' he says. 'You tend to buffer the blame off a bit to cover your own back, and there was a lot of that going on and the players were very aware of it.'

Shilton's form in an Argyle shirt was generally excellent and occasionally outstanding during his early days at the club, but the game had moved on since Shilton's heyday and the England legend was being left behind.

'The backpass law had just come in and he wasn't used to it,' remembers Martin Barlow. 'A centre-back would give him the ball when there was no pressure whatsoever, he could have taken ten touches if he wanted. But he wasn't a very good kicker of the ball so he used to sidefoot it out of touch – then he'd look at the centre-half and shout, "You fucking cheat!" I used to think it was hilarious. During a match sometimes I'd be running up the field laughing my head off because I could hear him going off on one behind me.'

'He was great at shot-stopping,' says Naylor. 'His kicking went a bit towards the end, though. If the wind was against you, you were shafted. You'd have to stand on the eighteen-yard line because you knew the ball would be coming straight back in your face.'

For Gordon Sparks, the manager's inability to cope with the new law was uncomfortable to watch. 'The backpass law really killed him,' he says. 'If he had a nippy forward coming down on him, he would just slice the ball out of touch. It got to the stage where the crowd were groaning in anticipation and I thought that was sad, I didn't see the funny side of that. To think he had been reduced to that because of a change in the laws was a real shame. I don't know if he dropped himself because of the backpass rule, but it certainly would have influenced his thinking.'

Regardless of his goalkeeping abilities, most observers agree that Shilton was ultimately missing several of the key ingredients required to forge a career in management – never mind reaching the giddy heights of his guiding force, Brian Clough. 'I suppose his big weakness was his man management,' says Alan English. 'Ultimately, he was never going to make it as a manager because he didn't have what it took to motivate players and, as harsh as it may sound, I don't think he had the emotional intelligence that you need to make it as a manager. He had some of the qualities, but you need a lot more and I think he was a long way short at the end of the day.'

Shilton's players believe that their manager took his autonomous status a step too far, and was too distant from them to convince as a leader. 'He was actually quite quiet with the lads,' says Ray Newland. 'People used to say he was an arrogant man, but I never thought that — he just kept himself to himself and was a bit shy.'

'He was always reasonably aloof,' adds Steve Castle. 'He was always like that throughout his career from what I've heard. He used to just focus on his goalkeeping, and was very rarely involved in the outfield stuff. But as a manager I don't think you can be too distant from the lads, and that was a problem that he never really dealt with.'

Shilton was an efficient machine, fearsomely programmed to achieve perfection in his chosen field, and replacing that robotic persona with a managerial refit was always going to be a complex, time-consuming and ultimately impossible task. 'I don't think he was cut out to be a manager as much as he was a player,' says Dominic Naylor. 'It was just the way he was, he was one of a kind.'

Chapter Six

SUPER STEVIE

Argyle fans were back on familiar territory in the summer of 1993. The previous year's close season had seen expectations reach unheard-of levels after Peter Shilton's Messianic arrival and his unprecedented summer transfer splurge. But the campaign that followed delivered the familiar mix of sucker punches and knock-out blows, and Argyle's famously fatalistic supporters were on standby for another season of sedentary spectating.

Twelve months earlier, all the focus had been on the Home Park ins rather than the outs, but with the mediocre waft of 92/93 lingering in the air, all eyes were on the players most likely to jump ship for more prosperous climes. Dwight Marshall, Jock Morrison, Warren Joyce, Martin Barlow, Ray Newland, Paul Boardman and Mark Edworthy were all tipped to leave in what Harley Lawer of the *Sunday Independent* was calling 'The 1993 Transfer Games', while Steve Morgan had been on the transfer list for more than a year and had taken to personally faxing managers of other clubs in a saga that rivalled *The Great Escape* for failed breakouts.

But the name on everyone's lips was club captain and outstanding performer of the first half of the previous season – Gary Poole. Leeds United had failed with a hefty bid several months earlier, but with Shilton having to sell in order to plug the gaping holes in his squad, the right-back was a certain departure.

The transfer merry-go-round eventually led to Poole being reunited with his former Barnet boss Barry Fry at Southend United. With the Shrimpers having sold Stan Collymore to Nottingham Forest for £2 million, Fry was able to meet Argyle's asking price of £350,000 – that after a player-plus-cash deal involving pacy forward Andy Ansah broke down over the player's personal demands. 'In the end, a combination of circumstances made it difficult for the Board not to go ahead with the deal,' said director and club spokesman Ivor Jones.

> Poole is one of the last players we would choose to sell, and the decision was taken with a great deal of reluctance. But Gary has a close relationship with Barry Fry and it was an opportunity he was very keen to take, especially as he comes from that area of the country. I think that if we had refused to let him go, we

would have been left with a very unhappy player. But there is a positive side to it. The cash puts us in a very good position financially and Peter Shilton is now in the position to tie up some of his own deals.

But the manager was putting any potential acquisitions of his own on ice while he still had much-needed unrealised value in his squad. The unsettled Joyce was next out the door when he joined Burnley for £150,000 after an insipid twelve months in Devon, quickly followed by Morgan – who despite being considered and snubbed by a whole host of lower division clubs, eventually moved to Premier League club Coventry City for a rather eyebrow-raising £110,000, plus £40,000 based on appearances.

However, if Shilton assumed the £650,000 the departures had raised would form the basis of his summer warchest, he was quickly put right by a Board desperately trying to fend off Barclays Bank's calls to reduce the overdraft. 'The gross figure [raised by player sales] is nowhere near the amount being bandied about,' said Jones in a public admonition of the media. 'In one transfer in particular, the actual fee wasn't the one widely quoted and we must stress that the club will not be receiving anything like £650,000 in total for the three players we have just sold. Initial payments are rarely more than 45 per cent of the transfer fee, and the rest is spread over time.' Jones also revealed that Shilton had been called to a Board meeting at which he was informed of his actual spending power. 'We had an amicable and very businesslike meeting to go into detail over what cash was now available and the manager is happy to take it from there,' he said. 'A lot of money has been put into the club and because gates fell off towards the end of last season we had to get some cash in to balance the books. We all have to be financially realistic about things because otherwise this club could end up like Barnet.'

It was to the crisis-torn London club that Shilton turned to secure his first signing of the pre-season. The Football League had granted eleven Barnet players free transfers after they had gone unpaid for three months, and for the second season in succession Shilton raided Underhill for a player valued at much more than the zero pounds he was signed for.

'We weren't paid for twelve weeks, we all got free transfers because of breach of contract so we all went our own way,' remembers Dominic Naylor – the specialist left-back Shilton had been seeking since his arrival at the club. 'In the end, we were getting half cheque, half cash on a Friday. You'd pay in your cheque, which would bounce on the Monday, and the cash you got was counterfeit. It was typical Stan Flashman. We got promoted that season as well. It was a good team, and it was a shame for it to break up.'

Naylor already knew the Plymouth area after visiting his former Barnet team-mate Gary Poole on several occasions during the previous season. 'While I was playing for Barnet I used to pop down to Plymouth to see Gary,' he says.

'We played Torquay once and I stayed down there for a couple of days and it was good fun. There were a few London clubs interested in me, Brentford was one, but nothing came of that. The first time I spoke to Peter Shilton I was actually working – I'd got a part-time job in a leisure centre in Watford to earn some cash. So one Sunday evening I got called down to reception and told it was Peter Shilton on the phone – I thought it was one of the Barnet lads on the wind-up.'

Once he was convinced of the call's provenance, Naylor headed west to discuss the move with his potential new manager. The deal looked nailed-on until the Board stepped in with a veto based on Naylor's demands for a signing-on fee equivalent to his market value. 'To pay him what we would have paid Barnet for his signature is out of court and undesirable,' said McCauley. 'Why should we treat outsiders differently to the players who had supported Argyle for several years? They are every bit as important as any free transfer.' Naylor was forced to reconsider his expectations, and eventually signed after receiving a more 'reasonable' signing-on fee.

With his first addition of the summer in the bag, Shilton took one eye off the transfer market to deal with a crucial matter closer to home – that of the club captaincy. With Poole no longer at the club and with other possible candidates Warren Joyce and Jock Morrison having also left or on the verge of doing so, Shilton and McGovern turned to the outstanding candidate already in their squad: Steve Castle. 'Gary thoroughly deserved the captaincy in that first season,' reflects the former Leyton Orient skipper. 'I believe I was one of four or five as candidates when I arrived at the club, but it wasn't a problem for me when Gary got it. He's a good friend of mine and started off that season like a house on fire – I think Leeds were bidding silly money for him at one point. But then he moved on, as did Joyce. Morrison eventually moved on too and I was very happy to take the mantle of being club captain.'

On 13 July, the day after the Argyle squad returned for pre-season training, Shilton filled Poole's right-back slot by returning to his former club for a player who went on to provide the club with almost as much value-for-money as Steve McCall. 'I was at Derby with Peter, and I remember rooming with him one night before an away game,' remembers Mark Patterson – who cost Argyle £65,000. 'The conversation came up, I don't know how or why, but he was talking about possibly becoming a manager sometime and he said, "Would you be interested in joining me if I did get a club?" I don't know if it was just a passing comment or what, but obviously I said yes because he was such an influence. Without really thinking about it, probably one of the major reasons that I went to Plymouth was because of Peter.'

The former Carlisle defender had been plagued by a serious injury since moving to Derby in 1987, and was granted a move by Rams boss Arthur Cox, who was keen to reduce his wage bill. 'I snapped my medial ligament in a cup game in January '92, and I was out the rest of that season,' says Patterson.

I played again towards the end of the following season, but obviously I was no longer needed. It was a great learning curve being up there with the likes of Peter and Mark Wright though, it was almost like a second apprenticeship. I'd gone there at nineteen, and walked into the dressing room with people that I'd only ever seen on television, that I'd never played against, never even met before, and there I was sitting among them thinking, 'Shit, what am I doing here? Should I be getting his kit? Should I be cleaning his boots?' It was a great experience, but it was obviously time to move on.

With two parts of his revamped defence in place, Shilton opted to boost his goalkeeping options by making a move for Cheltenham Town's nineteen-year-old prodigy, Alan Nicholls. Shilton was just nine games away from reaching the magic marker of 1,000 league appearances, but increasingly frequent injuries combined with his failure to successfully adapt to the backpass law meant the record books would just have to keep waiting.

But with the Board refusing to sanction both the signing of Nicholls and the pay increase requested by Shilton's existing deputy Ray Newland, something had to give. 'It was me being naïve and a bit thick that led to Alan coming to Plymouth,' admits Newland.

> I played twenty games in my first season, and I remember Craig Skinner saying to me one day, 'Make sure the gaffer doesn't mug you off with your new contract – you want a two-year deal, and try and get him up to £400 a week.' I was only on £250 a week at the time. I remember sitting down with Peter Shilton to sort out my new contract, and he said, 'You did absolutely fantastic for me last season, Ray. I was struggling and couldn't play, but you've come in and in your first season as a professional you've done fantastic.' He told me he didn't want to play that year, and that he'd found a young kid called Alan Nicholls who he wanted to bring in as cover for me so he could concentrate on management. He basically told me that I was the first-team goalkeeper, but then he said, 'The only trouble is, Ray, if I give you the contract that you deserve, I can't bring this young kid in. So could you do me a favour and sign a one-year contract with a £50 a week raise?' I went, 'Okay,' and that was that. All the lads gave me hell, asking me what the bloody hell I'd done.

Newland admits he had been taken for a ride by his illustrious manager. 'If I could go back in time, to what I feel was the defining moment of my career, I'd have told Peter Shilton where to go when he offered me that deal,' he says. 'I had been thrown in at the deep end the previous season and I'd done well. I should have gone somewhere else rather than accept a £50 pay rise and give him the nod to bring in the guy who replaced me. But I was a naïve kid up against Peter Shilton, and I think he knew that and took advantage of it.'

Nicholls was duly signed from Cheltenham for £20,000 in a complicated deal that included payments to his first club, Wolves, who still held the keeper's Football League registration after the former Molineux apprentice had left the Black Country club under a cloud three years earlier. 'I think it would be good for the club to have them [Newland and Nicholls] competing against each other,' said Shilton after swelling his contingent of goalkeepers to three. 'It should help them to bring the best out of each other. Nicholls has looked confident and he also has a very good attitude,' added the manager, spot on with one observation but resoundingly wide of the mark with the other.

Argyle's first two pre-season friendlies produced a dozen goals – a 5–2 win at Tiverton Town was swiftly followed by a 5–0 home defeat to FA and League Cup finalists Sheffield Wednesday. But a developing row over the future of Jock Morrison provided most of the entertainment at Home Park that summer.

At the end of the previous season, Shilton had instructed the Board to negotiate a new deal with the popular centre-back. When an agreement was finally reached several months later and Morrison's decision to sign made public in the *Western Morning News*, Shilton himself opted to go public over a covert deal he had been working on to sell the twenty-three-year-old to Blackburn Rovers. 'Morrison was about to sign a new contract,' says Alan English, the reporter who broke the story of the defender's initial decision to stay at Home Park.

> But Shilton wanted to sell him because he needed the money to bring in his own players, and he didn't take to Morrison's personality. So one Saturday night, Harley Lawer of the *Sunday Independent* got a call from Shilton. It was the first phone call he'd ever got from Shilton, and he told him Jock was attracting interest from a Premiership club. Harley was naturally delighted to get the story. But the whole point of it was that Shilton was trying to destabilise Morrison as he was about to sign his new contract. He was just trying to stir it, and it worked because Morrison didn't sign his contract and he left for Blackburn.

Morrison himself bemoans the way his exit from his hometown club was handled. 'I was treated very, very poorly that season,' he laments.

> I was promised a lot of things during the season when I went in to see the manager, but I obviously know in hindsight that I'd been lined up to be moved on. The service I'd given and the wages I was earning in relation to the other players that had been brought in didn't tally. To be fair, Dan McCauley said that he'd sort me out. He rang me at home and told me he was going to give me a three-year deal to put me on a par with the top earners at the club. Obviously as a Plymouth lad who had come up through the ranks, the chairman wanted me to stay. But I'd fallen out with Shilton by then. I didn't particularly get on with him that well and I didn't agree with certain things he did, so I was going to go anyway. McCauley told the press that I'd be signing, but the following week I was gone.

Shilton kept the identity of the interested club out of the public realm while he tried to persuade the Board to accept a cash offer from Blackburn of £150,000 plus a player in exchange (later revealed to be midfielder Wayne Burnett) and a further £50,000 based on appearances. The manager had already identified £200,000-rated Derby centre-back Andy Comyn as Morrison's replacement, but the complex transfer merry-go-round threatened to stall over McCauley's reluctance to lose Morrison for what he saw as a paltry cash sum and another Blackburn reserve to join Craig Skinner and Keith Hill at Home Park. 'If Blackburn can buy another Premier League-quality player for £150,000 then show me him,' said McCauley, by way of revealing the interested party to the public. 'He's too cheap at that price. I just want a fair return for a decent player. There's another player involved in the deal too [Burnett]. I'm not saying he's a bad player, but I don't want us to be labelled Blackburn Rovers Reserves.'

McCauley was forced to soften his stance when Morrison was finally informed of the identity of the club casting amorous eyes in his direction. 'There were three or four clubs at the time and it was whoever was willing to pay the most money,' says Morrison. 'But once I knew it was Blackburn I was off. I spoke to Dalglish, signed there and then and that was it.'

For Morrison, Shilton was the reason he left the club; for Burnett, however, the legendary goalkeeper was the reason he joined. 'I spoke to Kenny Dalglish and said, "Look, I need to be playing." I thought I was ready to play at the top level, but Kenny said that Peter Shilton had shown an interest in me and, when someone like that is interested in you, you just can't give it a miss. I spoke to Peter and he was really the reason I went to Plymouth to be honest.'

With a Warren Joyce-shaped hole in central midfield, Burnett was widely expected to be a like-for-like replacement by a local media as yet unfamiliar with his subtle talents. But as the player himself says, he was signed merely to add to the squad. 'Shilton said he wanted me to come in and add competition for places really,' he says. 'I think he was just bolstering his squad, he was making healthy competition for places. It wasn't a case of, "Come down and you'll be doing this or doing that," it was, "Come to this football club, we're going to be successful and hopefully you can be a part of that." That was enough for me.'

Burnett's signing added to the burgeoning Blackburn/Leyton Orient alumni at Home Park, which now numbered five: Burnett from an Orient and Blackburn background, Skinner and Hill from Rovers, and Castle and Nugent from Orient. 'I already knew a few of the lads at the club,' says Burnett. 'Even though Peter Shilton was the main reason I signed, it always helps when there's some familiar faces at training.'

With talismanic defender Morrison now Home Park history, Shilton stepped up his interest in Comyn – a 6ft 1in former Manchester United apprentice who had played in the European Cup during his spell at Aston Villa. 'He has got a little bit of pace,' said the manager, a former team-mate of Comyn's at Derby. 'He's useful in the air and will be a good character to have around the club.'

The twenty-five-year-old was purchased in a deal that would eventually cost the club £200,000, to take Shilton's summer spending to £455,000 [including payments based on appearances]. But with £850,000 bolstering the balance sheet and three high earners off the books in Poole, Joyce and Morrison [based on the new contract he never signed], the manager was a happy camper as he prepared for his second full season in management. 'We have replaced the four players who left with the four players I wanted and we made enough on the deals to put some money back into the club,' said an upbeat Shilton. 'It's worked out well for all concerned and we are now looking forward to making it work on the pitch.'

If pre-season friendlies are a barometer of a club's future prospects, then Shilton was making it work ahead of schedule. Notwithstanding the 5–0 home defeat to Premier League high-flyers Sheffield Wednesday [in which three goals came in the last seven minutes], the summertime living was easy for the men in green. A handful of victories against the usual local worthies was a mere warm-up for a simian-removal exercise of some significance during the week before the season began in earnest. Shilton was desperate to evict the monkey that had clambered onto his back over the course of three painfully embarrassing Devon derby defeats the previous season, and the return of the Devon Professional Bowl gave him and his charges an immediate chance to do just that. A convincing 3–0 home win over Exeter in what was effectively a meaningless friendly may not have given the monkey the head-clubbing Shilton would have liked, but when a 1–0 win at Torquay a week later confirmed the men from Plymouth as 'champions' of Devon, the normally reserved Shilton did allow himself some mild crowing. 'It's always nice to win a trophy and the fans deserve it,' he said with typical understatement. 'There was a lot of pride at stake, especially after we lost here [at Plainmoor] last season. We're not going to get carried away, but let's hope this is the start of better things for us.'

The bookmakers certainly didn't think so – pricing Argyle at 25–1 to win the Second Division title. That troubled Barnet – a club with just five senior players on its books going into August – were offered at the same odds illustrated just how much confidence the Shilton-McCauley axis was inspiring in the football community.

Shilton, however, was more concerned with a more immediate obstacle facing his side: that being the towering figure of Kevin Francis, who would be an unwelcome guest when Stockport County dropped by to kick-off the season proper on Saturday 14 August 1993. The 6ft 7in leviathanic hitman had plundered five goals against his generous Westcountry friends the season before, and Shilton was clearly feeling jittery over the prospect of his new-look defence taking on the challenge that had been so feebly passed up by the previous incumbents. 'We have got a pair of step-ladders in the dressing room,' joked the manager when asked how he was planning to stop his former Derby County colleague. 'He is obviously a handful, but we have got to cope with that and handle him a bit better this time.'

But it wasn't step-ladders Shilton's men needed. A brace from Francis took his tally against the Pilgrims to seven in just three games in County's 3–2 opening-day success at Home Park – six of those seven coming via his boots rather than his cloud-level bonce. His striking partner Andy Preece made it 3–0 to the visitors ten minutes from time, before Mickey Evans lashed home a cracker in injury time to give the score some respectability. Comyn scrambled home a debut effort to make it 3–2 with the last kick of the game, but by then Home Park was half empty and the goal was greeted at a volume normally reserved for travelling tumbleweed.

Skipper Steve Castle suggests confidence was high going into the new season, and is at a loss to explain why his side were such willing victims for the lethal Francis. 'Pre-season went very well,' he remembers. 'We scored plenty of goals and won plenty of games, so we were looking forward to getting started. But Stockport was always a tough one for us, they were a little bit of a bogey side and we just couldn't contend with Kevin Francis. My two-year-old has got more talent than him, but he was somehow very, very effective. We just couldn't get to grips with him, though we weren't the only ones.'

The defeat marked a day to forget for debutant Wayne Burnett. 'I got injured in that game,' he says. 'I did my medial ligaments in my knee. It wasn't really a great day for anyone really, and it certainly wasn't a great day for me – not only was it a defeat but I got injured and I was out for eight weeks. Not a good start to my Argyle career.'

An unhappy Shilton ordered his players in for an ad-hoc Sunday training session the day after the game, but it failed to have the desired effect. Three days following the Francis fiasco, Argyle were comprehensively beaten in the first-leg of their Coca-Cola Cup first-round tie against First Division Birmingham City at St Andrew's. With youngster Darren Garner in for the injured Burnett in midfield, Argyle were overrun and the 3–0 scoreline left them down and pretty much out ahead of the second leg a week later.

Shilton, though, remained admirably optimistic despite two defeats and six goals conceded from the first two games of a season that was widely expected to be his last should promotion remain elusive. 'While I've been disappointed with the first couple of results, I'm not totally unhappy with the performances,' he said. 'I believe we are still going to have a very good season, but there are just a couple of things I feel are letting us down.'

Despite the poor start to the campaign, some supporters were more concerned with the threat to a sacred club tradition. New commercial manager Peter Friend wasn't the first outsider to doubt the qualities of 'Semper Fidelis', the marching-band ditty that had long signalled the arrival onto the pitch of Argyle teams and their opponents. Friend made enemies of Argyle's hardcore traditionalists by ditching 'Semper Fi' in favour of an ear-splitting number by Frankie Goes To Hollywood – though was eventually forced to back down in the face of a passionate reaction from fans.

Home Park lost another institution that August – though there was no chance of this one returning, whatever the clamour. Youth-team coach and promotion-winning full-back Gordon Nisbet quit his role to join the police force, though had made up his mind some time before to leave the club. 'When I didn't get the manager's job with Alan Gillett, I applied for the police,' he says. 'It took a long time for my application to go through, it was well over twelve months in the pipeline, so obviously I had already made my mind up very soon after Peter Shilton arrived that I was going to go. The unfortunate thing was that it took so long for my application to go through, but I resigned the moment I got the job.'

Nisbet believes Shilton welcomed the news of his resignation. 'I think he was relieved in a way because it meant he could get his own man in. He didn't want to sack me because I wasn't doing a bad job. We worked long hours – though McCauley didn't think we did – for what was not a lot of money. Mind you, we enjoyed it, so we didn't worry too much about that. We got Paul Wotton through, Mickey Evans through, Marc Edworthy through, lads like that, and they all provided great service to the club and brought a lot of money in too.'

With Nisbet gone, the Board's attentions turned towards finding his replacement. McCauley was determined to cast for local candidates, someone with knowledge of the game in Devon and Cornwall. Former midfielder

John Matthews and ex-defenders John Uzzell and Danis Salman were linked with the post, but Shilton and McGovern were keen to bring in a man they both knew they could work with. 'I think John had put my name in to Peter,' remembers Ian Bowyer, a former Nottingham Forest colleague of the Argyle managerial duo.

> If you're going to employ someone, you'd like to think that you can trust them and that they're on the same kind of wavelength as you in terms of what you're going to be looking for in players. It's no good appointing a youth coach with a totally different philosophy of playing style than the manager. He'd have a great youth coach, but then it'd take him six months to knock out of a player what the youth coach had taught him. So the fact that Peter knew me and knew where I came from was a big plus for me, so I think that was a big part of the reason why I got the job.

With McCauley pressing ahead with his bid for a local candidate, Bowyer sensed the chairman's reluctance to go for an outsider. 'McCauley had someone called John Impey there at the interview [former Torquay defender and manager], and it was pretty obvious to me that McCauley was pals with him,' remembers Bowyer. 'John Matthews was also at the interview. I'm not surprised at all that the chairman wanted someone else, that would just be McCauley wanting one of his own so that he could have at least have one person in the camp that might take the odd story back to him.'

Bowyer, who had been manager at Hereford United and a coach at Dundee United before coaching American youngsters in the UK, was keen to return to the professional game. With McCauley favouring either Impey or Matthews, though, Bowyer believes his appointment was a close-run thing. 'I would imagine that Peter and John would have had to push him a little bit. It's not right for the chairman to make appointments, where does that stop? Do they then sign players too? It's a recipe for disaster, so you can't have that.'

'Ian has a great understanding of the way football should be played,' said McCauley on confirming Bowyer's appointment. 'He has quite a pedigree and was the best choice.'

But the chairman sounded an ominous warning to Bowyer when outlining his expectations of the role. 'When you come into this sort of situation, you have to prove yourself,' he said. 'It is vital because the youth is our future. Without youngsters coming through, you have to buy in talent and we are not in a financial position to do that.'

The most recent batch of talent bought in by the club had so far struggled to adapt to their new surroundings, but all that was about to change. Almost exactly a year earlier, Shilton had seen red at Hull as Argyle succumbed to a 2–0 defeat that saw the wheels come off their bright start to the season. Fast forward fifty-three weeks and Boothferry Park was again the setting for a defining moment – but this time for all the right reasons.

Argyle twice came from behind to hold the Tigers to a 2–2 draw in a display of character and commitment that had been sadly lacking during the previous campaign – particularly on the road. Not even Keith Hill's late dismissal could dampen the spirits of Shilton's men, who out-tigered the Tigers to earn a draw of some significance. Castle grabbed both Argyle goals on Humberside, and the skipper still points to the draw at Boothferry Park as the turning point of the season. 'We were on the back foot going into the Hull game,' he says. 'We'd just been turned over at Birmingham, and so we were very happy to get a result up there. It's amazing that one game, albeit just a draw, kick-started the season for us from there on in.'

The inevitable exit from the Coca-Cola Cup followed several days later, but not before Argyle had wowed the Home Park crowd with an exhilarating display in a 2–0 second-leg victory against Birmingham. The home side created enough chances to have comfortably won both legs, but it was the confident performance of Alan Nicholls in goal that caught Shilton's eye. 'That was what pleased me most,' he said of his young protégé. 'It was a big plus for me, and we managed to score two goals at home again too. It was a good performance and now we must look to build on it.'

Build on it they did, with a fine 2–0 win over promotion candidates Port Vale at Home Park on the last weekend in August. After a quiet first half, the contest was lent a sheen of incandescent brilliance when Dwight Marshall – back at Home Park after a loan spell with Middlesbrough the season before – out-did Pele himself with a sublime opening goal. Mickey Evans played Marshall through on goal, and with Vale keeper Paul Musslewhite advancing, the nippy striker touched the ball wide of Musselwhite's left, ran around the stranded keeper's right and calmly slotted home to succeed where Pele had failed attempting the same trick at the World Cup in 1970. Marshall's manager was thrilled; the player he nearly sold after a disappointing 92/93 campaign was rediscovering the form that saw him grab fourteen league goals in his debut season. 'Dwight took his goal superbly well,' said the manager. 'He's looking the part and that's a big bonus for us. Hopefully he'll kick on from here.'

But Marshall took his manager's encouraging message too literally when Argyle travelled north for a Tuesday night test at Blackpool three days later. With Argyle already losing 1–0, Marshall was brought down and then strong-armed by Mich Cook, so he aimed a couple of kicks at the Blackpool defender and was promptly sent off for the first time in his professional career. Argyle fell further behind five minutes later, and Castle's rebound effort from his own missed penalty nine minutes from time was too little too late. It was later claimed that Marshall's uncharacteristic reaction was due to racist abuse from one or more of his opponents; but the striker was advised simply to ignore such taunts in future and no action was taken.

Argyle recovered from their seaside setback to claim their first away win of the season at Swansea the following Saturday – largely thanks to the gaffer's penalty save twelve minutes from time after a trademark effort from Paul Dalton had put the visitors ahead in style. Victory at the Vetch sparked a three-match winning sequence for the Pilgrims, which also included home wins over Leyton Orient and Rotherham United.

Castle – with four goals from the first six games of the season – led the way with a match-winning brace in a 3–1 win against Orient, and insists he felt no sympathy for his former team-mates. 'That was a good day,' he remembers. 'Most of the Orient team were lads I'd either played with or grown up with, but all this "you don't show joy when you score against your old club" stuff is a load of rubbish personally. I don't think it's disrespectful to any supporters – you score a goal and celebrate it like it's against anyone.'

Three days later, Rotherham had the audacity to take a 2–0 lead at Home Park after just twenty-three minutes thanks to a double from Imre Varadi. But by the half-time whistle, Argyle were 4–2 up after an attacking display of coruscating brilliance in which they blew away their visitors from Yorkshire. Goals from Nugent, Comyn, Castle (again) and Dalton ensured a vociferous reception from a delighted home crowd – sections of which were so entranced by their side that they continued chanting well into the interval.

Shilton's formula was simple. A stable back-four that included centre-backs Keith Hill and Andy Comyn was flanked by attacking full-backs Dominic Naylor and Mark Patterson – the latter of whom did the bulk of the forward foraging. Steve McCall, meanwhile, sat at the base of a midfield diamond, neutralising danger and providing sparkling passes with the efficiency of a pinball machine. Running the left channel was Paul Dalton, his rubber legs rendering many a Second Division full-back catatonic; while Craig Skinner or Martin Barlow fulfilled the right-wing shift and Wayne Burnett ploughed a classy furrow in a roving midfield role when called upon. Strikers Kevin Nugent and Dwight Marshall gorged on the deluge of opportunities that came their way, but the heartbeat of the side was undoubtedly Steve Castle. The captain scrapped, harried and harassed his opponents for possession, all the while searching for opportunities to unleash his lethal sting of a left foot – a devastating weapon that became the basis for Argyle's success that season.

The three-match winning sequence propelled Argyle into fourth place by mid-September, and Shilton was encouraged by his side's incipient progress. 'The spirit is really developing now,' said the manager. 'It was pleasing, after going two goals down at home, to see the players geeing each other up and getting each other going. We're in a good position, but it's early days yet.'

By early October, Argyle were still stuck in fourth spot. An impressive 3–2 victory at Cardiff was followed by a 2–0 win at home to Huddersfield – but that six-point haul had been preceded by a recklessly cavalier 3–2 defeat at Reading that underlined a season-long focus on scoring goals at the inevitable expense of keeping them out.

Winger Craig Skinner made his long-awaited comeback from injury with an impressive display on the right flank at Ninian Park, but does not have happy memories of his return from a nine-month absence. 'I was out for a full year if you count the time I was away for my brother,' he says. 'So to come back and be part of a winning side was a great feeling.' Skinner kept his place for the Autoglass Trophy home tie against Swansea three days later, but had more reason than most to resent a match that ended in a 3–1 defeat. 'I thought I'd keep my place in the side after playing well at Cardiff, and I did do. It was 0–0 at half-time, and Shilton brought me off. I just thought, "Could he not have just stuck with me?" I was trying to get match fitness back. When you're out for so long, it's not perhaps the first game you play but the one after that when you start to feel leggy. It was things like that that used to mount up and frustrate me, in terms of how he handled it.'

Skinner was only an occasional starter for the remainder of the season, much to his dismay. 'You want the lads to do well and you want the club to do well, because it's a really good club,' he says. 'But when you're in and out of the side and when you're not getting on with the management, it's tough. In your work life in general, if you're not particularly happy with the people you're working for it's going to have an effect on you.'

Up to the Swansea match, first-team strikers Marshall, Nugent and Evans had bagged seven goals between them, but Shilton was keen to add another targetman to his squad. The big presence he wanted was Bristol City's transfer-listed six-footer, Wayne Allison, but was thwarted in his attempts to sign the former Watford hitman by McCauley – as director Ivor Jones explains, 'Dan had backed the club by over a million pounds at that stage,' he says.

> It sounds like nothing now, but it was a lot of money in those days. The financial situation at the club was not that good. And although it would have been very nice to get more players in, we just couldn't afford it. When the name of Wayne Allison was brought to us, it was just out of the question because of the financial position of the club. The only way we could have bought him would have been if Dan had put the money up himself. So in fairness, Dan was thinking of the situation at the club. A lot of money had been spent, so we had a lot of value on the pitch and we were getting the benefits of that. So to get Wayne Allison down was, in Dan's opinion, a step too far.

With Shilton denied in his bid for more firepower, his side were given an untimely lesson in finishing by Burnley at Turf Moor on 9 October. The Clarets, imperious at home that season, were too strong for their visitors and emerged with a 4–2 victory that underlined both sides' attacking credentials (and lack of defensive ones). Argyle's second was scored by Paul Dalton in a typical demonstration of mesmeric dexterity; the former Hartlepool man slalomed his way around the home defence before firing home into the corner for the fourteenth goal of his burgeoning Argyle career. Of those fourteen, eleven were scored away from home, and most were visual treats. 'People always used to say that I didn't really score goals off my backside or simple tap-ins,' he says. 'I can't explain it really. They also used to say I'd only ever score those type of goals away from home, and they're probably right. In away matches I'd probably get a little bit more space, because the onus is basically on the home team to attack so we could then counter attack and have a bit more space as individuals. Home Park became quite a fortress so managers prepared their teams to close the space down and play tighter and not be too adventurous.'

Dalton was certainly catching the eye of the Home Park faithful, but the undoubted star of the season so far was Captain Castle. By the time Argyle travelled to Stockport County on Friday 17 December, the skipper had a dozen goals under his belt from central midfield and went on to make club history on a stunning night for the Pilgrims at Edgeley Park. The 3–2 victory – Argyle's first against County since relegation – was remarkable enough, but it was Castle's record-breaking hat-trick that made the headlines. Three goals – a close-range side-footer, a diving header from five yards and a nod-in at the far post – in just six minutes and seven seconds was the fastest hat-trick in the club's history. Stockport did their best to spoil the party by grabbing a pair of goals late on to set up a tense finale, but Argyle held on to record a defiant victory.

Castle has fond memories of his awesome display in Greater Manchester, but modestly gives most of the credit to his team-mates. 'That night was one of the highlights of my career – it was fantastic,' he says. 'I didn't really do an awful lot to get the hat-trick goals other than get on the end of them. There were two absolutely superb crosses from Paul Dalton, so he has to take all the credit for that. Then for the third there was a little bit of a melee in the box that just fell to me. It was a great result for us, especially against Stockport who we always struggled against, and it set us up nicely for the Christmas period.'

Midfielder Steve McCall, enjoying an influential season as Castle's wily chaperone in midfield, believes the Stockport result underlined Argyle's growing credentials as genuine promotion contenders. 'That was a big game for us,' he says.

Stockport were up there and it was a really big test, our biggest so far that season. Could we go to one of the top sides in the league and get a result? We proved that we could that night. It was a great hat-trick from Stevie, an absolutely stunning hat-trick in as much as it included some great team play, and he finished things off. Though after he scored the third I can't remember us having another attack, I think we just absorbed their pressure and they nearly got back into the game. Towards the end a couple of shots went just wide and we were hanging on.

For defender Andy Comyn, who was raised in Stockport, the result held particular significance. 'Playing Stockport was always a big game for me because

I grew up there, so going back home was always nice,' he says. 'They beat us in the opening game of the season, so it was great to get the win. Steve was certainly the heartbeat of the team. He was so difficult to mark, bursting forward from midfield. The way we played, the full-backs didn't get forward huge amounts, which allowed the midfield to go anywhere they wanted really. Steve in particular. It just made him very hard to pick up.'

Some of Castle's other team-mates hail the midfielder as one of the greatest they played with. 'Steve was the best. Unbelievable,' says Keith Hill. 'He led by example, a real man's man. He was Captain Marvel if you like, Captain Invincible. He was a great mate as well. Steve was one of the best team-mates I had. He knew the game very well, he was an incredible player, a real workaholic and a goal-scorer too. His goals were integral to our success that season.'

Mark Patterson agrees, 'Steve led by example and was a great captain to play with. Some captains I've played with over the years would say, "We'll do this and we'll do that," but in the end they don't lead from the front. But Steve actually did. To score twenty-one goals from midfield is some record. He was good in the changing room too, leading the team on and he took a lot of responsibility with talking to lads in the changing room, especially some of the younger ones.'

The victory at Stockport was the sixth on the bounce for the promotion-seeking Pilgrims, but they had to wait nearly two weeks to go for number seven after the Devon derby at Exeter was rained off on 22 December. Fulham therefore became Argyle's seventh victims on 28 December – in front of a bumper gate of 15,601 that had the chairman positively purring. 'The Fulham crowd was most unexpected,' he says. 'I said to the Board then, "If they would turn up every week like this we'd have no trouble." All we were worried about was the money all the time.'

Midfielder Wayne Burnett had made his return from injury just in time to tag along for the winning ride, and admits promotion fever was beginning to creep into the dressing room. 'I came back into the team in mid-October,' he says. 'We had a little inconsistent spell but then we went on a long unbeaten run. There was a real buzz around the city that Christmas, and it showed from the support we got. All players want to play in front of the biggest crowd they can, so it was fantastic to play in front of crowds of that magnitude. The players certainly rose to the occasion in that Fulham game.'

With heavy heads but hearty spirits, a bleary-eyed Green Army converged on an unsuspecting Bournemouth on New Year's Day, 1994. The 3,000-strong procession filed wearily along the A35 hoping that their side would provide them with the footballing equivalent of hair of the dog – and they weren't disappointed. The Pilgrims rode the storm against their rough-house opponents and carved out an eighth successive victory thanks to Dwight Marshall's near-post finish midway through the second half. As Argyle's weary supporters made their way home with the strains of 'Auld Lang Syne' still ringing in their ears, the concept of defeat was rapidly becoming an old acquaintance they were only too happy to forget.

Chapter Seven

DOCTOR DWIGHT

Of the twenty-eight professional footballers on duty at Dean Court that New Year's Day, none would have experienced a more circuitous or dispiriting journey to get there as Argyle's match-winner.

Dwight Wayne Marshall was born in Lucea, Jamaica, on 10 October 1965. Nicknamed 'Andrew' in his fledgeling years, the young Dwight was a shy individual compared to his boisterous older brother and didn't lace up a pair of football boots until he left the island when he was seven years old.

His mother, Lilas Riding, was eager to provide a better head-start in life for her two sons, so in the early '70s, the family took a path familiar to so many of her countrymen in that era and moved to the UK. 'My mum brought me and my brother over here when I was about six or seven,' remembers Marshall. 'She wanted to try and make a better life for us – like a lot of families who came over at that time. She got a job as a night nurse, a practitioner, and worked really long hours to try and support us.'

The three-strong contingent of Marshalls settled in North London, where they were eventually joined by Dwight's sister and their future step-father. 'Our first place was in Finsbury Park, near Highbury, so I grew up in Islington basically. It was difficult in those early years, maybe because my dad was over in Jamaica – when you've got a lone parent it's really not easy. My step-dad eventually came into our lives and he took on the three of us. So I didn't really have a father figure in my life until I was about eleven or twelve.'

Football figured in young Dwight's life for the first time as a schoolboy in his new country, and it quickly became evident that he possessed a rare talent. Discouraged by his parents from pursuing a career in the game, young Dwight dutifully concentrated on his qualifications, though he didn't entirely give up on pursuing a goal many of his schoolmates told him he'd be mad to ignore. 'My parents wanted to push me more into education and away from focusing so much on football,' he says. 'I was playing at school a lot, and I also got picked for the London County a couple of times, but I never signed with a professional club like most young footballers do. I drifted into the non-league football scene and got trials for league clubs that way.'

It was while he was still at school that Marshall was offered his first chance to try his luck at the lower end of the non-league pyramid. 'The referee in one school match I played in was part of a non-league club called Hampton,' he says.

He told me to go down there for a trial, so I did and they took me on – Hampton was my first non-league football experience. I was still living in Islington then, and I was travelling all the way down there via Waterloo, it was minging. But I was only about sixteen at the time, so I didn't really think too much about the travelling, it was just an experience for me. I was playing in their first team, the reserves and the youth team, so I was down there all the time. You can play that many games when you're that young.

After earning some cash doing shifts in a hospital for tropical diseases ('people used to get their jabs for going abroad there, so some of the lads at Plymouth called me Doctor Dwight'), Marshall began working for a training organisation based in central London. 'It was a company that laid on training courses for health, education and the local government sector. We set up the admin side of the training sessions.'

An ordinary life and career beckoned, but Marshall refused to give up on chasing his dream. 'Me and a mate of mine used to send off letters to pro clubs for trials,' he says. 'We went to Southend and Gillingham, and at one point I was actually with West Ham – not actually on their books, but I was going there regularly and training and they'd give me the odd game for the youth team. I was still playing for Hampton then as well, but left after a couple of years to go and play for a team called Kingsbury in Wembley, which was closer to my home. I played for them for a year or two before I ended up going to Grays, and that's when it all started to change.'

Grays Athletic, then of the Vauxhall Opel Premier League (today's Southern Premier League), were a completely different proposition to Marshall's previous clubs when he joined them in the summer of 1990. 'Grays were a pretty big non-league club compared to Hampton and Kingsbury. It was the first time I played for a club that actually tried to coach and train players – rather than us just turning up to play.'

Marshall scored thirty-two goals in his debut season in Essex, with strike partner Richard Cherry contributing the rest in a fifty-eight-goal partnership as Grays finished sixth. The twenty-five-year-old's scoring prowess alerted league clubs to his ability, and Marshall no longer had to resort to postal pleas for opportunities to impress at a higher level. 'I had a great season at Grays, scoring goals for fun,' he remembers. 'And that's when the trials started to come – even before the season ended. There was somebody at Grays who knew Dave Bassett, who was the Sheffield United manager at the time, and I was offered a trial up there.'

But fate – or rather, Mother Nature – intervened, and Marshall's big chance in Yorkshire eluded him. 'It was around January when I went there – not the best time to go as it turned out. Brian Deane was there then, and to meet him and all the other top players they had was a real experience. I trained with them for a couple of days and was due to play in a reserve game one evening – but because it was snowing the game was called off and that was the end of that. I thought, "Brilliant, I've come all this way for nothing." I never heard from them again.'

However, unbeknown to Marshall, his name had been circulating on the old boys' network in a trail that eventually led to his big break. 'I went to Crystal Palace next – there was some kind of connection between them and Sheffield United on the coaching staff,' he says. 'So I went to Palace on trial and that was actually quite good. I went on a three-match tour of France with their reserves, which included a few fringe first-team players. I played really well, scored in every game and things were going brilliantly. But they decided not to take me on. The coach said I did really well, but he thought I was more or less the same as they already had.'

With Palace flying high in the Premier League at the time, it was perhaps no surprise that boss Steve Coppell was unwilling to take a gamble on an unproven non-league striker in his mid-twenties. But Marshall did catch the eye of one of the Palace coaching staff who had connections with a certain club way out west. 'Luckily, one of the coaches at Palace, Wally Downes, knew Dave Kemp from their time at Wimbledon together. So he obviously told Kemp about me and before I knew it I was heading down there.'

Argyle were involved in an unusual three-team tournament in Cornwall in the summer of 1991, and it was there that Marshall's long pursuit of professional football finally came to fruition. 'It was a three-team tournament in St Austell,' he remembers. 'Tottenham and Manchester United were the teams we were playing. For me, it was the first time going to the south-west and I just remember this beautiful place with a nice little beach – totally different to what I was used to in London. I remember having the time of my life – I was with the first team, we were staying in this nice hotel, and having nice meals together and things like that. It was a whole new experience for me.'

Argyle manager David Kemp was looking for a nippy little striker to pair with big frontman Robbie Turner, and didn't take long to realise that he'd found his man. 'I knew after about ten minutes of watching him that I wanted to sign him,' he says. 'I told the Board I was bringing this kid down from Grays and that his club were asking £35,000 for him. So of course they're not doing somersaults about that. He went and scored in his first game against the United reserve team, and I decided that was my cue to start putting the pressure on to get the money.'

Marshall leapt to the very top of Kemp's wanted list in the space of just ninety minutes, but the manager didn't receive clearance from his Board to make the signing until the evening of Marshall's second game – against Tottenham. 'After the last game, Kempy came over to me and said, "Look, we want to sign you," and I just said, "Yes," straight away. I certainly wasn't going to say no! I knew without a shadow of a doubt that I wanted to sign and that was it. So that was the beginning of me as a footballer.'

With the reality of his astronomical rise still sinking in, Plymouth Argyle's newest professional headed back to London to break the news to his family and employers.

> I headed back to London after that tournament, and went in to see my bosses to tell them what had happened. They were really happy for me, I didn't even have to give my month's notice, I was off in two weeks. My mum and dad just couldn't believe it. They'd wanted me to try to get my education and start a career for myself – and I was doing that anyway while playing non-league football. But when I told them I'd got a professional contract they were absolutely stunned – in the Second Division too, so a very good level. My missus and I had one child at the time and we were living in a council flat in Angel, so it was a question of just packing everything up and heading down to Plymouth.

After a series of near misses, Marshall had begun to give up hope of ever realising his schoolboy dream. 'It was unbelievable to finally get there,' he says. 'After the failed trials with Sheffield United and Crystal Palace and all the others, I never thought it was going to happen. I had reached the point where I was happy doing what I was doing, everything was going fine in my life. You never think at the age I was, mid-twenties, that it would ever happen. It was just unbelievable.'

After settling into his club digs in Plymouth, Marshall's first week as a professional footballer was a stark demonstration in being thrown in at the deep end. 'Adapting to training was really difficult,' he reflects. 'I just remember feeling tired and jaded in that first week or so. I was used to training two or three times a week, so to train most of the morning every day of the week was tough. But obviously Kempy knew that so he would try and tailor my training in the early days, but it was still difficult. The thing is though, because I was still in a bit of a dream world, I wasn't really thinking about it too much, so I just got on with it.'

After a lowly league finish the season before Marshall's arrival and a pre-season in which Kemp's batch of new arrivals had hardly inspired, the atmosphere around the club – and particularly among the fans – had reached the bottom of the trough. But Marshall was oblivious to the sullen air surrounding Home Park, and could think of nothing other than his first chance to impress against his third top-flight opposition in the space of a fortnight.

> We were due to play Aston Villa in a testimonial for Tommy Tynan, and I remember spending the week or so before it just really looking forward to that game. I was actually on the bench because Tommy was obviously playing, but

in the second half Kempy subbed Tommy off and brought me on – that was another great moment for me because he was a legend down there. It was me and Robbie Turner up front and I actually managed to score. A ball came into the box, Robbie nodded it down to me and I tucked it away. It was just unbelievable. Can you imagine going from signing, to coming on as sub for a club legend and then scoring? It was just amazing. Seriously, it's difficult to explain. The whole thing was just incredible for me … the training ground was beautiful, like nothing I'd seen before, and the fans were just unbelievable, they really were.

With Tynan released, Marshall had been signed to fill the considerable void left by the great man, and Kemp was in no doubt that he was up to the task. 'He's a confident boy,' he said on the eve of the season. 'He doesn't need me to protect him, he believes he can do it and I believe he can do it. With Robbie Turner and Marshall, we're going to have one of the best strike forces in the Second Division. They're going to cause other teams no end of problems.'

The manager proved to be quite the soothsayer, at least as far as the opening day of the season was concerned. Marshall and Turner grabbed a goal each as Barnsley were beaten 2–1 at Home Park on 17 August 1991. Marshall took just nineteen minutes of his league debut to pay back a generous slice of his measly transfer fee when he pounced on a cross from the right to send the ball into the net with as low a bicycle kick as you are ever likely to see.

'Dwight Delight!' screamed the headlines. The king was dead, long live the king. 'I still remember that goal as if it were yesterday,' says Marshall. 'The ball came over at chest height and there wasn't much I could do with it, but I had a go and it went in. The whole day was amazing. Coming into a professional dressing room is a whole new ball game when you've only ever known non-league football. I remember going out to do my warm-up and seeing the crowd, those are the sort of moments where you just listen to the fans, you can get a feel for the atmosphere. I remember those moments as clearly as if they happened yesterday.'

Marshall may have announced his arrival in the best possible manner, but he was all too aware that he still had much to learn if his debut was to be more than a tantalising flash in the pan. 'I didn't have a great first touch when I started,' he says. 'I had great speed, enthusiasm and spirit, and obviously I could find the goal, but I was still rough in my early days. But through regular training and good coaching, I learnt a lot in terms of my technique and understanding of the game, more awareness, and gradually I became a better player touch wise. Obviously what you're trying to work towards is becoming a more accomplished player.'

Marshall continued to knock in the goals at an impressively frequent rate for a raw talent freshly off the conveyor belt playing in a struggling side. But his crowning glory in a green shirt that season came at Oakwell, with Barnsley once again on the receiving end of more 'Dwight Delight'.

After putting the home team to the sword with two clinically taken strikes, the Oakwell faithful in the main stand stood to acclaim Marshall's third – a delightful chip over the keeper. 'I always seemed to score against Barnsley,' he reflects. 'And that day was obviously brilliant for me. We worked a lot on Robbie Turner getting flick-ons and knock-downs for me, and it came off twice that day.'

And what did Marshall make of the manager's long-ball methods? 'I remember Kempy saying to us that we could get it down and play in an ideal world, but he just wanted to keep it simple for us. He felt that approach suited the players that he had at the time.'

With Marshall the leading light in a side fighting relegation, it was inevitable that bigger fish would soon start circling Kemp's prize bait. Chelsea were reportedly lining up a player-exchange offer for the former Grays man, and Manchester City also had him on their wanted list. 'I did hear about Chelsea,' says Marshall. 'It was quite bizarre really because one of my early trials was at Chelsea, but obviously it didn't come to anything. Fast forward a few years and there's a rumour that they want to spend money on me!'

Manchester City boss Peter Reid took his interest as far as making a formal enquiry, but Argyle resisted all attempts on their prize asset and Marshall stuck around for the arrival of Peter Shilton and subsequent relegation. 'I had a great season personally, but we got relegated,' he says. 'I look back at it and we just didn't score enough goals. We leaked in too many as well, so obviously we didn't have enough quality.'

As a disappointing 91/92 season came to an end, Marshall inevitably scooped all the plaudits. 'His goals have surely been the only thing that has saved Argyle from being relegated some time ago,' said London branch secretary John Coker on announcing Marshall as their choice for Player of the Year, ahead of the final match of the season. Coker was right. Marshall single-handedly won eighteen points for Argyle that season out of the forty-eight they ended up with. The player himself is in no doubt who to thank for his finest season in Argyle colours. 'Dave Kemp remains my ultimate, all-time favourite manager,' he says.

Without Kempy taking me on, I may never have experienced League football. Up to this day I've got enormous respect for him, he was a very nice person, a good manager to work with and he tried to help me, not just on the field but off it too. So I'll always remember David Kemp for the rest of my life. I remember the first time I saw him after he got sacked. I was at Luton then, and we were playing Wycombe – where he was assistant manager. I walked past the dugout and heard someone calling me. When I realised who it was I went over and just started hugging him and all that because I was so grateful to him – people watching must have wondered what on Earth I was doing! Kempy's style of football at Plymouth wasn't to everybody's taste and in the end it didn't really work, but I'll always remember that season fondly despite how it ended for us.

For his part, Kemp wasn't at all surprised his non-league discovery had adapted so well to the professional game. 'If you're prepared to work hard, nice things will happen to you,' he said. 'Dwight works hard, he listens, so nice things happen.'

However, with Kemp dismissed, Marshall's fortunes at Home Park took a turn for the worse. New boss Shilton was keen to utilise the nippy striker's pace on the flanks instead of in his preferred role of playing off a targetman, and the effect on his goal-scoring contribution to the team was devastating.

Unbelievably, Argyle's third goal in the 3–0 victory over Bradford on 22 August was Marshall's only Second Division strike of the season. He did manage three in the FA Cup, but Shilton gave the striker precious few opportunities to lead the line – preferring to partner Kevin Nugent with Mickey Evans, Dave Regis or Tottenham loanee Lee Hodges at various stages of an inconsistent campaign.

Fans were dismayed to witness the decline of a player they had taken to their hearts, and the *Sunday Independent*'s Postbag was inundated with letters in defence of Marshall. 'Dwight is given a game here and there,' wrote one, 'playing even when taking antibiotics for tonsillitis and running up and down the wing, far away from his striker's role of last season. Where is Mr Shilton's faith in Dwight?'

Marshall admits he struggled to adapt to the new manager's playing methods, which were in stark contrast to the more rugged style he had been schooled in under Kemp. 'I just wasn't able to get to grips with the new style of play,' he says.

> The season before, the long ball would go to Robbie and I would feed off him – we had it down to a tee. But when Shilton arrived, I'd be up front watching the defenders pass the ball across the back and I remember thinking, 'What's going on here? This isn't the Plymouth Argyle I know.' As well as the change in style, I played out on the wing a lot – either side really. I also had a few injuries and just couldn't score to save my life. So I experienced both sides of being a footballer in the space of two seasons.

With Marshall recovering from an injury in the reserves while his manager desperately tried to convince Spurs to part with Hodges, his future at Home Park appeared terminally bleak. But with the former Grays man not deemed good enough for a side struggling in the Second Division, a Premier League manager with struggles of his own came calling to catapult Marshall into the big time in a move that shocked everyone – the player most of all. 'Lennie Lawrence was Middlesbrough manager at the time,' he says. 'He remembered me from the season before when I played against the three north-east teams away and did really well. They were battling relegation, so he took me there on loan for the rest of the season. One minute you're down in the dumps in the reserves, the next minute you've got a call from Middlesbrough saying we want you to go the Premiership. I was just thinking, "What is going on!"'

Lawrence revealed that Marshall's name came up out of the blue in discussions with Peter Shilton about another matter. 'The opportunity to take him on loan was there, so we took it. We've got nothing to lose and it's the same situation for the player. He's quick, strong and can score goals, and we'll take a good look at him before deciding whether to keep him.'

Marshall was not exactly welcomed with open arms by sceptical Boro fans, but earned a place in their affections for his tireless running and refreshing attitude over the three matches in which he appeared in a red shirt.

> I remember reading the paper when I first got there, and they were saying, 'Why are we signing somebody from Third Division reserve team football at Plymouth Argyle?' But they seemed to take to me in the end. My first game was at Stamford Bridge against Chelsea. It was just a different level, the fans were unbelievable and the whole experience was amazing. I came on after about seventy minutes when we were 3–0 down, but that didn't matter to me because I was just glad to be there. It was like a weight had been lifted off my shoulders.

Boro were in dire straits by the time Marshall arrived on Teesside, and were eventually relegated – by now a familiar feeling for their loanee from the Westcountry. 'I played away at Sheffield Wednesday a few games after Chelsea. We won 3–2 but we were already down by then,' he remembers.

> Then I came on in the last game of the season at home to Norwich. We drew 3–3, but obviously our heads were down because we'd already been relegated. Lawrence came into the dressing room after the game, and as he was speaking there was a knock on the door. There was a steward there telling us we had to get back out on the pitch because they were worried about the crowd, all the fans were still out there. So we had to go back out, it was unbelievable, they were still cheering us. I'd only been with them a short period of time, but I felt I did quite well. I didn't score, but the crowd took to me. It was a great experience, even though I got relegated two seasons in a row!

In the summer of 1993 Marshall returned to Home Park, but was considered almost as much of a certain departure as the eternally transfer-listed Steve Morgan. Shilton was pursuing the signature of Southend's Andy Ansah, an almost carbon copy of the striker he had just welcomed back from a loan spell in the Premier League, and Lennie Lawrence was keen to talk terms on a permanent transfer. However, Marshall insists his future at Home Park was never in doubt once his loan spell in the north-east was over. 'I remember having a conversation with Peter about coming back to the club, and he said he wanted me to be part of the team,' says Marshall. 'If he wanted to get rid of me he could have done. I know I went out on loan, but that didn't work out and I came back keen to do well. There were no problems between us at all.'

With Ansah rejecting a move to Home Park, Shilton finally gave Marshall an extended run in his preferred role up front – and the decision paid dividends. 'The manager gave me opportunities to work alongside Nugent as an out and out striker to see how that worked,' he remembers. 'What helped was that we had other players scoring goals, so it took the pressure off the strikers. The whole system just clicked.'

Marshall ended the season with fifteen league and cup goals, and was relieved to bury the ghosts of second-season syndrome. 'I was so glad to turn it around and show, not just myself, but the fans too that I could still do it,' he reflects. 'That season was just brilliant for me and the club. The players Shilton brought in were all ball players, and the football we played was brilliant and we were winning games. When everything's going for you, you've got great team spirit and it was a good place to be that season.'

Marshall's first goal of the 93/94 season was his sublimely crafted effort against Port Vale, a goal that finally signalled his arrival in the affections of the manager. 'That goal was just instinct really,' he says. 'The ball was played through to me, the keeper's coming out and instinct takes over. I put the ball around him, ran round the other side and tucked it away. I remember going back into the dressing room afterwards and Peter Shilton said to me, "That was just like Pele, only you managed to score." That was a real bonding moment for us.'

Ultimately, the season would end in disappointment for the club, and Marshall decided it was time to move on. His three years in professional football had taken him to the age of twenty-nine, and he was keen to make the most of the years he had left. 'I had reached a crossroads in my career at the end of that season,' he says. 'I had three seasons at Plymouth and it was time to move on, time to take my career in a different path. I'd joined the pro game at a late stage, and you just try to achieve as much as you can.'

Marshall signed for First Division Luton Town in a £150,000 deal, and dismayed Argyle fans were forced to wave goodbye to a player who had worn their colours with his heart on his sleeve and a smile on his face. 'Plymouth will always be a part of me,' he says. 'It was the first League club that I played for and the fans were always good to me. They would always shout my name, even after I left the club. I remember I played against them for Luton, and when I was substituted they all started chanting my name – it's those sort of moments that you look back on. You look at your highs and lows on the pitch, but it's moments like that with the fans that you really remember. At least I can say I made some people happy.'

Chapter Eight

THE NEARLY MEN

For Peter Shilton, the first few days of 1994 would turn out to be the blissful zenith of his reign as manager of Plymouth Argyle. Second in the table after eight straight league and cup wins, locals shaking off their apathy to return to Home Park in their droves, a chairman prepared to open the purse-strings once more and a richly-deserved managerial award all added up to one exceedingly happy gaffer. 'There are still things we can improve on,' said Shilton after the win at Bournemouth, 'but after eight wins on the trot, if I'm not happy now, I never will be.'

Less than a year after Dan McCauley called for Shilton and his squad to return a portion of their wages to the club after the deplorable home defeat to Exeter, the chairman found himself issuing a 'hands-off' warning to potential suitors casting amorous eyes in Shilton's direction. 'They couldn't afford him anyway,' said McCauley – after insisting any approaches for his manager would be given a dose of Irish-flavoured short shrift. McCauley continued:

> But seriously, the fans have demonstrated in recent weeks that they want success for the club and that there are enough of them out there to help make it happen for him [Shilton] and the Board. When you can attract crowds of over 15,000 [as the Christmas double-header against Fulham and Brighton did], it only goes to prove that there is no limit on what we can achieve together. Peter Shilton knew that before he came here and now he's seen the evidence first hand, he's being given every incentive possible by the fans to carry on his good work.

For his part, Shilton was keen to assure supporters that he had no intention of going anywhere. 'I never wanted this to be a stepping-stone to a bigger club,' he said.

> You do that when you're at a club with attendances of four or five thousand and know it's not going to get any bigger. Our last two league gates have proved what I always hoped would happen here, and the crowd will go even higher if our plans for the future materialise. I always knew it was going to be a hard job, but we can

now see the light and the fans are beginning to share it with us. There is still a lot to be done, but I am convinced we can achieve real success and that means eventually being part of the Premier League.

In his New Year's address [actually an interview with the now long-defunct *Today* newspaper], Shilton also spoke of his side's flowing football as a source of great pride. 'Many of our supporters tell John and I that it's the best football side they've had in years, and I've also been receiving letters from fans of other clubs saying how good they think we are, which confirms we are doing it the right way.' Shilton also revealed the extent to which he had taken the job to his heart. 'I eat, sleep and think of nothing but this club,' he said, before revealing how he plots Argyle's fortunes on the sand close to his South Devon home in Bigbury. 'The only free time I have is spent walking on the beach on my own. It's my only form of relaxation, my only real hobby. I suppose there were people who might have thought I was daft going into management, well, goalkeepers are supposed to be daft. But it was something I had to do and I am glad it has turned out to be at Plymouth. Words like "challenge" can be misunderstood, but that really is what this is for me and I'm loving every minute of it.'

Shilton's sense of nirvana was complete when he was awarded the Manager of the Month award for December, even though his side only played three league matches in the final month of 1993 – beating Hull, Stockport and Fulham. The postponement at Exeter denied the Argyle boss a full house, but with no other Second Division manager possessing a 100 per cent record – the decision was straightforward.

Shilton was quick to reach for the hymn sheet often used by managers from which to recite their gratitude in such circumstances. 'This award isn't just for me,' he said. 'John McGovern, in particular, is very much part of it, and there's Ian Bowyer and the players as well. The award is recognition for all of their efforts.'

With that recognition came the almost inevitable interest from other clubs in Argyle's high-flying talents. Barry Fry, having left Southend and Gary Poole for David Sullivan's ambitious Birmingham City before Christmas, was employing a scatter-gun approach to player recruitment that saw most of the lower leagues' leading stars end up at St Andrew's.

Fry signed no fewer than thirteen players in less than four months after taking charge in December, seven of them for six-figure sums, and was reportedly keen to add Steve Castle and Paul Dalton to his stable of lower-league pedigree performers.

Castle got wind of Fry's interest, but with no official offers forthcoming he was content to continue leading the Pilgrims in their quest for promotion. 'Yep, I knew about Birmingham's interest,' he says.

I think they talked about a bid, and I'd heard of a few others – Coventry and West Ham were also interested but nothing had got back to me and I knew nothing about any bids. I probably would have considered it had it been something from a league higher – you always want to play in as high a league as possible, that's why I moved to Plymouth in the first place. It's like anyone's job situation, if you get offered a promotion you have to at least look at it. But at the same time I was enjoying my football at Plymouth, loving the area I was living in, and had no problems at all with anything football-related down there.

Castle was eventually sucked up by Fry's giant player hoover eighteen months later, as was Poole, but in January '94 any prospective deal was a complete non-starter in the Argyle chairman's eyes. 'Barry Fry has been dropping names left, right and centre recently,' said McCauley. 'He's mentioned just about every player in the country, but I don't see why people have been getting excited about this because I can't believe any of our players would be interested in joining a second-rate team like Birmingham. It would be crazy to try and promote any sales at this stage,' added McCauley when asked if the club needed to raise funds by selling key assets. Shilton, said the chairman, was for once actually in a position to add to his squad without having to sell first. The bumper Christmas gates had raised almost £170,000, and McCauley was eager to talk signings, not sales. 'Success feeds success,' he said. 'Hopefully, the higher we go the more fans we can attract to see us – and that will bring in more income, which would mean more funds becoming available for the manager to spend in the transfer market. We have got to push it home while we are in this strong position, and that could mean giving it a crack sometime this month. Now the money has started coming in, it's up to us to show the manager he has our full support to keep the momentum going.'

In the end, Shilton displayed admirable frugality in response to his chairman's generous, no-strings-attached offer. With his first-choice striker partnership of Dwight Marshall and Kevin Nugent having scored just eleven league goals between them by early January, the manager took another leaf out of Brian Clough's book and plucked an untried striker straight out of non-league football. Shilton and McGovern had witnessed first hand the impact Gary Birtles had at Nottingham Forest after moving from Gresley Rovers for £2,000 in 1976, and were confident of repeating the trick themselves.

Richard Landon was a prolific twenty-three-year-old striker with Bedworth United, and had been attracting interest from Middlesbrough and Celtic – among others – after scoring twenty goals in nineteen games so far that season. But only Argyle showed any serious interest in the former Stratford Town player, and made their offer before Landon's head was turned by more illustrious suitors. 'Richard Landon was a young boy that I was very influential in signing,' says McGovern. 'I went up to see him at Bedworth. He wasn't the greatest, but I knew he would get us a goal or two. And he cost next to nothing too.'

Landon was kept in the dark about a potential move, and only became aware of Argyle's interest when a friend read about it in a local newspaper. 'It was in the local rag apparently,' remembers Landon. 'A mate of mine rang up and said, "What's this about Plymouth watching you?" Bedworth hadn't told me there was anyone interested. I wasn't aware of it – so I just carried on playing and scoring. Then they came to watch a trial game against Northampton and that was the first time I knew of any proper interest.'

While waiting for the green light to head south, it was business as usual for office worker Landon. 'I had a day job at the time as an estimator with a building company,' he says.

> The secretary rang through one day and said, 'It's Peter Shilton on the phone.' I've gone 'You're having a laugh, don't be stupid.' But I picked the phone up and it was actually him. He said, 'It's Peter Shilton here, could you come to Plymouth for a few days?' So I went down there for a three-day trial. I must have done quite well because when I got back they asked me to go back down again. The Bedworth chairman wouldn't let me go, but about a week later there was an offer on the table from Plymouth. Maybe interest from another club had forced their hand, I don't know, but they put a bid in without me going back down there. I think Peter was happy to go with John's instincts and his impressions of me.

Argyle agreed a modest fee of £30,000 with Landon's Warwickshire club, and Shilton's transfer business for the season was complete – leaving a rather significant sum sitting in the Home Park coffers. 'I was told after I signed that Shilton had a lot of money to spend,' says Landon, 'but he went and bought me for £30,000 rather than going out and getting an established player for a lot more. So it was nice he put that faith in me, and I'll always be grateful to him for that.'

Shilton was thought to have renewed his interest in Bristol City's Wayne Allison and also made an enquiry for Brighton striker Kurt Nogan – who Dan McCauley later suggested the Board were keen to see brought to the club and had thus made the funds available. However, the manager was keen to emphasise his faith in his existing personnel. 'We are always looking to strengthen the side, but I certainly don't want to rush out to spend a lot of money just for the sake of it. Whoever we go for must be an improvement on the players we already have here – and they have done a very good job for the club so far.'

'Very good' swiftly became 'must do better' as the mythical manager-of-the-month curse struck Shilton's men in their pomp. Just one win in six followed the New Year's Day victory at Bournemouth, and by late February the Pilgrims had dropped to fourth place – fourteen points behind leaders Reading and firmly back in the sights of the chasing pack.

Despite the lack of three-point hauls, Argyle were still unbeaten in fifteen league and cup matches when they travelled to bogey ground Vale Park on 19 February. The 2–1 defeat to a side with their own promotion ambitions may not have raised too many eyebrows among Argyle fans well-used to Vale Park vexations, but, unbeknown to Shilton, the battle in Burslem had tremendous significance for his side's promotion prospects – not to mention his own future as manager of the club.

With the score at 1–1 two minutes into the second-half, Paul Dalton latched onto Dwight Marshall's pass and waltzed around Vale keeper Paul Musselwhite. With the goal gaping and Dalton cocking the trigger, defender Peter Swan arrived out of nowhere to take the ball off Dalton's toe with a perfectly-timed tackle and deny Argyle the lead.

A 2–1 victory for the men from Devon would have proven decisive in the final-day race between Argyle and Vale for the second automatic promotion slot; as it was, Vale themselves went on to snatch a winner that would itself prove significant in separating the sides when they crossed the finish line four months later.

As for Swan, his match-winning intervention was fatefully logged in Shilton's notebook for future reference. His manager at the time, meanwhile, sang the praises of his big defender, saying: 'It looked as if all Dalton had to do was tap the ball in and, lo and behold, Swanny has come from nowhere with a magnificent covering tackle. It was the turning point of the game, without doubt.'

As for Dalton himself, he insists an ankle injury he sustained early on in the game led to his failure to put the ball in the net. 'I got done by Neil Aspin in the first five minutes,' he explains.

> It wasn't a bad tackle, he won the ball fair and square, but I did my ligaments in and I tried to carry on but was really struggling. I didn't say anything though, I just tried to get through it. I remember the open goal as if it was yesterday. I had two decisions to make: the keeper was coming out so one was to hit it first time to try and score that way; the other option was to knock it past him, run around him and tap it into the empty net. I went for the second choice, but with my ankle the way it was, I didn't get there and Swanny came in and tackled me. If my ankle wasn't as bad as it was then I probably would have made it and got the shot away. But it was the wrong decision. I should have passed it into the net rather than be a bit too clever and try to knock it past him.

Knocked out of their stride but not flattened altogether, Argyle recovered from their Vale Park setback to bag a pair of narrow 2–1 home wins over Blackpool and Swansea – two much-needed shots in the arm that sent Shilton's men back into second spot ahead of an unnerving trip to St James's Park, where Exeter City were keenly awaiting the arrival of their high-flying Devon cousins.

The Grecians were enduring a tepid campaign and were firmly entrenched in the bottom four. Talismanic manager Alan Ball had been poached by Southampton, and the players he left behind were without a league win at home for a full four months. Despite all that, the fixture was still a cause of immense concern for all connected with Argyle. The Greens had gone sixty-six years without a win in the Devon capital, and despite their promotion-chasing form, memories of the previous season's home and away capitulations were still nibbling away at Pilgrim pride. 'We've got a bit of a score to settle with Exeter,' said Shilton on the eve of the sixty-first meeting between the two sides. 'We appreciate it's a local derby and something the supporters look forward to, but as far as we're concerned there are three points at stake.'

New Exeter manager Terry Cooper – embarking on his second spell as City boss – sounded an ominous warning to his nervous visitors. 'We're the underdogs, but we're quietly confident about the game and we're really looking forward to it,' he said. 'I watched Plymouth against Blackpool the other day and they're a good footballing side. But I've seen a slight improvement in us in every game since I came back here.'

Cooper witnessed another slight improvement in his side when Argyle came to town on Wednesday 2 March, but it wasn't enough to take the spoils in one of the most pulsating Devon derbies for many a year. Despite going into the break 1–0 down, Argyle emerged from the dressing room in voracious mood to storm into a 3–1 lead – a winning position they protected until the final whistle despite being pegged back to 3–2 seven minutes from time. Argyle's equaliser came just three minutes after the break and was credited to City defender Mark Gavin – who deflected Mark Patterson's shot into the far corner of the net after the popular Argyle right-back had made a rampaging run into the box. 'I'll have that one,' says Patterson – who failed to find the net that season. 'Even though it was deflected in I'm still claiming it even now. I created a few goals down there, but I didn't score many so they could have given that one to me.'

Wayne Burnett side-footed Mickey Evans' cross past Peter Fox for the second, and the midfielder admits he was surprised that the victory meant so much to the club's fans. 'I was having an absolutely torrid time, not the best of games,' he remembers. 'But then the ball came across from Mickey and it just ended up in the back of the net, it wasn't a wonder goal by any means but it put us 2–1 up. I remember there was a real big thing about us playing Exeter, we hadn't won there in decades and when we beat them they actually had T-shirts made to celebrate. I knew it was a big game judging from the build-up, but I didn't really appreciate just how big until afterwards. I just didn't realise the magnitude of it all.'

Evans sent Argyle's large travelling support into raptures with the third goal, before David Adekola made the Pilgrims sweat with what turned out to be a late consolation. For Shilton, the victory provided a large dose of satisfaction and a small measure of justice. 'It was a good night for the supporters, it's been a long time coming,' he said in the St James's Park tunnel after the game. 'Exeter have had the best against us since I've been at the club, but they have had a lot of luck in that time and I thought we thoroughly deserved the victory tonight.'

It was perhaps inevitable that a section of Argyle's travelling support would let the occasion get to them, and so it proved. More than 1,200 away fans filled the St James's Road end of the ground, but a further 500 secured tickets for the Big Bank home terrace. Sporadic scuffles during the game itself threatened to boil over after the final whistle, when a number of Argyle fans gleefully ran onto the pitch and began clambering onto the goalposts – provoking a predictably irate reaction from the home supporters still in the stadium.

It was left to assistant manager John McGovern to restore order when he approached the exuberant supporters and appealed for calm. 'At first, I was more concerned about the safety of our players,' he said.

> It was only after I rescued Dominic Naylor from the scrum of celebrating fans that I realised the situation could get out of hand. They shouldn't have been on the pitch to start with, and when I saw some of our supporters swinging on the crossbar, I thought they wouldn't stop until they broke the goal down and all the TV and media coverage afterwards wouldn't be concentrating on our excellent victory. But with gentle persuasion the majority took the hint and gradually moved back behind the barricades. They would be letting themselves and the club down if they caused any damage inside the ground.

The fervour that surrounded the derby win was rapidly extinguished when Argyle were beaten 2–1 at Leyton Orient three days later, but the Brisbane Road result was a mere distraction with the biggest match of the season so far just around the corner.

Mark McGhee's Reading had begun the season at a frightening pace the previous summer, with eight wins from their first ten games propelling them to the top of the table – a position they still occupied as they prepared to visit Home Park on Saturday 12 March.

Argyle had eaten away at Reading's lead, which at one stage stretched to fourteen points, and were just five points adrift of the Royals going into the first-vs-second match at Home Park. McGhee had cast an eye over the Pilgrims as they laboured to a 1–0 last-minute win over rock-bottom Barnet four days before, and wasn't impressed by what he saw. 'Plymouth deserved to win,' he said, 'but what I saw was a team who weren't that convincing. They have had some decent results, but I still see Stockport as the team that can get closest to us at the top of the table.'

McGhee, in the third season of his first managerial post, cranked up the stakes ahead of the Second Division's crunch clash. 'It will be the biggest game of my managerial career,' he said. 'Both teams have an awful lot to play for. If we beat Plymouth it would put us in a tremendous position, but if Plymouth win they'll claw themselves right back into the race for the title. There's a lot at stake and it's the sort of game I was involved in as a player and want to be involved in as a manager.'

Shilton, who landed his first job in management just two months before McGhee, preferred a typically restrained approach to the pre-match build-up. 'It's obviously the match of the day,' he said, 'but there are only three points at stake. We hope to take the points that would put us within touching distance of the top, but I don't think the winner of this game will

'You are feeling sleepy, very sleepy, you will put all thoughts of promotion out of your mind for a few more weeks ... oh, forget it!!'

automatically be promoted. There's a long way to go and plenty of points still to play for.'

McGhee should have known better than to doubt Shilton's men – who hadn't lost at home since the opening day of the season, winning twelve and drawing four of the sixteen games they had played at Home Park since Stockport's 3–2 victory. Despite a promising first-half in which Alan Nicholls was tested to the very limits of his considerable goalkeeping prowess, Reading faltered after the break in the face of a tidal wave of home attacks and Argyle emerged with a morale-boosting 3–1 win thanks largely to a Kevin Nugent brace, to move just two points behind their visitors. Paul Dalton grabbed Argyle's second to put the home side 2–1 up, and recalls a second-half display of the highest quality from his team-mates. 'When Nuge got the first goal to put us 1–0 up it should have taken a bit of pressure off us,' he says. 'In that type of game, whoever gets the first goal settles quicker and is the more likely to win. But they came back at us and it wasn't until our second goal that we started to play. From then on we really clicked and just steamrolled them, they didn't know whether they were coming or going.'

McGhee denied that his pre-match assessment of Argyle's qualities fired up his opponents, but admitted his side were deservedly beaten. 'All I said was that I saw a side that didn't look all that convincing,' he said. 'And I think anyone at the Barnet game would agree with that. Plymouth struggled but deserved to beat Barnet, and I thought that was also true in the first-half today. They didn't look a team that really should have frightened us, but in the second-half they got about us and we didn't play well at all. In the end, they thoroughly deserved their victory.'

Shilton was naturally delighted with the three points, but was already turning his attentions to the midweek visit to struggling Rotherham. 'It was a good game in front of a big crowd and we got a good result,' he said. 'But as far as I'm concerned, the big test comes at Rotherham on Tuesday night. The players have got to prove to me that they can come away, very tired, from a big game like this and follow it up by getting a result at a place like Rotherham.'

Shilton's players didn't let him down – a three-goal burst inside the last fourteen minutes secured a 3–0 win at Millmoor and, more significantly, first place in the Second Division.

With the Pilgrims sitting pretty on top of the pile for the first time since they had been relegated almost two years earlier, Shilton perhaps predictably refused to get carried away ahead of the visit of relegation-haunted Cardiff. 'We don't even discuss it [promotion],' he said. 'The only thing I am interested in is getting three points against Cardiff tomorrow; nothing more and nothing less.'

Mark Patterson admits to having more than one eye on the table with just eleven games of the season remaining. 'We went to Rotherham and we absolutely murdered them,' he says. 'I know you shouldn't count your chickens, but we were playing so well and we were so confident, I remember thinking – we'll never get a better chance. We'd hammered Reading and we'd hammered Rotherham, but then we just imploded. I don't know what happened, but all of a sudden it was crash, bang, wallop.'

Cardiff, a side with just one win from their fifteen away games, travelled to Home Park on Saturday 19 March and started a three-match chain of events for the table-topping Pilgrims that they would live to bitterly regret.

Argyle's 2–1 loss that day to a Cardiff side who went on to avoid relegation by just two points marked the beginning of a disastrous string of defeats – with Huddersfield and Brighton the other Second Division sides only too happy to take advantage of a loss of form that nobody could quite put their finger on.

'When you reach the top of the league, sometimes it becomes that little bit harder to stay there and I think that's what we found,' says Steve McCall, who sat out the Cardiff defeat through injury. 'Teams decided to shut up shop against us – they became a bit more negative, harder for us to break down. Earlier in the season they would come out and take us on, but once you get to the top of the league they start to keep it tight and we had less space to play in and found goals harder to come by.'

Adrian Burrows, a steadying hand in the table-topping victories over Reading and Rotherham, believes Shilton's failure to add to his squad before the transfer deadline contributed towards the costly run of defeats. 'I remember that little spell,' he says. 'The squad was crying out really for a loan player or two just to give us a boost and keep us up there. It was a fairly small squad

'It's no puzzle to me – isn't that where Steve McCall usually does his bit of magic?'

and an extra player or two would have helped, but that didn't materialise and ultimately it cost us.'

Centre-back Andy Comyn ponders whether the management should have adjusted the team's tactical approach to ride out what was an inevitable loss of form from some of the side's usually potent attacking talents. 'Perhaps we could have done with a bit more solidity at that stage,' he says. 'Maybe that was the time when we should have perhaps curbed our attacking instincts a bit. If we had even just got a couple of draws in that run then we would have been in a much better position to push on. So maybe we should have altered some of our tactics at that point to fit in with the stage of the season and our position in the league.'

McCall believes the team had begun to take Steve Castle's goals from midfield for granted, and suffered for it when the captain's strike rate dried up after Christmas. 'Probably the only difference was Steve Castle not getting the goals in the second half of the season. We'd come to rely on them, which we probably shouldn't have done. We looked good for the title and it was just so frustrating.'

Castle himself suggests the goals dried up throughout the side, something that exposed the team's lack of solidity when defending. 'After such a good season we were always likely to misfire in front of goal,' he says. 'We'd got a fair level of consistency going, but unfortunately when we weren't putting the ball in the net, which happens sometimes, you've got to be a little bit more solid defensively – and we weren't. That's what we were consistently bad at, even with that great result at Stockport we still conceded two goals and had to hang on. No way should you score three goals and have to hang on. We were always very vulnerable at the back.'

After a 1–0 defeat at Huddersfield, Argyle were on course to steady the ship at Brighton's Goldstone Ground with the score at 1–1 late on, when Paul Dickov beat Patterson to a low cross into the box and fired a looping shot over Alan Nicholls with just seconds on the clock. 'I made the tackle on Dickov, but it's looped up off his foot and gone in over the top of Alan,' says Patterson. 'That was in injury time, and I remember sitting there thinking, "I don't believe this has just happened." That was our third defeat on the bounce but there's nothing you can do about it once it's happened.'

Dalton also laments the part Lady Luck played in Argyle's south-coast heartbreak. 'I think luck plays a big, big part,' he says. 'I remember Dickov's shot seemed to take a wicked deflection over Alan Nicholls, it spooned just over his hand – a freak goal really. That was a cruel blow to us, but being top of the league you wouldn't expect to lose three on the bounce, maybe one or two, but not three. I'll always go back to those three games as being the turning point of that season.'

For Shilton, a run of defeats wasn't exactly new territory as Argyle boss – but finding a way to recapture a once-potent winning formula certainly was. The manager allowed himself a rare lapse into frivolity following the cruel defeat at Brighton that suggested he was becoming increasingly desperate. 'I have told the players they have got to keep their heads up and keep battling and believing in what they are doing,' he said. 'Perhaps we could do with being 10 per cent more ruthless in both penalty boxes. The only other thing I can think of is to get out the prayer mat and sit in the garden for ten minutes.'

Despite the bothersome blip, Argyle were still second in the table with eight games to go – but Reading had moved into a commanding eight-point lead and Stockport were just a point behind the Pilgrims with three games in hand. Rivals Exeter would normally have been very last on the list of opponents Shilton would have picked to halt such an alarming loss of form, but the Grecians were no longer the threat they had been when they had sacked Home Park so ruthlessly almost exactly a year earlier. Six points adrift of safety, Terry Cooper's feckless charges had won just twice in their last twenty-three games, and had conceded four or more goals on five occasions that season. Even with the added pinch of derby spice, Exeter were the ideal opponents to awaken Argyle from their ill-timed slumber – and so it proved when a lacklustre home side emerged with a desperately-needed 1–0 victory thanks to a defiant Dalton effort just after half time.

The three points may have prompted a huge Home Park sigh of relief, but the manager was far from happy. 'To be honest, we will have to play a lot better than that to even think about promotion,' said Shilton in an unusually forthright post-match interview. 'There's seven games to go and we're in a position where we can start talking about promotion, but if we don't play better than we did today I can't see us going up.'

Shilton's warning fell on largely deaf ears, though his players did at least stop the rot on the road by earning a 1–1 draw at relegation-threatened Fulham. Bournemouth were the next lowly opposition in Argyle's faltering sights, though some semblance of a promotion-winning aura was restored thanks to the fourth own-goal scored in the Pilgrims' favour that season and Steve Castle's first goal in nine games: 2–0 Argyle.

With just three weeks and five matches of the season remaining, Shilton's men were occupying a precarious position. Second in the table they may have been, but Stockport had a stack of games in hand – and were seven points behind Argyle with twelve up for grabs from their bonus schedule. Port Vale were another potential thorn in Argyle's side – a point behind Stockport with three extra games of their own with which to make up the deficit.

With the sharks circling, Shilton's side picked the worst possible moment to start thrashing around in the promotion waters – and once again it was left to Cambridge United to sink their teeth into Argyle's ambitions. A little more than two years after they had done for David Kemp, the Us inflicted a mortal blow on the Pilgrims' promotion hopes when they emerged with a shock 3–0 victory at Home Park on 16 April. Goals from Matthew Joseph and two from future PL2 resident Carlo Corazzin, combined with Stockport and Port Vale victories, left Argyle practically needing snookers to go up on Reading's coat-tails.

Assistant boss John McGovern was stunned by his side's biggest defeat of the season, and admits it came completely out of the blue. 'The Cambridge game really shocked me,' he says. 'It was one of those results when you just think, "How the hell has that happened?" And you do a post-mortem on it, and you think, "No, that was right, that's what we always do," and you analyse the whole thing – more so than when you win, because when things are going right you don't have to analyse as much. We were quite adept at reading situations, but Cambridge was one that blew us all away.'

With Argyle's season dangerously running out of steam, Shilton turned to the young striker he had hauled out of non-league football three months earlier in a desperate last throw of the dice. First-choice strike partnership Kevin Nugent and Dwight Marshall had two goals between them in the last seven games, and despite a below-par start to his professional career, Richard Landon was the ace up the manager's sleeve. 'At first, I was a bit in awe of the management and the players,' he remembers.

> It was difficult coming in from non-league into a team of professionals who were doing really well, and I didn't start off that great. It took me a few reserve games to get my first goal and I wasn't particularly training that great. Peter Shilton called me into his office one day and said, 'What's the problem? What's the matter

with you?' I said, 'Well, I've just come from non-league, I'm here with all these top players and you and John McGovern, and it's all a bit overwhelming.' He told me I was there because of my ability and to just get on with it. 'It doesn't matter who we are or what we've done,' he said, 'just get out there and show us what you can do.' So I decided to pull my finger out and make a real go of it, and that was the turning point for me. From that day on, things turned around for me.

Landon knuckled down in training and earned a place on the bench for the away trip to Brentford on Saturday 23 April. With the Greens 1–0 down and just ten minutes remaining on the clock, Shilton told Landon to remove his tracksuit and enter the fray – which he did with dramatic effect. 'Scoring my first goal was a fantastic moment,' he says.

> It was great, I remember it so vividly. I had only been on for three minutes, and I got on the end of a ball into the box from Paul Dalton. I think it was about two yards out, but for me it could have been a thirty-yarder. Whenever I went back to Brentford throughout my career, I always looked around the stadium and remembered it fondly. I used to look over at the stand where all the Argyle fans were that day – they filled the bottom and top tiers, there must have been at least a thousand fans there.

In fact, close to 2,000 boisterous Argyle fans had packed into the away end at Griffin Park, and it must have felt like a home game for the visiting players. 'They were terrific,' said Shilton. 'They really kept us going and the reception they gave the lads at the end was superb.'

Whether it was the relief at having rescued a draw from the jaws of defeat, or the tremendous backing of their fans, Argyle suddenly got their mojo back. A superb 3–0 win at Wrexham on Tuesday 26 April was the first evidence of genuine promotion form by the men in green since the victory at Rotherham by the same scoreline six weeks earlier. The home side were outplayed in all departments by the Pilgrims, who earned the victory thanks to strikes from Martin Barlow and Dwight Marshall, and a trademark individual effort of sublime quality from Paul Dalton. The winger had scared the life out of the Wrexham defence all night long, and four minutes from time he beat three men in red shirts on a hypnotic run from the corner flag that ended with two defenders on their backsides and the ball nestling in the back of the net. 'We did our best but Plymouth were better than us on the night in all departments,' said Wrexham manager Brian Flynn. 'I told my players after the match that if we are to achieve anything next season, we have got to remember how Plymouth played against us tonight.'

With just two matches of the season remaining, Argyle maintained an increasingly fragile grip on second spot – and Port Vale and Stockport were winning their games in hand. By the time Bradford City had been dispatched

3–1 at Home Park on the penultimate day of the season, the three promotion rivals were chasing for the line almost arm-in-arm. But crucially, Vale and County each had an extra ninety minutes in midweek with which to engineer a decisive thrust across the tape.

Argyle had practically made second place their own after seizing it in early February and vacating it for just a fortnight during their brief stay in top spot and that three-match blip. But midweek wins for Port Vale and Stockport dumped the Pilgrims down into fourth place, from where they were forced to enter the final day of the season on Saturday 7 May.

The equation was simple: Argyle had to win at Hartlepool and hope that Vale lost at Brighton and Stockport failed to win at home to Hull. 'We didn't know what was going to happen,' reflects Steve McCall. 'Port Vale were at Brighton that day, and we were crossing our fingers that something was going to happen – that was a much tougher game than we had at Hartlepool. We just knew we had to do our job. If we won there was a chance, if we didn't then we'd kick ourselves if Port Vale lost'

McCall's assertion that Brighton were a tougher proposition than Hartlepool was a sizeable understatement. A decent start to the season by the Monkey Hangers had been long since forgotten, with an Inland Revenue demand of £300,000 threatening to bring the club down to its knees. United's relegation had already been rubber-stamped by the time Argyle arrived at Victoria Park, and the squad hadn't been paid in months. Players were threatening to strike ahead of the final day, but in the end decided to play out their season despite having boycotted training during the week in protest. Gordon Sparks remembers the troubled build up to the game for Argyle's final-day opponents. 'It was a poor Hartlepool side anyway,' he says, 'but they didn't train that week, they were in dispute over pay and apparently it came to light that there was some doubt whether they were even going to turn up for the game. But they did and we stuffed them – so maybe they shouldn't have bothered.'

It took Argyle half-an-hour to get off the mark – Dwight Marshall stabbing home a cross from former Hartlepool winger Paul Dalton. Less than an hour later, the home side had been completely rolled over and the Pilgrims had ruthlessly raced into an 8–1 lead – a joint club record. For one player in particular, the game will always hold special memories. After his equaliser at Brentford, Richard Landon had grabbed his second league goal against Bradford and capped his debut season off in fine style with a hat-trick at Hartlepool. 'Those were great times,' he reflects. 'The end of that season just seemed to get better and better for me. Kev Nugent had an injury but was ready to come back for the Hartlepool game. Even so, the boss decided to stick with me and I'm obviously glad he did. It was a fantastic day – I remember the whole game vividly. And coming back on the bus afterwards, despite it being one of the longest journeys in football, was just fantastic for me. I'd come from a tiny non-league club to the Second Division play-offs – it was brilliant.'

For Dalton, the result evoked mixed emotions.

> I remember the manager saying, 'Just make sure you win the game, don't worry about what goes on at Brighton. Keep it out of your minds, let's just win this game first and foremost.' Hartlepool were already down, so they had nothing to play for, but we had plenty to play for so we were bang up for the game. Once the first goal went in it was just wave upon wave, attack after attack. We just battered them. It was mixed emotions for me, I spent three good years there and I don't think I really celebrated any of the goals just out of respect for Hartlepool.

In the dying moments of the match, the Green Army launched into a defiant refrain of 'Que Sera, Sera, Whatever will be will be, We're going to Wemberlee,' and the players realised that automatic promotion was a distant dream. 'The fans obviously had radios on them,' says Dalton. 'We knew from their chants that we were going to have to settle for the play-offs. So we went back in the dressing room after the game, basically dusted ourselves down and tried to remain professional because we knew that potentially we still had three huge games left.'

Stockport did their best to provide Argyle with a helping hand by drawing with Hull, but Port Vale shattered Devon dreams by comfortably beating Brighton 3–1 to take a decisive hold on second place. 'We kind of knew from the crowd that Port Vale had won,' says McCall. 'That was obviously frustrating, but credit to them – they'd had a phenomenal run-in so we just pretty much held our hands up and accepted it. We'd had a great result at Hartlepool, but now we had to go and win the play-offs. The season still had another couple of games to go at least, so we were very much thinking, "Let's get it right."'

Martin Barlow had come back into the side for the final seven games of the season, and remembers the manager insisting his players remained focused even on the long coach journey back to Plymouth. 'Our next game wasn't until more than a week later against Burnley,' says Barlow, 'so Steve Castle, being captain, said, "Right, we're getting some beers in." We were all disappointed, even after winning 8–1 away from home, so he got a few cans in – but Shilton's come on and absolutely slaughtered us. We were trying to hide it, but Steve just stood there with a beer, and Shilton said, "What are you doing? No drink allowed." A few of us tried to put our cans in between our legs, but he cottoned on straight away and came up through the coach looking down at the seats.'

Old head McCall accepted his manager's hard-line stance. 'You want to celebrate a good season, but at the same time you knew you had a couple of games left,' he says. 'And that was Peter Shilton all over – professional to the end. We hadn't finished the season yet, and we wanted to make sure we finished it right.'

Chapter Nine

WE ONLY NEED TEN MEN

Plymouth Argyle finished the 93/94 season in third place in the Second Division, a mere three points off automatically-promoted Port Vale. They scored eighty-eight goals – more than any other club in Britain that season – but conceded fifty-six, just eight fewer than the relegation side of two seasons before.

Had just one of Argyle's eleven defeats that season been a victory by the odd goal, it would have been the Pilgrims and not the Valiants looking forward to receiving their First Division timesheet. Peter Shilton was in no doubt where to point the finger: the mad March blip of three matches that returned zero points. 'If you lose three games on the trot then it's going to affect you,' said the manager at the end of the season. 'Everybody was delighted when we went top of the league at Rotherham, and thought that was it. But then we lost to Cardiff when their keeper made a number of saves, we lost at Huddersfield when we really should have won – they had two chances and scored from one of them. Then we lost to a last-minute goal at Brighton when we deserved a point. It's fractions really.'

Old schemer Steve McCall was voted the club's Player of the Year for the second successive season, with Alan Nicholls coming second and Kevin Nugent third. Steve Castle, somewhat surprisingly, didn't even make the top three despite leading the club's scoring charts with twenty-one from midfield. 'It was strange, I did raise my eyebrows a little bit,' he says. 'I don't mean this to be big-headed, but I went through a barren spell and people were maybe expecting me to keep scoring and performing. I did have a few personal issues just after Christmas, and by my own admission I didn't really play as well as I had been. I still ended up with twenty-one goals though, but I think it was maybe the fans looking at the whole season and I hadn't been having the best of times when the voting was done.'

Argyle's final position of third meant that they would face a two-legged play-off semi-final against sixth-placed Burnley, with Stockport meeting York City in the other tie.

Had Danny Bergara's Stockport beaten Hull City on the final day of the season, or had Argyle contrived to draw at Hartlepool, then it would have been Shilton's men facing York – a side from whom they had taken four points that season – leaving Stockport to face a double-header against Burnley. But, on paper at least, the Pilgrims had drawn the longest straw. Jimmy Mullen's Burnley claimed the final play-off place just three points ahead of seventh-placed Bradford City – finishing a massive twelve points behind Argyle. Their presence in the end-of-season lottery was almost solely down to their form at Turf Moor, where they had lost just twice all season, winning seventeen and scoring fifty-five goals in the process. The Achilles heel that Argyle would be aiming for was the Clarets' away form – which was wretched for a side with designs on promotion.

Mullen's men had lost thirteen of their twenty-three matches on the road that season, including embarrassing 4–1 hidings at relegated Exeter and Hartlepool and a 3–2 reverse at Fulham – who also fell through the Second Division trapdoor.

The head-to-head record between the Lancashire outfit and the men from Devon suggested a play-off tussle of mouth-watering potential. The sides had shared eleven goals between them that season, and had also filled the top two spots in the attendance charts. Indeed, Football League officials were lamenting the fact that the two weren't meeting in the final at Wembley. 'It would have made a marvellous final,' a League spokesman told the *Herald* in the build-up to the game. Burnley had taken 35,000 fans to the national stadium for the Sherpa Van Trophy final in 1988, and the League anticipated similar numbers travelling from the Westcountry should Argyle make it that far. 'I think we've got to be looking at 30,000 fans at least coming from Plymouth. They've twice had 15,000 for a league game this season, and it's such a huge catchment area.'

But a first ever appearance beneath the Twin Towers was still at least 180 minutes away, and Argyle first had to negotiate a daunting trip to Turf Moor – where they had been soundly beaten 4–2 earlier that season. Far from urging caution, however, the manager was adamant that his side would be heading north with victory in mind. 'We will be trying to win the match,' said Shilton. 'Some sides might approach the game looking for a draw or a narrow defeat, but we are full of confidence and will be looking for a win. With away goals counting double, it's almost like a European tie and it's important we try and get a goal to take into the second leg.'

Shilton had the rare luxury of an almost fully-fit squad to choose from for the trip to Lancashire, but one player who missed out was the unlucky Dominic Naylor. The left-back had been almost an ever-present going into the visit to Wrexham in late April – but was surprisingly dropped for the trip to the Racecourse in favour of Keith Hill, and failed to regain his place in time for the play-offs. 'I don't know what happened there,' he reflects. 'Obviously something did because Shilton didn't play me in the play-offs. If I look back, it was probably the most disappointing thing for me that happened down there, but we were a really close bunch of lads. Hilly played left-back in my place and

I was more than pleased for him. It was more important for me that we won. Obviously I would have liked to have played, but we were such a good bunch of lads that going up was the most important thing for me.'

Argyle were allocated a section of Turf Moor's Longside Terrace, with 3,800 tickets available for £6.50 each, though in the end just over 2,500 made the pilgrimage from Plymouth for the 3 p.m. kick-off on Sunday 15 May. Even with a reduced travelling contingent, the atmosphere inside Turf Moor as kick-off approached was as electric as it was volatile. The Argyle supporters were separated from the home fans by an unstewarded wire fence, and the Burnley faithful laid down the gauntlet by hoisting an Argyle scarf above their heads on a pole and setting it alight.

Down in the away dressing room, the Argyle players were preparing to enter the lion's den for a match that was to be a particularly poignant occasion for one of them. Centre-back Adrian Burrows was to leave the club that summer, and fittingly had made his debut in a green shirt at Turf Moor ten years before. 'I remember thinking before kick-off that it could be my last match, because I wasn't a regular by any means under Shilton and I didn't know if I'd be selected for the second leg and beyond,' he says. 'I knew I wasn't going to be staying at the end of the season. Almost six months prior to that match I was told that I wasn't going to be offered a new contract, but I just wanted to play as many matches as I could and then get another club come the end of the season. So I just went into the match wanting to finish on a high note.'

With Burrows taking his place in the centre of defence alongside Andy Comyn, Argyle dug their heels in from the off and could have snatched a first-half lead when Dwight Marshall latched onto a Landon dink over the top. The striker rounded Burnley keeper Marlon Beresford, only to trickle his shot agonisingly wide of the far post with the away fans already celebrating. 'I somehow missed giving us the lead,' says Marshall. 'I took it round the keeper and, even today when I look at the angle I was at, I know I should have scored. I think I tried to be too precise but put it just wide. I remember talking to Steve McCall afterwards, and he agreed with me that I should have just got my head down and put my foot through it.'

But Marshall's misery was overtaken as the main talking point of the match when Burrows was controversially dismissed by referee Keith Cooper just after half-time. Cooper had already set the tone for the contest by booking six players in the first half, and though a sending off was perhaps inevitable in such an explosive battle, no-one would have anticipated the circumstances in which it duly came.

Burrows was chasing a long ball over the top with an opponent in close pursuit, but stumbled as he was about to control the ball – which bounced up and hit him on the shoulder. Cooper showed Burrows a red card, a decision that was to have far-reaching consequences for the Pilgrims' fortunes in the tie. 'The idiot who was refereeing that day was Keith Cooper of Pontypridd,' remembers Gordon Sparks, commentating that day for Plymouth Sound.

> He was this little baldy Welshman. I enjoyed watching him up to a point because when he sprinted at full speed he was like a cartoon character, his legs went so fast you couldn't see them, just circles. When Burrows was sent off, I said on the radio that he was pushed from behind and his body struck the ball at the point where the top of the arm meets the body. No way was that intentional handball, but he was sent off. I was livid and made that clear in the broadcast. I did notice, and this is where I made an assumption, and an incorrect one on the radio, that a couple of Burnley players were really sarcastically rubbing it in, walking alongside him towards the tunnel with their arms around him and I thought they were trying to wind him up. But speaking to Adrian afterwards, they were actually saying there was no way he should have been sent off, because they knew it wasn't a deliberate handball.

For Burrows himself, the dismissal was a heartbreaking way to end his Argyle pilgrimage and, as it turned out, his career as a professional footballer. 'It was the first time that I'd ever been sent off,' he says. 'So I was sent off in my last ever match as a footballer. My brothers were in the ground that day to see my final game. They'd not really been able to see me that often, but they knew I wasn't going to be playing many more games so they came along, but they didn't quite see me as long as they hoped.' And of the sending off? 'I was in front of the striker with the ball coming over the top. It reared up a little bit and I felt as though it hit me … more ball to shoulder really, but the ref saw it more arm to ball and I was gone.'

Midfielder David Eyres was the Burnley player in hot pursuit of Burrows, and understands the Argyle reaction to Cooper's decision. 'I was closest to Burrows when it happened, and I did think it was quite harsh at the time,' he reflects. 'When he was going off I asked him if there was anything I could say to the ref that might help, but Cooper had already made his mind up and I just said to Adrian that it was pretty harsh. The fact that he'd miss the next game and probably Wembley as well … I could understand him being upset.'

Burrows returned to an empty dressing room and the reality of what the dismissal meant began to sink in. 'I must admit I shed a tear or two when I got back into the dressing room, because I realised that was it for me. I thought that even if we made the final I still might not get another game. It was a sad way for my Argyle career to end, but I've got no complaints. I had ten years at Argyle and it was great.'

Out on the pitch, Burrows' team-mates were facing more than forty minutes without their most experienced defender. Keith Hill filled in for Burrows in the centre of defence, while Steve McCall switched to left-back. When Adrian Heath went close to opening the scoring for the home side soon afterwards, Shilton and McGovern decided to shut up shop – sending Wayne Burnett on for striker Richard Landon in a bid to pack the middle of the park with bodies and fence off a Burnley midfield that had been largely anonymous up to that point anyway.

Paul Dalton believes Shilton learned a valuable lesson from the side's previous Turf Moor encounter earlier that season. 'We went to Burnley in the league and we got stuffed 4–2,' he says. 'I think that had a lot to do with our approach in the play-off match. We knew we had to be a bit more disciplined defensively, especially when Adrian was sent off, because they were so dangerous at home – as they had proved against us before.'

With time running out, the Clarets resorted to speculative long-range efforts as they desperately sought a goal to take with them to Devon.

As the home fans began to voice their frustration at their side's inability to forge an advantage, the travelling Argyle fans in the Longside Terrace paid tribute to the heroics of the short-handed Pilgrims with an impromptu number that became the overwhelming soundtrack of the final stages of the first-leg. 'Ten men, we only need ten men!' went the passionate refrain over and over again, at which point many in the home stands decided they'd seen and heard enough.

Shilton was naturally the happier of the two managers with the goalless draw, but inevitably refused to accept that his side were home and dry. 'It's only half time and there's a long way to go,' he said. 'We are happy but we won't be complacent and there is still plenty of work to be done.'

Meanwhile, his opposite number, Jimmy Mullen, was fuming at what he saw as a roughhouse approach to the game by Argyle. 'Anybody who knows football knew in the first two minutes when the first tackle went in what they were trying to do,' he said. 'Some of the tackles that went in on my lads in the first quarter of an hour I thought were an absolute disgrace.'

Shilton disagreed, insisting his side had only given as good as they had got. 'I think Burnley put it about a bit too, but we stood up for ourselves and that's what you've got to do sometimes. It shows we can mix it with the best. If the opposition fancy a few tackles then so will we – it shows that we're not soft.'

David Eyres believes the contest simply reflected the competitive nature of both sets of players. He says:

It was a physical, scrappy game, but from playing against Plymouth in the league that's the sort of game we had come to expect. We were a hardworking, physical side and they had some strong players too, and none of us shied away when it came to putting in challenges. But in a two-legged semi to get to Wembley you expect it even more – it was a typical cup tie really. The gaffer was probably just upset that we only drew 0–0 and were going to Home Park as underdogs. Once the whistle went I'm sure Plymouth thought that they had one foot at Wembley.

Indeed, while the atmosphere in the away dressing room was far from complacent, there was certainly a heavy air of confidence surrounding the

Argyle players as they prepared for the long coach journey back down to Devon. 'It was a great occasion up there, a full house,' says Mark Patterson. 'We played with ten men and we still should have won. We played really well, and I remember coming back down the motorway and thinking, "We've got a great chance now of getting to Wembley."'

'I remember finishing the game just delighted with a 0–0 draw,' says centre-back and man-of-the-match Andy Comyn. 'To have had ten men for so long and got a draw against a very good home side was terrific. We were a decent home side too, and Burnley were poor away, so even though we didn't think we were through, we certainly thought we had got through the hardest part.'

Martin Barlow agrees. 'It wasn't particularly a great game,' he says. 'But it was a good result, we'd have been happy with that before the game. We were so strong at home, so obviously we thought we had a great chance.'

However, Wayne Burnett reflects on a dangerous undercurrent of over-confidence among the squad. 'It was probably the worst result we could have had if I'm honest,' he says. 'We went back into the changing room thinking that we only had to go back home to Home Park and the rest would take care of itself. I'm being perfectly honest, we thought as a group of players, just among ourselves, that getting that 0–0 draw made us favourites to win the tie and that we would win it. We thought we'd be in the final.'

Steve McCall was satisfied with what was mission accomplished, but reveals how one member of the Argyle squad took the muted celebrations a step too far.

Before the game we were saying, 'Let's keep it tight, let's get a good result to take back to Home Park and get our win there.' We got the result we wanted and we couldn't see any problems ahead, we were going to go down there and we were going to beat them. But the turning point for me was the behaviour of Alan Nicholls. There had been something going on with him and a couple of their players during the game. Then after the match, he started winding them all up. He got involved with a few of their players, saying stuff like, 'We're going to Wembley.' Things like that can just focus players a little bit – where the disappointment of them being held 0–0 all of a sudden gives way to a little bit more determination to stick one on us, which was a motivation that they didn't need from our point of view. Alan was told off, 'We've still got a job to do, be professional and don't get involved with them.' It was a stupid thing to do though.

With ticket sales for the return leg going through the roof and with fans already making tentative arrangements for a trip to Wembley, Shilton publicly implored his players not to start dreaming of the Twin Towers just yet. 'Anyone who thinks we have reached Wembley already is daft,' said the manager. 'It's only half time and there's still a lot of work to be done.'

Mullen – all too aware of his side's frailties on the road that season – was pinning his hopes on the score-draw that would send Burnley through on the away goals rule. 'The second leg is just like an FA Cup semi-final,' he said. 'After there were no goals on Sunday, a score draw will get us through to Wembley.'

With Burrows suspended, Shilton was forced into an untimely reshuffling of his defence for the club's most crucial match of the season. Keith Hill partnered Andy Comyn in the centre of defence, while Steve McCall was pulled out of midfield to fill the left-back slot at the surprising expense of specialist full-back Dominic Naylor. Wayne Burnett, meanwhile, was given the considerable task of taking on the playmaker role vacated by McCall.

Burnley had a selection headache of their own as they headed south in preparation for the match. 'We travelled down and stayed just outside of Exeter, a lovely hotel out in the sticks,' remembers Mullen.

> But one of my best players, Ted McMinn, was a major doubt. He was on the end of a really crunching tackle from one of the Plymouth lads in the home leg, and I thought he was 90 per cent sure of missing the game, but he was adamant that he was going to be fit so he travelled with us. I always remember getting to the hotel, and Ted getting off the bus limping and me thinking, 'Jesus Christ, he's got no chance.' But to be fair to him he desperately wanted to play. He had a fitness test at the hotel, and he admitted to me that he wasn't 100 per cent right, but he asked to play for at least half-an-hour so I took the gamble because I knew how much he wanted to beat them.

On the morning of the game, the *Western Morning News* was one of a clutch of newspapers delivered to Burnley's hotel, and Mullen naturally turned straight to the back pages. The headline on Nigel Walrond's match preview caught his eye immediately – 'Argyle have the taste for weak Clarets', it said. In the preview itself, Walrond dutifully fulfilled his brief as a local reporter, talking up the home side's chances in that night's second leg: 'Argyle must start as strong favourites,' he wrote. 'Even after being reduced to ten men at the start of the second half [at Turf Moor], the Pilgrims still looked a class above the Clarets and showed why they finished the season with a twelve-point advantage over the Lancashire side.'

Mullen, evidently unaware that regional bias exists in local newspapers, was not pleased. 'All the directors were at the hotel, the chairman, all the staff and of course the players, when the newspapers arrived,' he remembers. 'And it was there for all to see – "Weak Clarets" it said, or something like that. The papers were basically saying Plymouth were already at Wembley. Someone at the hotel also told us that Plymouth had booked every bus here, there and everywhere for their trip to Wembley. That made my players a little bit angry, and a lot more determined to make sure that when we got to the ground we were going to do it properly.'

'It certainly spurred us on,' says David Eyres. 'When we got to Home Park there was a carnival atmosphere going on. There were a lot of supporters saying,

"Unlucky" and things like that. A lot of them had Wembley banners that they were holding up against our coach.'

Mullen had tucked the *Morning News* story away in his pocket for later, but on his arrival at Home Park he was provided with another gem to put towards his pre-match team talk – thanks to the brand new green and black-striped shirt Argyle would be wearing for the first time that night. 'We got to the stadium and I went in with my chairman to meet Mr McCauley,' says Mullen.

> We shook hands and were having a chit-chat about the game, and what a big occasion it was. Out of the blue, in walks one of McCauley's directors with a Plymouth shirt, and says, 'This is the shirt we're going to wear at Wembley, Dan.' I just said, 'Thank you very much, you've just given my players the best team talk that anyone could ever give them.' I could see Mr McCauley's face drop, as if to say, 'Oh no – do you realise what you've just done?' I walked out and went and told my players exactly what had happened, and also reminded them about the buses that were being booked up to go to Wembley. I told them, 'You've got an incentive now because they think they're already there, so don't disappoint those travelling supporters out there, and don't disappoint yourselves.'

Mullen's claim is news to Argyle director Ivor Jones. 'I think that might have been Jimmy Mullen psyching up his team, because I don't remember any of that going on,' he asserts. 'There might have been some provisional coach bookings because people were obviously hopeful, but to say something like that … none of us expected us to roll them over. That's good psychology by Mullen.'

His players certainly thought so. 'The gaffer had seen a couple of local papers,' says Eyres. 'So he just put these articles up on the dressing room wall, saying, "I don't need to do a team talk, just look at the headlines in the local papers. They think they're there already. It's a chance for us to put them back a step or two."'

'It was a good move from Jimmy,' reflects Burnley keeper Marlon Beresford. 'It actually did the trick because it gave us more of an incentive to prove them wrong.'

Over in the home dressing room, the Argyle management team were doing their best to keep a lid on the heightened expectations of their players. 'Obviously everyone's thinking about Wembley,' says John McGovern.

> But you're trying to keep the players' feet on the ground, so we told them, 'Hey, we've got a job to do now, this is when we do it. You've earned the right, now go and get it done.' Of course, they do hear certain things from the outside about what the fans are saying, and it's your job on the management team to remind them that it's never over till it's over. Peter and I had had similar experiences. We'd gone to Wembley against Wolves in our third consecutive League Cup final as red-hot favourites, but Peter ran into David Needham and Andy Gray walked

the ball into the net and we lost. Everybody's looking at each other afterwards and thinking, 'How have we done that?' We could have played Wolves ten times that season and beaten them nine times, so we were trying to pass that kind of experience on to the players.

Unknown to the expectant supporters basking in the early summer sunshine, the battle between the two sides was already unfolding underneath the packed main stand. 'There was a bit of a ruckus in the tunnel before the game,' remembers Burnley striker John Francis. 'There were a few words said between the two teams, started by the Plymouth goalkeeper actually. He was being a bit of a tosser, going around threatening us. There were a few chuckles and nervous laughs at a couple of comments he made. So things were already quite heated before we even got out onto the pitch, but we went out there with that little bit more of an incentive to prove him wrong.'

'It goes with the game really – a bit of banter, a bit of winding up in the tunnel,' says Eyres. 'There was a little bit of argy-bargy in the first leg but we tried not to let it affect us. So there were a few niggles down in Plymouth before the game, but it was probably more handbags than anything else. The Plymouth players seemed really confident going onto the pitch, but that and the carnival atmosphere at the ground just inspired us.'

Mark Patterson remembers walking out onto the Home Park pitch to a real sense of occasion. 'It seemed to take ages before the second leg came around, even though it was only three days,' he says. 'We walked out there into a beautiful summer's night and it was a full house – a hanging off the rafters job. We were all really fired up and were just keen to get the job done.'

Despite the feverish atmosphere and the confrontation in the tunnel, the match started at a sedate pace with neither side willing to take the initiative. But with fifteen minutes gone, the home side got a lucky break. Paul Dalton curled a free kick low into the box that Dwight Marshall flicked on with the back of his head. The change of trajectory threw Burnley defender John Pender, and he could only sidefoot the ball straight back out to Marshall who smacked a fierce rising drive straight into the roof of the net via Marlon Beresford's outstretched gloves. Cue pandemonium inside Home Park. 'The ball's come back to me and I just smashed it,' says Marshall. 'I remember thinking, "That makes up for that miss in the away leg." I didn't normally score from that distance, but we were 1–0 up and nearly there.'

Beresford admits Marshall's goal left him wondering if the Wembley dream was over. 'Marshall took a shot from near the edge of the box, a really powerful hit that flashed past me,' he remembers. 'I got up and thought, "Christ, we're up against it here."'

Over in the away dugout, Mullen was carefully studying his players to see how they would respond to the early setback. 'I was sat there thinking, "Well, we've got to do something now that we haven't done all season, and that's come from behind away from home." Going a goal down obviously didn't help us, but normally when that happens you look at your team and you can see one or two heads go down and you think, "Here we go again." But I looked at my players and there was none of that at Plymouth. I didn't see anyone put their head down.'

Prior to the game, Shilton had publicly warned his players to guard against Burnley's attacking threat on the counter. 'We have got to get forward without leaving the back door open to allow Burnley a goal which could give them the initiative,' he said, before adding with ominous foresight, 'We need to have total concentration at the back when we are attacking.'

With a decisive 1–0 advantage to protect, Shilton's cavalier players failed to heed their manager's advice and pushed up in search of a killer second goal. After twenty-nine minutes, Adrian Heath prodded a ball over the heads of Argyle's static back four, who had been watching the play unfold in Burnley's defensive third from the halfway line. Centre-back Andy Comyn looked odds-on favourite to reach Heath's hopeful punt, but John Francis tore past him to steal the ball, before evading the challenge of the onrushing Alan Nicholls and slotting home to give his side the upper hand in the tie.

Home Park was stunned into silence, but worse was to come just two minutes later. Paul Dalton lost possession midway inside his own half and another Heath pass found Francis lurking dangerously inside the centre-circle. With Comyn and Hill blocking his path to goal and with no team-mate up in support, Francis went for broke. Running straight at the pair of centre-backs, he dumped Comyn on his backside and outpaced Hill before prodding the ball into a gaping goal after Nicholls had once again raced out in a futile attempt to narrow the angle.

Sat in the stands watching on in disbelief was the suspended Adrian Burrows, who couldn't help but wonder what might have been had it not been for his cruel sending off at Turf Moor. 'Who knows what would have happened if I hadn't been sent off? John Francis actually played out wide in the first game, but in the second leg he played down the middle and I think it was his pace through there that undid us in the end. I like to think that if I'd played it might not have happened. But it's all conjecture.'

Comyn also laments the absence of the most experienced member of Argyle's squad just when they most needed his calming presence. 'Adrian had a great few months towards the end of that season and had been playing really solidly,' he says. 'But with him suspended, Burnley changed their tactics accordingly and we didn't handle it at all. They put John Francis up front and it caused us major problems. We obviously weren't at all happy with those goals from a defensive point of view. Not happy at all.'

Steve McCall shares the view that Burrows' Turf Moor red card sealed Argyle's fate. 'The big disappointment of the first game was obviously the sending off of Adrian,' he says. 'That affected the balance of the defence. We had a settled side going then with me in midfield and Hilly at left-back. But for the second leg it was a case of, "Hang on, we've got to shuffle a few things around and come up with a new back four now," and obviously it just didn't work.'

Wayne Burnett, who was sacrificed after Burnley's second goal in a tactical reshuffle, felt the goals were the fault of Argyle's young goalkeeper rather than the two centre-backs. 'Alan Nicholls had been our hero so many times that season,' he says. 'But he wasn't the hero that night. Those two goals were down to him, he came rushing out when he shouldn't have, but that's football. We went 2–1 down and it was a mountain too far to climb really.' Steve McCall agrees. 'We got a great start, just the start we wanted,' he says.

> I didn't see any problems coming from anywhere, and then all of sudden it's 1–1. Then Alan starts getting involved with their players because they're obviously winding him up, makes a rash decision to come off his line and it's 2–1. After the second, he came out of his goal up to the halfway line and took his gloves off, and I was like, 'Get back in your goal and concentrate on what you're doing – we haven't finished yet, get back!' But he wanted to complain to the referee for some reason. It was strange where his head was at. He was young and inexperienced and he probably couldn't deal with the occasion.

With a home support watching on in outraged disbelief, Francis further stoked the flames of an already volatile atmosphere. 'When I scored, I ran around the side of the pitch doing a monkey impression,' he remembers.

> I was getting a lot of racist stick from the supporters at the time, which obviously wouldn't go on nowadays. It wasn't as bad in the first leg with the bigger Burnley crowd, but down there as soon as I got the ball there would be monkey sounds. If you watch the video, just before I get the ball you can hear them. So that's the reason why I did that. It wasn't a good thing to do, it isn't something that I would encourage anyone to copy, but it's one of those things you do on the spur of the moment.

Mullen was naturally delighted with the goal-scoring contribution of a player who hadn't even managed double figures in regular league action that season. 'John Francis was absolutely fantastic on the night,' he says. 'I remember him running from near enough the halfway line for the first goal, and he was almost carrying the centre-half on his back. His strength and his power, not to mention his pace, took him through. He wasn't the most clinical of finishers when he got in front of goal, but both of those goals that night he finished fantastically well. He ran riot, he was on fire.'

The half-time whistle was greeted by resounding cheers from the 1,000 or so Burnley fans standing on the Barn Park terrace, but stony silence from the other three sides of the ground. Argyle had to score twice in the second half against a side that would inevitably sit deep and leave the lethal Francis lurking on his own up front – or their promotion dream was over.

In the home dressing room, assistant boss McGovern was in no doubt of where the blame lay for his side's predicament. 'We were having most of the play,' he remembers, 'but all of a sudden they break away and get a goal, and then they go and do exactly the same thing two minutes later. I said to the two centre-halves at half time, "You two should be fucking shot, getting caught twice like that. Okay, you fall for the three-card trick once, but you've somehow fallen for it twice." The thing was, we got caught for the second because we were pressing, trying to get a goal back.'

The home crowd did their best to lift the deflated Pilgrims after the break, but it soon became clear that Argyle's attacking talents had no answer to the claret and blue wall that had sprung up in front of them since Francis had inflicted his double-blow.

Kevin Nugent was brought on for Richard Landon with precious time ticking away, but Argyle could create nothing more than a handful of half-chances against their resolute visitors. 'At 2–1 up they can just sit back,' says McCall. 'We got our lead and they're having to come out, giving us space to counter-attack them. But all of a sudden it's us trying to chase the game. We had a lot of possession in the second half but we couldn't convert it into chances. Credit to them, they did a good job on us.'

'As much as we huffed and puffed in the second half, it wasn't going to happen,' says Patterson. 'And then Alan dropped a shot, Joyce fired it into the net and it was all over.'

Indeed, Burnley's Wembley invitation was rubber-stamped nine minutes from time when Ted McMinn's angled shot was fumbled by Nicholls, leaving ex-Argyle midfielder Warren Joyce to rub salt in the wound by tapping home Burnley's third. 'Even at a goal down we could still have got one back and pushed on from there, so we were doing most of the pressing,' says McGovern. 'But then they scored again and at the end of the game the ground's like a morgue, it was like a graveyard. Usually you'd have some kind of reaction from the crowd at the final whistle, but it was just total silence. I think stunned was probably the best word to describe the atmosphere in the dressing room afterwards. We were just stunned that we'd gone up there and got a result but couldn't get one at home. It didn't work out on the night, sometimes in football that does happen, but it's really hard to bear.'

For captain Steve Castle, the final whistle brought with it the painful realisation that he hadn't contributed as much to the play-off cause as he perhaps ought to have done. 'The first thing I thought when the whistle went was that I hadn't done myself justice,' he reflects. 'I don't think I played that well over the two legs, but saying that, I didn't play well in any of my play-off games. It was just an empty, gutted feeling as I walked off. All that hard work … gone just like that. We'd got so far and done all the hard work up at Burnley, but not managed to finish it off. It was just devastation in the dressing room.'

Castle believes the manner in which the two John Francis goals were conceded was a microcosm of the season. 'We started off well, but then we had two or three minutes of madness and we couldn't come back from it. It was those defensive frailties that maybe should have been addressed way before the play-offs – it should have been addressed during the season. A lot of work should have been done on making us less attractive going forward but much more solid, and had we done that we'd have gone up without a doubt.'

Right-back Mark Patterson echoes his captain's account of a disconsolate dressing room. 'I remember the final whistle going and thinking, "We've shot ourselves in the foot here, we've done ourselves a disservice." I remember walking into the dressing room and sitting there thinking, "Jesus Christ, how has that happened?" It was very much an anti-climax when you look at how well we'd done to get there and the football we'd played. If you could say anyone deserved to go up I think we did deserve it, but it doesn't work that way.'

After the game, Patterson was presented with a belated man-of-the-match award for an earlier away game, and remembers wanting to get the bottle of champagne he received out of his sight as soon as possible.

I got a bottle of champers given to me after the game and I thought 'I don't want this.' I didn't want to walk around with it and have people asking me what I had a bottle of champagne for. So I went up to the Burnley dressing room and went in to see Ted McMinn because we used to live together in Derby. I went in and said, 'There you go, have a drink with your mates and I hope you win at Wembley,' and walked out again. What did I want a bottle of bubbly for? It was almost like it was the wrong way around, I didn't want it because we hadn't won. We had a chance to go up automatically but blew that, and we had a chance to go up through the play-offs but blew that as well, and I was obviously in no mood to celebrate.

'We were shellshocked because we should have gone up automatically,' adds McCall. 'We did the job in the first leg, we were miles better than Burnley and should have been going to Wembley with a chance of promotion. But all of a sudden it was cut off, the season is finished and that was it. That's us then, we don't get another chance – absolutely shocking way to finish the season.'

Martin Barlow was similarly choked. 'It was a massive shame really because the whole season's just a waste because of one night,' he laments. 'To finish twelve points above them, it was ridiculous. You forget the whole season, everything we had achieved, and the football we played was the best Argyle fans had seen for years – but it was all for nothing.'

Paul Dalton remembers being particularly frustrated at being denied a chance to play at Wembley. 'We all thought that Stockport would win their play-off game,' he says, 'and that the bigger pitch at Wembley would suit our attacking style better than it would Stockport's, so we thought the Burnley game was our play-off final if you like. And whoever won it would get promoted – and that's how it turned out with Burnley beating Stockport at Wembley to go up.'

Richard Landon recalls Shilton and McGovern's final team talk of the season. 'They were very despondent,' he remembers, 'but they said to us, "It's done with now, forget it, we have to start again next season. Go off on your holidays, enjoy yourselves but come back ready to work and we'll go again." And we all went off gutted but looking forward to the new season at the same time.'

For Burnley boss Jimmy Mullen, the victory still holds special memories. 'I'll never forget that night,' he says. 'Because of what was said before the game, the coaches to Wembley, John Francis, and that bloody new green and black shirt.'

Just a few months later, Mullen wasn't the only one bemoaning that bloody green and black shirt.

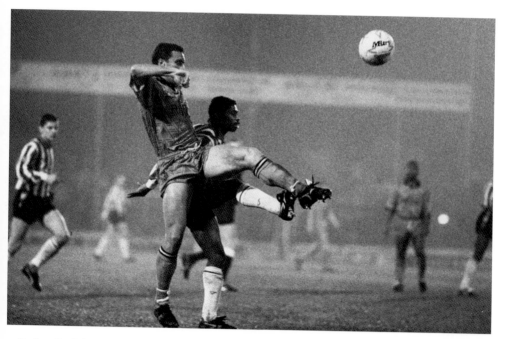

1. Striker Dwight Marshall attempts to hold off the attentions of future Argyle team-mate Mick Heathcote during the 1–0 home defeat to Cambridge United in February 1992. Marshall led the scoring charts in 91/92 with fourteen goals in his debut season in league football.

2. Tony Spearing launches into a typically crunching tackle. The feisty left-back fell out with Peter Shilton over his committed approach to the game in a friendly at Bodmin Town, and he was shipped out of the club soon after.

3. Peter Shilton poses on the Home Park pitch hours after his high-profile appointment as Plymouth Argyle player-manager was announced on 2 March 1992. Different versions of this picture appeared on the back pages of most national newspapers the following day.

4. Shilton makes his dugout bow alongside new number two, John McGovern, during the 1–1 draw at home to Derby County in March 1992. Jock Morrison's equaliser ensured the pair's Argyle tenure got off to a steady start.

5. Winger David Smith puts Argyle 1–0 up in the crucial home encounter with Blackburn Rovers in May 1992, before three unanswered goals by David Speedie condemned Argyle to relegation after six seasons at the second level of English football.

6. Victorious Blackburn manager Kenny Dalglish consoles Argyle skipper Nicky Marker – a player he would sign for the Lancashire club just three months later. Blackburn would go on to win the Premier League title three years later, though not a single one of Marker's fifty-four Rovers' appearances came during that season.

7. Strikers Kevin Nugent (left) and Dave Regis (centre) celebrate a rare goal in their short-lived partnership up front (winger Craig Skinner is pictured in the background). Regis would be sold to Stoke City less than a year after signing from Notts County for a club record £200,000.

8. Peter Shilton leaves the field after keeping a clean sheet in the 2–0 win over Chester City on 10 October 1992. Despite occasional brilliance between the posts, ageing limbs and an inability to cope with the backpass law meant the former England keeper managed just forty-three appearances in three years at Home Park.

9. The manager and his assistant take a breather on the Harpers Park training pitch in the summer of 1993. McGovern admits he occasionally felt restrained by the manager when it came to coaching the club's outfield players.

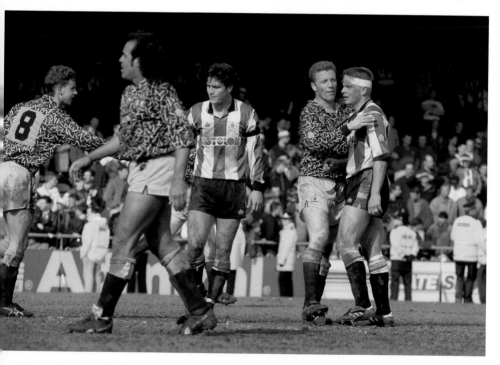

10. Skipper Gary Poole (centre) and centre-back Jock Morrison (right) retreat to the dressing room to a chorus of boos following the 3–0 home defeat to rivals Exeter City on 10 April 1992. Despite the abject performance, Argyle won 5–2 at promotion-chasing West Brom just two days later.

11. *Left:* Steve McCall receives the club's official Player of the Year trophy for 1992/93. The former Ipswich Town utility man also scooped the honour the following season, becoming the first player since Paul Mariner in the mid-1970s to win the award in consecutive seasons.

12. *Below:* Argyle's 92/93 captain Steve Castle in typically barnstorming form at the heart of the action. Castle was the only Argyle player to hit twenty league goals in a season over a twenty-year period from 1988/89 (Tommy Tynan) to date (2008/09).

13. Flamboyant winger Paul Dalton in full flight down the Argyle left. The former Manchester United apprentice made 111 league and cup starts in his three years at Home Park and scored twenty-nine goals – but missed thirty-nine games through injury.

14. Maverick goalkeeper Alan Nicholls spent just two full seasons at Home Park – an eventful spell during which he made seventy-nine appearances, kept twenty-two clean sheets, won eight player of the season awards, was sent off twice and was capped by his country once.

15. Steve Castle throws himself at the ball to score the second of a double-strike in a 3–1 win against his former club Leyton Orient on 11 September 1993. Castle was in sensational goal-scoring form in the calendar year of 1993, scoring twenty-six goals in fifty-one appearances.

16. Kevin Nugent and Paul Dalton celebrate Nugent's first of two strikes in a 3–2 win against Cardiff City at Ninian Park on 25 September 1993. The brace added to a flurry of four goals in three games for the former Leyton Orient striker – who ended the 93/94 season with seventeen league and cup goals to his name.

17. Dwight Marshall celebrates in front of 3,000 travelling Argyle fans after scoring the winner in a 1–0 victory at Bournemouth on New Year's Day 1994. The victory was Argyle's eighth in a row in all competitions, and their fifth league away win of the season.

18. Kevin Nugent arrows home a left-foot shot to put Argyle 2–1 up against Reading in a fine 3–1 victory over their promotion rivals on 12 March 1994. Future West Ham, Newcastle and Portsmouth goalkeeper Shaka Hislop (in the purple jersey) endured a torrid afternoon at Home Park.

19. Nugent is congratulated by team-mates Andy Comyn (left) and Steve McCall (right) after his Devonport End strike. Argyle were prolific goal-scorers at Home Park in 93/94, scoring forty-six goals in twenty-three games. They failed to find the net just once on home turf – against Cambridge United on 16 April.

20. Richard Landon, a striker signed from non-league Bedworth United in January 1994, celebrates his hat-trick strike in Argyle's thumping win at Hartlepool United on 7 May 1994. Landon scored five goals in the last four games of the 93/94 season – but managed just seven the following campaign and was sold to Stockport County.

21. Referee Keith Gifford shows Argyle centre-back Adrian Burrows (in yellow shirt, far right) a red card for deliberate handball in the first leg of the play-off semi-final against Burnley at Turf Moor on 15 May 1994. The dismissal was the first of Burrows' ten-year professional career.

22. Peter Shilton passes on instructions to his players during the Burnley first leg. The sending off of Burrows threatened to derail Argyle's play-off bid, but a smart reshuffling of his pack stifled the home side and earned an encouraging draw for Shilton's men.

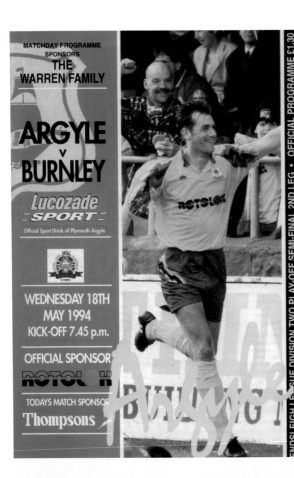

MATCHDAY PROGRAMME
SPONSORS
THE
WARREN FAMILY

ARGYLE
v
BURNLEY

Lucozade
SPORT
Official Sport Drink of Plymouth Argyle

WEDNESDAY 18TH
MAY 1994
KICK-OFF 7.45 p.m.

OFFICIAL SPONSOR
ROTOLOK

TODAYS MATCH SPONSOR
Thompsons

OFFICIAL PROGRAMME £1.30 • ENDSLEIGH LEAGUE DIVISION TWO PLAY-OFF SEMI-FINAL 2ND LEG

23. *Left:* The match-day programme from the second leg of the play-off semi-final against Burnley at Home Park. The crucial fixture was attended by 17,515 spectators – the club's highest gate since 27,566 packed into Home Park for the 1–1 FA Cup fourth-round draw against Everton in January 1989.

24. *Below:* A bleeding Keith Hill looks shellshocked as he leaves the pitch following the play-off second-leg defeat to Burnley at Home Park. Hill and fellow centre-back Andy Comyn were given a torrid time by Burnley hero John Francis, but it was Hill who ultimately carried the can for the defeat.

25. *Right:* Chairman Dan McCauley shakes hands with Peter Shilton after agreeing the manager's new contract the day after the Burnley defeat. But despite the smiles, the pair's relationship was already crumbling and was soon to break down irretrievably.

26. *Below:* Peter Swan signs on the dotted line to complete his club record £300,000 signing from Port Vale on 20 July 1994. The Yorkshireman claims Argyle attempted to deceive him over the terms of his contract, insisting the discrepancy was only resolved after he threatened to walk out of the press conference.

27. Swan shares a joke with his new manager on the Home Park pitch. Shilton was renowned for his ability to convince sceptical players to sign for the club, but simply had to match Swan's opportunistic wage demands to get his man.

28. Shilton puts his players through their paces in the summer of 1994. Argyle were among the favourites to go up in 94/95, but lost most of their key players to injury during the pre-season friendly programme – by which time Shilton had already spent most of his transfer budget on Peter Swan.

29. An exasperated Shilton attempts to rally his hapless troops during the disastrous 5–1 defeat to Brentford on the opening day of the 94/95 season. The manager's post-match press conference included the infamous line, 'Things can only get better.'

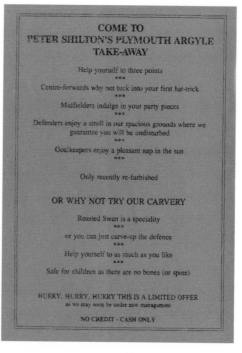

30. The front and back covers of Argyle fanzine *Rub of the Greens* from the autumn of 1994. The front cover takes a cynical look at the financial disagreement that led to John McGovern's resignation, while the back mocks the dreadful start to the 94/95 season at Home Park.

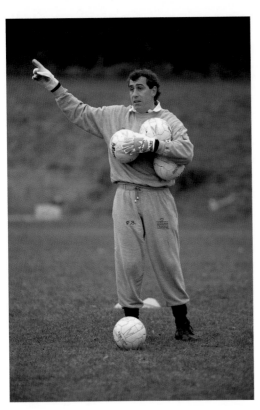

31. *Left:* Peter Shilton endured an arduous final few months as Argyle manager. Having lost his assistant, he was also forced to juggle an appalling injury list, a tempestuous chairman, an unhappy dressing room and the breakdown of his personal finances.

32. *Below:* The headstone of Alan Nicholls at St Paul's Parish Church in Blackheath, Birmingham. The former Argyle keeper was buried at 3 p.m. on a Saturday afternoon, a stone's throw away from a park football pitch.

Chapter Ten

NICO

The atmosphere around Home Park in the summer of 1994 was largely one of missed opportunities. But for one member of Peter Shilton's squad, the greatest opportunity of them all was just around the corner.

Despite his moments of madness in the second leg against Burnley, Alan Nicholls was still considered the club's most exciting prospect in years after an electrifying debut season in league football. The bargain signing from non-league Cheltenham Town had already received one richly deserved call-up to the England Under-21 squad that year, but had been forced to withdraw to line-up for his club side against Barnet at Home Park. A second chance wasn't long in coming, however, and senior England boss Terry Venables was keen to assess the nineteen-year-old's qualities by including him in the Under-21 squad for that summer's Toulon Tournament in France.

For the young Brummie, the call-up completed a startling rise from the depths of non-league football that would dazzle like the brightest of comets but fizzle out in the worst way imaginable.

Alan Nicholls was born on 23 August 1973 in Sutton Coldfield, Birmingham, the first and only child of Alan and Celia Nicholls. A pupil of King's Norton Boys' School in the south of the city, Nicholls was an early learner with a football – and his father soon spotted a unique ability. 'He was five or six when he first started to properly kick a ball around,' remembers Alan senior. 'The first thing I noticed was that he was left-footed and had a hell of a kick on him. He was the only one in the family who wasn't right-footed, so where he got that from, I don't know.'

Nicholls decided to don a pair of gloves despite being rather useful with the ball at his feet, and his progression between the sticks was rapid. 'He was the Birmingham schoolboys Under-11 goalkeeper at the age of nine,' says Alan. 'They always said he'd make it. We were told a long time before that potentially he would play for his country if he wanted to.'

The budding youngster's potential was quickly spotted by eagle-eyed scouts in the Midlands, and before long he was training with West Bromwich Albion. 'We got to know a lot of scouts,' says Alan.

> They would be chasing after every promising kid in the country, offering them free trainers, all sorts of things. I got fed up with the Blues [Birmingham City], they were pestering him all the time, they never stopped. Alan was playing for Erdington Star at the time, which was one of the best clubs in the Birmingham Boys' League. At one match, I was told an Albion scout was there and he wanted to have a word with me – apparently he wanted to take Alan on. I said, 'How do you mean?', and he replied, 'Sign him up for the club.' Alan would have been eleven then.

Nicholls' stay with the Baggies was a short one, but the young keeper didn't have to wait long for the offers to start flooding in once more. 'Nobby Stiles was one of the West Brom coaches then,' says his dad. 'But it was a bit of a waste of time. Stiles wasn't a goalkeeping coach, so Alan had six weeks there and that was enough.

'So he left Albion and, of course, once one club has been sniffing, they all start sniffing. So the Villa came in for him then. He was with [former Villa keeper] Nigel Spink there for eighteen months, he took him under his wing and they got on really well. Nigel was a case, a nice fella.'

Villa boss Graham Taylor was keen to sign Spink's protégé on schoolboy forms, but the headstrong youngster had other ideas. 'It was pre-season at Bodymoor Heath, Villa's training ground,' remembers Alan. 'Taylor called him into the office to get him to sign schoolboy forms, which would have been a two-year deal. But when Taylor said he couldn't guarantee that Nigel would be coaching him, Alan said no. It was his decision, not mine or anybody else's. He was his own person even back then.'

With Villa and Nigel Spink now history, the fourteen-year-old Nicholls spread his wings in search of a professional club that would nurture his talent with the necessary care. 'We had loads of clubs sniffing when he left Villa,' says Alan. 'He spent Christmas week one year at Crewe with Dario Gradi. The set-up there was brilliant, but it was just too far for him to travel. They trained every Monday and it wasn't really possible for him to get there every week. He also went down to Tottenham, it was just after the hurricane in 1987 and all the tops had been taken off the trees. Maybe that was what put him off, but he didn't fancy it down there.'

With scouts offering Nicholls and his dad all sorts of incentives, it was Wolves who finally won the race with a rather more spartan approach. 'Wolves offered him none of the crazy stuff,' says Alan.

> All they were going to give him was a proper kit and proper training. But more importantly they were also going to employ an international coach just to look after his training – I was very impressed by that and the set-up there. Graham

Turner was the Wolves manager then. I couldn't go to Al's first week of training because I was on shift, but I took him to the second. I remember Turner shouting over, 'Alright Al?' He'd only met him the week before and he remembered his name, that was really impressive. After a few weeks, Alan was coaching the eleven- and twelve-year-olds, he wasn't worried about his own training.

A year into his schoolboy contract at Molineux, Nicholls had progressed in such great strides that he was considered for first-team duty at the tender age of fifteen. 'Mark Kendall was the first-team keeper at the time,' says Alan. 'He'd cut his hand, so Graham Turner set a practice match up just to watch Alan against some of the first-team pros. He must have done well because he was put on standby for the first match of the season. He was a £28-a-week YTS lad when he was the second-choice keeper – at fifteen!'

With his career about to explode into life, disaster struck for Nicholls when he became involved in a ticket-touting scam with some of the other schoolboys at the club. 'The Wolves used to give him free tickets, and Alan and some of the others were flogging them,' says his dad. 'Of course, they eventually got caught. Wolves took them all to court and kicked them out. They kept Alan's registration though, so basically he couldn't play first-team football for any other league club without their say so.'

Banished by Wolves and unable to sign for another league club, Nicholls could have drifted into a life outside of football, but decided to get straight back on the horse. 'Getting kicked out would finish some lads,' says his dad, 'but it just made Alan even more determined to make it. He wanted to prove a point to himself and everyone else.'

Nicholls signed as a semi-pro for Cradley Town FC of the Midland Football Combination – nine levels below the Conference – in a bid to kickstart his faltering career. In his first season the club finished top of the West Midlands League Division One and were promoted to the Premier Division.

After displaying the effusive form that had taken him to the verge of the Wolves first team, Nicholls nearly ended up in the south-west a lot sooner than he eventually did. 'Torquay United used Cradley as a sort of nursery club,' says Alan. 'A lot of players went there from the Birmingham area, they were always up here sniffing.'

Nicholls was pencilled in to play five games for Torquay's reserves while on trial at Plainmoor, but Wolves pulled the plug on any potential deal because they still held his registration and presumably felt Nicholls deserved a longer spell in Midlands League obscurity.

His one and only match in Torquay colours came in a 5–2 win at Cheltenham Town, where a former Wolves stalwart was watching on from the Whaddon Road stands.

Ally Robertson had been a veteran centre-back at Molineux while Nicholls was trying to make his way in the reserves, and had made a note of the youngster's ability for future reference. Spurred into action by his solitary appearance for Torquay, Robertson tried to sign Nicholls while manager of Worcester City, but the trail went cold.

However, when he later took over as Cheltenham boss, Robertson tried again with more success. 'Alan came down and played in the reserves for me,' remembers Lindsay Parsons, Robertson's then assistant manager at Cheltenham. 'After just a couple of games I could see he had ability in spades.'

But with the Robins struggling in the lower reaches of the Conference, Robertson was sacked in January 1992 and Nicholls was facing up to another return to Cradley. 'Ally got the boot just after Christmas, and they put me in as caretaker boss,' says Parsons. 'The first thing I did was put Alan in the first team. Because like I said to Ally, the Board wasn't going to pay a fee for a player to come in and play in the reserves. If we're going to pay two or three thousand he'd have to be in the team. We signed him on Conference forms so we didn't have to pay Wolves for the league registration and he never looked back.'

Parsons was eventually given the job on a permanent basis, and set about providing the team with an influx of youth. 'I went to Cheltenham originally to run the youth team,' he says, 'and the first thing I wanted to do when I got the manager's job was to get rid of quite a few of the older players. Alan was a player of youth-team age who fitted the bill.'

Cheltenham were relegated from the Conference in May 1992, but under Parsons the Robins had begun to play more exciting football with a team of hungry young talents and optimism was high under the new regime.

'We had a bad season that year,' remembers long-serving Cheltenham club secretary, Paul Godfrey. 'We'd been near the bottom of the Conference all season and we ended up getting relegated. We'd had a terrible time of it, but Lindsay took over as caretaker in January '92 and he steadied things down a bit. He's a good judge of a player, particularly with young lads, and Alan was his first signing. We finished that season with a much better side than we started it with, even though we got relegated.'

Nicholls began 92/93 as Cheltenham's first-choice goalkeeper as they prepared for life in the Southern League. With Parsons at the helm, the Robins' fortunes took a much-needed U-turn and they went on to secure second place in their new division. 'It was a difficult introduction for Alan in his first season with us because we were crap and we conceded a lot of goals,' says Godfrey. 'But the following year we finished second and Alan was very good that season. He didn't play every game, but he was the regular keeper and played well.'

However, it wasn't all plain sailing. Still living in Birmingham, Nicholls would occasionally skip training sessions claiming he couldn't arrange transport. But Parsons decided to teach his young goalkeeper a lesson when he knew it would hit home the hardest.

'We played Bournemouth in the FA Cup,' he remembers, 'which was a huge game for us at the time. We drew the first game 1–1 at home, and Alan told me he couldn't make it to training the following Monday because he didn't have a car available. I just told him to get there however he could, and that if he didn't turn up he wouldn't be playing in our league game at Rugby the following Saturday.'

Nicholls ignored his manager's warning and didn't show up for training, but did report for duty at Rugby on the day of the club's Southern League fixture. 'I announced the team and I'd left him out,' says Parsons. 'He's waited until all the lads have gone out, then he's said to me, "I've been ill all week." Apparently he couldn't reach me. So I said to him, "If you've been ill all week, you're not fit to play then are you?" And he said, "I feel okay now." But I put my foot down with him and said "No, Nico, you're not playing." I had to show him he couldn't mess me about like that.'

Cheltenham prepared for their replay at Bournemouth by romping to a 5–0 win at Rugby without Nicholls in goal – and his replacement didn't have a single save to make.

Alan comes to me after the game and says 'Am I playing in the replay?' I said, 'Well, if you come in on Monday, you'll find out won't you?' So I go in on Monday to take the YTS lads for training, and Dennis Deacon the chairman asked me to play him. And I said 'No, Den, we've got to set an example here. As much as I want to play him, he's not playing. He's not going to be a big time Charlie and get away with it.' So Alan comes down for training on the Monday night, and he says, 'Before I train, I just want to know if I'm playing.' I couldn't believe it, and said, 'You're asking me that before you train? You want to know now do you?' He said, 'Yeah, now.' So I said, 'Okay, you're not playing,' and he stormed off back to Birmingham. Anyway, we were beaten 3–0 down at Bournemouth and the lads went out for a drink afterwards because we stayed the night down there. In fact, Nico came down with us and even stopped a couple of the lads doing something stupid that night. He never caused one ounce of trouble in football terms after that.

Nicholls was a popular figure at the club, according to Godfrey. 'He was a bit of a jack the lad,' he says. 'I've known a few footballers like him – on the outside you might think he was a bit brash, but once you got past that he was a nice kid really. He was obviously a bit of a character, but there were never any disciplinary problems. He was very, very popular at the club.'

But it was pretty evident to Parsons that wherever Nicholls went, trouble was always close by. 'There was never a dull moment with Nico,' he says. 'Things just seemed to follow him about. I always had a lot of time for Alan, but incidents seemed to happen with him all the time. There were a couple of things at the club that Alan got blamed for, and to be truthful I was always very wary of what he would do. Anything that went wrong I blamed him for, though I wasn't always right. But if he had someone with him who would get a bit carried away – then Nico was in his element. He was always game for a laugh.'

Despite his off-field antics, Nicholls was in sparkling form between the posts for Cheltenham, and it was only a matter of time before Peter Shilton got wind of the precocious youngster. The Argyle boss was at the Robins' FA Cup replay at Bournemouth, but was stunned to discover Nicholls wouldn't be playing. 'Shilton turned up at Bournemouth,' remembers Parsons. 'He couldn't believe that Nico wasn't playing. He was gutted. I only spoke once or twice to him about Nico after that. I spoke to John McGovern many times though – and I knew they did really, really rate Alan.'

Shilton stepped up his interest in the young keeper, despite his no-show at Bournemouth, and eventually invited him down to Plymouth for a trial in the summer of 1993. 'I remember the whole thing rumbling on for quite a while,' says Godfrey. 'You always get rumours with young players at non-league clubs who are doing well – but the Plymouth thing had a bit more of a ring to it because it was Peter Shilton involved. I remember going to Halesowen for a friendly in August 1993 and all the talk being of Alan going to Plymouth. I certainly seem to remember it being rumoured and talked about for quite a while before it happened.'

'When he went to Plymouth, I let him have my club car,' says Parsons. 'He probably drove down there on two, maybe three occasions. He had the car for the best part of a week to get himself to and from Plymouth to have a couple of games for the reserves and for training.'

Nicholls made an immediate impression on the Argyle management, particularly assistant boss John McGovern. 'I'd done my homework on Nicholls,' says McGovern.

> That was one player where I insisted to Peter, 'We need this kid in now. I know you're looking to get a thousand appearances but I think it's more important that we sign this boy.' I knew he would be a handful; I spoke to Dan McCauley and said we'd probably have some trouble with him, but let's just judge him on how he does on the pitch. I just knew after having seen him a couple of times that the boy had a lot to offer. I thought he literally was the final added ingredient to give our recipe a bit of spice.

Once Shilton had been convinced of Nicholls' ability, a deal had to be worked out with Cheltenham and Wolves – who were refusing to sign over his Football League registration without recompense. Argyle agreed a fee of £10,000 with the Robins, while Wolves settled for a staggered payment of £5,000 depending on appearances. 'We didn't get a big fee,' says Parsons.

> It wasn't very much at all, but Dennis [Deacon] said just to take whatever they're going to give us and that'll be it. He didn't want to stand in Nico's way because he had a lot of time for him. So anyway, the deal had just been done, when Alan called me one night from his home in Birmingham. I asked him why he wasn't

down in Plymouth. He said, 'I haven't got your car any more, how am I supposed to get down there?' I couldn't believe it, I just said, 'I haven't got a clue mate… train, bus, whatever!' He said, 'I want you to take me down'. I told him I wasn't budging. That was typical Nico really.

Despite not rushing down to join his new club, Nicholls was understandably thrilled to be linking up with England's legendary goalkeeper. 'To hear that Shilton was interested was amazing,' says his mum, Celia. 'Alan was over the moon. But all I kept getting after he signed was, "How am I going to get down there, mum?" In the end he went by taxi – paid for by Shilton himself.'

It was perhaps understandable why Shilton was so keen to whisk his man straight down to Home Park. Ray Newland had endured an erratic 92/93 campaign, and the manager himself had finally admitted defeat in his battle to come to terms with the backpass law.

Nicholls' signing, which was completed on Thursday 5 August 1993, hardly merited a mention in the pages of a local press uninspired by the signing of another untried rookie keeper, just twelve months after the arrival of Newland. The youngster was ostensibly signed as back-up to Newland and Shilton himself, or at least that's what he was led to believe by Shilton. 'He was signed as third keeper,' says his dad, 'that's what we were told anyway.'

However, after Newland conceded eight goals in the first three games of the 93/94 season, Nicholls was thrust into the spotlight. The nineteen-year-old had impressed Shilton in reserve matches with his eagerness to bawl at his defence if he thought they were neglecting their duties. Not even rugged pros with years of Football League experience were safe from the youngster's wrath – an attribute that sparked a glint in the eye of his watching manager.

In fact, the similarities between the gifted Brummie and his new boss were obvious to almost everyone. 'When Alan first joined Plymouth, people used to call him Shilts' toyboy,' says his dad, 'because he looked like him, he was built like him, and obviously he was brilliant in goal.'

'As far as I'm concerned,' says Parsons, 'Peter Shilton saw a lot of himself in Alan – the build, physique, they did look very similar, neither of them were the biggest of keepers height wise. And the first time I saw Alan play he was just seventeen, but there was no fear there at all with him – and Shilton was the same when he started out.' Steve Castle agrees. 'Alan had unbelievable ability,' he says. 'I'm pretty sure that Shilton would have looked at him in those early days and been reminded of what he used to be like. There were so many similarities between the two of them – it was obvious to everyone really.'

'Alan was an immense keeper, technically brilliant – as good as any I've seen with his hands,' says Steve McCall. 'I think the first thing that struck me about Peter Shilton was that any shot that went towards him stuck in his hands, and Alan Nicholls was probably the closest I've seen to him in my entire career.'

Whether Shilton recognised a kindred spirit or not, the master took to his apprentice almost instantly, reveals Dwight Marshall. 'Shilton absolutely loved him,' he says. 'Alan was a young lad at the time, a little bit arrogant, kind of flash, but Shilton just took to him straight away, like a son really. They got on really well.'

Nicholls made his debut in the second leg of the Coca-Cola Cup first-round tie against Birmingham City on Tuesday 25 August – a low-risk baptism considering Argyle were already 3–0 down from the first leg and on a hiding to nothing. A first win of the season – by a 2–0 margin thanks to goals from Marshall and Martin Barlow – created the headlines, but it was Nicholls who took the plaudits. The man-of-the-match award he received was thanks in part to a fine double-save from Paul Moulden and Carl Shutt, but it was the constant barracking of his defenders that really caught Shilton's eye. 'He's a very good talker and instils confidence in those around him,' he said, before adding the obligatory: 'But he's still got a lot to learn.'

Mark Patterson had watched on in amazement from his right-back berth as the rookie goalkeeper made his bow in professional football. 'One of the first things I can remember about Alan was in that Birmingham game,' he says. 'Somebody crossed the ball and he came out and caught it one-handed on the edge of the area. I remember thinking, "Bloody hell, you don't often see that." He was supremely confident for such a young lad.'

Over in the dugout, the manager was proclaiming the arrival of a formidable talent to a small audience. 'I remember being in the dugout during that Birmingham game,' says physio Paul Sumner. 'After Alan made a save, Shilton said to no-one in particular that he was one of the best goalkeepers he'd ever seen of that age.'

Another onlooker that night with a particular interest in the performance of the newcomer was the man who began the season as the club's number one keeper. 'I remember watching Alan,' says Ray Newland, 'and thinking, "I'm going to have real trouble getting my place back off this kid." I remember looking back to my contract talks with Shilton and thinking, "What the hell have I done!" I really messed up there because it was me who was responsible for Alan being there in the first place.'

After such an impressive confirmation of his rookie credentials, Nicholls was a shoo-in to keep his place for the home match against Port Vale the following Saturday. The game against promotion-hopefuls Vale produced a rousing 2–0 victory for the Pilgrims, in which Nicholls turned in another hugely encouraging performance to chalk up his second successive clean sheet.

However, despite a thrilling afternoon for club and player, the headlines focused on a mass brawl between home and away fans that was supposedly sparked by Argyle's new goalkeeping discovery. Rick Cowdery takes up the story, 'The Barn Park End was a big terrace in those days,' he says. 'The away end was packed, and Nicholls went behind the goal to retrieve the ball. He had a habit of winding up away fans, and on this occasion he allegedly exposed himself, pulled down his shorts – certainly he did something that sent the Vale fans absolutely spare.'

Whether it was Nicholls' indiscretion or provocation from some of the more colourful Argyle fans in the Barn Park corner of the Lyndhurst, a significant section of the Vale fans decided to take matters into their own hands. 'A few Vale fans got over the fence,' continues Cowdery. 'Some of the Plymouth boys were giving it the "come and have a go gestures", and then all of a sudden they did – the Vale fans just started pouring over. The Plymouth boys realised that they'd bitten off more than they could chew, so turned around and legged it with Vale in pursuit. And that whole thing kicked off because of something Alan did.'

With no police presence inside the ground due to a cost-cutting measure by the club, it was left to a handful of hapless stewards to try to restore order. But the fighting was still going on twenty minutes after the final whistle, much to the chairman's horror. 'We have pleaded with the fans to help make this stewarding scheme work,' said McCauley after the match. 'But the message is falling on deaf ears. They are just hell bent on causing trouble, and we don't want them or their money.'

For Nicholls, it was an unsavoury twist to his propitious first week as a professional footballer, and McCauley was in no mood to give him special treatment. 'We know he's only a young goalkeeper getting his first experience of league football,' he said, 'but these accusations are serious enough to be investigated by the manager, and I'm sure he will be anxious to find out what happened.'

As it turned out, only a small number of visiting fans had reported Nicholls for his alleged indiscretion and nothing came of the club's internal enquiry. In any event, Argyle's stewards claimed the young keeper was merely reacting to provocation from the Vale fans in the first place. 'We collected about twenty coins that had been thrown at him,' said one.

Whether he was to blame for the Vale riot or not, it was clear to most onlookers that Alan Nicholls was something of a showman who relished the interaction with supporters as much as his role between the posts. 'He always used to play up to the crowd,' says his dad. 'I saw him play at Oxford once, and the fans were throwing coins at him for some reason. He was putting them in his pocket and asking them to throw some more. We went in the clubhouse after and their fans were absolutely brilliant, they loved him.'

Like most goalkeepers, Nicholls was a frustrated Maradona and would often have his managers tearing their hair out over his antics with the ball. 'He tried to be a bit of a showman all the time,' says Parsons. 'He'd come out with the ball, touch it and touch it and bring it out almost to the halfway line – and I'd be stood there hoping that one day someone would close him down, give him a right old tackle and that might teach him a lesson. But they never did.'

'Alan would always try and do things with the ball that most keepers wouldn't,' says Marshall. 'I remember once, the ball was coming towards him with an attacker bearing down. Alan just flicked the ball up in the air and the forward ran straight past it. That was Alan, he was a character alright.'

McGovern prefers more parochial parlance. 'Nicholls was a complete and utter nutcase,' he says. 'But for a young player with no experience whatsoever, he was magnificent as a goalkeeper. Once we put him in the side we couldn't leave him out. He was the best keeper I've ever seen at dealing with people knocking the ball back to him, considering he was all left foot. Because if they knocked it back to him on his right foot he didn't have to run round it, he just hit across it with the outside of his left foot to bend it and keep it in play.'

Nicholls' performance against Vale left Shilton hailing the non-league capture as the bargain he undoubtedly was. 'He did everything I asked of him today,' said the manager. 'It is still early days and he's still got a lot to learn, but we signed him for only £5,000 [without appearance payments] and it's looking like a good piece of business at the moment.'

Nicholls missed the next three games owing to a suspension carried over from his non-league days, and a pair of matches in October when he sustained a broken toe, but eighteen consecutive appearances followed and it was clear that he was indisputably no longer the club's third-choice goalkeeper.

By late December, Shilton's men were in the midst of their long winning run, and Nicholls' form seemed to run along a rising parallel with that of the team as a whole.

Steve Castle may have been the man in the headlines after his lightning-quick hat-trick at Stockport on 17 December, but amazingly it was Nicholls who scooped the man-of-the-match honours. The youngster almost single-handedly repelled the home side as they launched wave after wave of attacks on his goal in an attempt to overturn the 3–0 deficit, at one point fearlessly launching himself at the never-ending limbs of Kevin Francis with the giant striker clean through.

Nicholls' brilliant form prompted Harley Lawer of the *Sunday Independent* to dedicate his entire column one week to the discovery of the season. 'He looks the best young goalkeeping prospect to emerge from Home Park since Martin Hodge nearly two decades ago,' he wrote. 'Successive performances oozing confidence with his agility, safe handling and sure-footed kicking made each selection decision that much easier for his manager – who needs just five more appearances to reach the magical 1,000. He has been reticent to lavish excessive public praise on the young pretender, which suggests that he is deliberately trying to shield Nicholls from too much publicity during his formative years in the same way Alex Ferguson has protected his star protégé Ryan Giggs.'

With rumours circulating that Newcastle boss Kevin Keegan had his eye on the young keeper, Shilton and the Board moved quickly to tear up the contract Nicholls had signed just a few months before and present him with a huge pay rise and an additional two years.

One man thrilled with the progress Nicholls was making was his former chairman at Cheltenham, Dennis Deacon. 'Every football supporter in Cheltenham is talking about him,' he said. 'They have seen him on the telly and think he's fantastic. I was always convinced he would make it and have got several bets with friends that he will end up playing in the Premier League. I told Mr Shilton from the start that, once you got him on your side, he would move Hell and Earth for you. Underneath that rough exterior he's a decent lad and has a heart of gold.'

Nicholls' 'rough exterior' had certainly made an impression in the Argyle dressing room. 'Alan came across as an arrogant, loud-mouthed so and so, and to be honest he was,' says fellow keeper Ray Newland.

But when you got to know him he was actually quite a quiet, insecure guy. We used to hang around together quite a lot in the early days, because the likes of Steve Castle, Paul Dalton and so on were older than us and would go out on the town and buy flash cars to try and impress each other. Whereas I wasn't really into that scene, so he used to let his guard down with me. We'd go bodyboarding together down in Cornwall, just me and Alan. For the first ten to fifteen minutes of the journey he'd be typical Alan Nicholls, going 200 miles per hour down country lanes and telling everyone in his way to 'eff off.' I used to try and get him to slow down, and to stop mouthing off at people. You could almost see him thinking, 'Hold on a minute, I don't have to impress Ray here,' and then we'd get on really well. So in the morning I'd be in the changing rooms with him, watching him carrying on and I'd be thinking, 'This guy's a prick.' But then I'd be with him in the afternoon and thinking, 'What a nice guy.' Honestly, he was like Jekyll and Hyde. But if he hadn't had that arrogant edge I don't think he would have been such a good goalkeeper. He wasn't the biggest, or the strongest, but he made himself big through that arrogance. Basically when he went onto the pitch he just didn't care.

Another member of the Argyle squad who experienced the softer side of Alan Nicholls' personality was Mark Patterson, who took the headstrong young keeper under his wing. 'I had a lot of time for Alan, I liked him,' says Patterson.

Probably because I was one of the older ones around he used to come round to my place for a chat. I'd go home from training when he'd been sent home for whatever reason, and he'd be there chatting to my wife, pouring his heart out. As soon as I got home the bravado kicked in, 'I don't care, I don't give a shit about this and that,' but deep down I think he did. He wasn't one of those kids who could take it on the chin and get on with it, he needed to get things off his chest. So he used to go up to my place quite often if he was in trouble or something had happened, and I used to think, 'Christ, I know where he is now.' I'd get back home and there he was. I didn't mind, it was someone for him to talk to – but it always came back to the same thing: it's your own fault, nobody made you do it.'

Many of Nicholls' team-mates believe he was exempt from the management's strict disciplinary regime at the club. 'Alan used to get away with murder with

Shilton,' says Martin Barlow, 'but none of the other players would. I think Shilton saw a lot in him of himself when he was younger so he used to let him off. He had a bit of special treatment. If he found out one of us had been drinking the night before a match, it was normally a two-week fine. But with Alan it'd be swept under the carpet because he was performing and playing so well. And to be fair he had an outstanding season that first year he was at Argyle.'

Dominic Naylor agrees, and paints a surprising picture of England legend Shilton taking verbal abuse from his young apprentice. 'Alan was the only one who could tell Shilts to fuck off,' says Naylor. 'He used to hammer him, "Shut up", "Fuck off" and all that. He just didn't give a damn about what he said to him, he was just his own man. I'd go out with him the night before games when I'm suspended but he's playing and he'd just get absolutely hammered, then he'd get up the next day and be man of the match. Everything was just a laugh and a joke with him, but he was a great lad, very funny. He just lived for the day, lived for the minute.'

But some members of the squad believe Nicholls would have benefited from more guidance from his immensely experienced manager. 'Nicholls was a great goalkeeper,' says Keith Hill. 'But he was given too much of a leash, he should have been reined in a little bit. He was the real deal and I think Shilton saw that in him, but I think he should have been a bit more disciplined with him rather than treating him like a happy-go-lucky character who could just do what he wanted as long as he played well.'

Striker Paul Boardman lived with Nicholls during his time at the club, and remembers watching on in amazement as his new housemate spent the night before his debut out on the town. 'When Alan came to Plymouth he moved into my place,' says Boardman. 'Shilton knew I had a spare room in my house, so he asked me if Alan could move in. He stayed with me for a few months in the end. I remember my debut, I was in bed early two nights before, eating all the right things and everything else. But on the night before Alan's debut, he didn't get in till about two or three o'clock in the morning. But by the way, he was man of the match the next day, he played an absolute blinder.'

Boardman was later on the receiving end of a more sinister side to Nicholls' personality, which culminated in a violent encounter. 'While he was living with me, I'd lent him some money for something,' he remembers.

I think it was about a four-week period when this was going on. He'd just signed a new contract and one day he drove into the car park with a new car. So I asked him for the money back and he told me to eff off in front of all the lads. So I went to see Shilton and told him about it, I asked him if there was any way we could get it off him – and he said, 'Well, it's a private matter.' To be fair to Shilton, it was. I'd gone up to Lilleshall for two weeks to get an injury looked at. You just feel bottom of the pile when you're injured, but when I came back Alan waltzed in and said, 'You're effing injured again?', and I'd just about had enough by that stage

— it wasn't even about the money anymore. It came to a head at St Mellion [golf course] one day. I went into the dressing room and said, 'I've had enough of this,' and he stood up and said, 'What are you going to do about it?' So we had a scrap. The physio was the only one there, so I've gone up to see him and said, 'I think you'd better come down, me and Alan have just had a fight.' When he was okay, you could have a laugh with him and he was great company. But if he was off for whatever reason, he could really be quite verbally aggressive. The funny thing was, after the scrap me and Alan got on great.

Making an impression on and off the pitch, Nicholls' rise from obscurity was crowned in March 1994 when he was called up to the England Under-21 squad for a friendly against Denmark at Brentford. But somewhat cruelly, Nicholls was forced to put club above country and turn out for Argyle in their home encounter with Barnet on the same night as his scheduled international debut.

Despite the call-up ultimately ending in disappointment, Alan Nicholls senior still remembers the moment he found out his son had been summoned by his country. 'The first I knew about England,' he says, 'was sat at home looking at Teletext and I saw his name in the squad. I phoned everybody I knew straight away!'

Shilton himself was naturally thrilled that his young goalkeeper had received the call from his country, despite withdrawing him from the squad. 'We are very pleased with Alan's selection,' he said. 'It is a great tribute to him and the club and shows the strides he has made recently. I have spoken to [England U-21 manager] Dave Sexton, and he did not realise we had a game the same night. He understands the situation and has assured me that Alan will get another chance.'

That second chance did not take long to materialise. Following the club's aborted bid for promotion against Burnley, Nicholls was drafted into the Under-21 squad for the Toulon Tournament, and on Friday 27 May he jetted out to France with the likes of Robbie Fowler, Sol Campbell and Jamie Redknapp to take on the cream of Europe's young crop.

Paul Gerrard of Oldham Athletic was first-choice keeper for the Under-21s going into the tournament, but he suffered an injury in the opening game against Russia, a 2–0 win, and Nicholls was given the nod ahead of Aston Villa's Michael Oakes for the second group game against France.

The first Plymouth Argyle player to represent the England Under-21 age group had already made quite an impression on his illustrious team-mates, all of whom were with clubs in the Premier League. Peter Fear was a budding young midfielder with Wimbledon at the time and, like Nicholls, was on his first tour of duty under an international banner. 'I remember meeting Alan at the airport, and it seemed to me that he just couldn't believe he was there,' Fear recalls. 'I wasn't aware of him before I went to the tournament. I was aware of the other players and who they played for, but Alan was new on the scene. He came across as a very excitable lad and enjoyed every minute of being out there. I was from a lower Premier League club, and obviously he was at Plymouth, so we sort of bonded through that really. A lot of the other lads were top stars already. Also, I roomed with Michael Oakes, another Brummie keeper, so I saw quite a bit of Alan on that tour.'

'He seemed to be a really nice guy,' remembers Ian Selley, then of Arsenal. 'All the lads on that tour were genuine guys, we all enjoyed a laugh and a joke and it was just a thoroughly enjoyable tournament. You had some decent players there, and Alan certainly didn't look out of place at all.'

Alan Nicholls earned his first and only cap for England against France on Tuesday 31 May 1994 in Aubagne, near Marseille. The England line-up that day was: Alan Nicholls (Plymouth Argyle), Chris Makin (Oldham Athletic), Stuart Nethercott (Tottenham Hotspur), Sol Campbell (Tottenham Hotspur), Dean Gordon (Crystal Palace), Trevor Sinclair (Queen's Park Rangers), Peter Fear (Wimbledon), Jamie Redknapp (Liverpool), Chris Bart-Williams (Sheffield Wednesday), Bruce Dyer (Crystal Palace), Robbie Fowler (Liverpool).

According to Fear, the Argyle keeper was 'a bit excitable in the dressing room before the game,' and he carried that excitement out onto the pitch in what turned out to be a nightmare debut for Nicholls in front of the watching Terry Venables.

The twenty-year-old conceded a penalty after just two minutes when he brought down Lyon's Florian Maurice – and was beaten from the spot by Johan Micoud to give France an early lead. Nicholls settled down after that, but lost concentration ten minutes after the break when he strayed off his line and was lobbed by Olivier Baudry from 30 yards. Ten minutes later it was 3–0 to France when Nicholls – his confidence now in tatters – picked up a backpass from Stuart Nethercott inside his area, and Samassi Abou fired home from the resulting indirect free kick.

Substituted in the seventy-eighth minute for Michael Oakes, Nicholls was understandably crestfallen after the game. 'I don't deserve to be picked again on that form,' he said in a rare media interview. 'I would like to play in the next match, but now I'd say I don't deserve to be in the team.'

England head coach Dave Sexton offered words of support for the youngster, insisting he had taken him off simply to give Oakes a run-out. 'It's a squad thing, you've got to get the people on when you can and it's nothing to do with Alan's performance,' he said. 'He's feeling a bit sick in there, but this is something he has to get through and he has to learn from it.'

Fear admits Nicholls was at fault for one of the goals, but refutes suggestions he was responsible for the crushing defeat. 'We got pretty much played off the park as a team in that game,' he says. 'I think Alan might have been a wee bit at fault with the penalty, but he didn't make any goalkeeping mistakes, no bad howlers or anything like that. He was just nervous.'

However, Sexton had seen enough, and Nicholls was replaced by Oakes for the third group game against the USA – a match England won 3–0. In fact,

Sexton's youngsters went on to win the tournament itself, beating Portugal 2–0 in the final, but Nicholls' only involvement came in their only defeat.

Nicholls' dad believes it was over-confidence rather than nerves that led to his son enduring a torrid international debut. 'We always knew he'd end up playing for his country, but he didn't have a very good game,' he says. 'He was his own worst enemy that night – I think he was just too cocky.'

News of the young keeper's stuttering start for his country reached the media back in Plymouth, who reported a 'nightmare' debut for the Argyle starlet. But Nicholls' team-mates over in Toulon were impressed with his ability. 'He was an extremely good goalkeeper,' says Selley. 'To get called up in the first place he would have to be of a certain standard – and it was understandable why he was called up because he knew what he was doing, and was very capable of doing it.'

Fear was so impressed that he was keen to spread the word when he returned to England. 'When we got back, I spoke to our manager at the time and I told him Alan was a good keeper who he should keep an eye on,' he says. 'I think a few clubs were looking at him at the time. I just think maybe he should have gone to a bigger club, got himself settled down, had some good coaching and the rawness taken out of him and who knows what he could have done?'

Almost inevitably, stories of Nicholls' behaviour off the pitch began to appear in the Plymouth media. The Argyle keeper had reportedly led a group of players in vandalising a taxi, but Fear denies all knowledge of the event and insists Nicholls was impeccably behaved on the tour. 'Alan never once did anything that was remotely out of order,' he says. 'We had the odd night out where we came in at 2 a.m. when the curfew was midnight, but that was all of us, not just Alan. We had the press with us when we were out having a drink so they might have wanted to bend the truth a little. But Alan didn't do anything out of order, he was just a bit excitable, a bit mad – but that's goalkeepers.'

The taxi incident is also news to Ian Selley. 'I don't recall anything happening with a taxi,' he says. 'I know that we had a couple of nights out, but I can't remember anyone getting into trouble, and I think I'd remember if something like that happened.'

Alan Nicholls senior insists the taxi incident did happen, but that his son was not involved. 'Some of the players did wreck a taxi, but Alan wasn't in it,' he says. 'He got the blame though, some of the players tried to pass the buck onto him and the crowd he was with. Alan told me all about that – he said, "I didn't wreck it, I wasn't in there." The FA just whitewashed it … paid the taxi driver off and kept it quiet.'

FA bosses were said to have taken exception to Nicholls' general behaviour at the team's base – particularly at one gathering when he threw food at the England coaching table. 'Now that one definitely happened,' laughs Selley. 'It was at a meal one night. A bread roll flew across the room and hit Dave Sexton I think. But that was just a laugh and a joke, a group of lads enjoying themselves and no-one got into trouble for it.'

Nicholls returned to Home Park for pre-season training two months after his ill-fated trip to France, but decided to keep the details of what went wrong to himself. 'We obviously didn't see him for a while because it was summer,' says Mark Patterson. 'But when we all went back for training, he never said anything about the Under-21s, none of us had a clue what had happened.'

Nicholls had noticeably gained a few pounds over the summer, and almost immediately picked up a knee injury in training that would dog him for the remainder of his time in Plymouth. Barely had the Argyle squad reconvened to begin their preparations for the new season, when Nicholls was once again making headlines for all the wrong reasons.

Fined £150 by Torbay Magistrates, Nicholls had threatened a police officer outside a nightclub in Torquay three days before he was due to fly out to France with the Under-21s. He had been leaving a nightclub with a group of friends when police intervened to ask them to settle down; Nicholls and two other men were arrested when the incident turned ugly.

For his Argyle team-mates, there had been a noticeable change in Nicholls over the summer. 'Because he had a bit of success he became a little bit above his station,' says Patterson. 'He just had this self-destruct button inside him – everything had to be going at a million miles an hour. I think he was just on a freefall from when he got into the Under-21s and life had been so great for him. He was living this life that he loved, and then all of a sudden it got a little bit out of hand.'

The local media were quick to pick up on the recalcitrant starlet's apparent fall from grace. Harley Lawer, the *Sunday Independent* writer who just months before had predicted such a bright future for Nicholls, pilloried the youngster a week before the 94/95 season was due to kick-off. 'Nicholls appeared to have a highly-promising career ahead of him,' Lawer wrote. 'But he has put it all at risk following a disastrous England Under-21 debut and a succession of off-field incidents. Judged on his self-destruct stupidity – without the Gazza-international playing pedigree to get away with it – Nicholls is set to remain indefinitely in the promising category.'

Injuries punctuated Nicholls' appearances as the season got underway, but the gathering storm above his head drew another black cloud when the management of the Far Post Club – the social establishment inside Home Park – reported the increasingly wayward star to chairman Dan McCauley for 'unacceptable behaviour' on their premises. The complaint followed a series of anti-social incidents around the city's nightspots and restaurants, but Nicholls' latest misadventure was the first to make its way to the door of the chairman.

Disciplinary action was averted when Nicholls personally apologised for his indiscretion with a bunch of flowers, but several of his team-mates had already made up their minds that the previous season's star performer was persona non grata when it became evident his lifestyle was affecting his form on the pitch. 'When we were going well he was tremendous,' says Patterson.

But he got more and more confident, more and more full of himself, and when he lost his confidence there weren't many people who were going to help him because he'd really pissed a few of the lads off with his attitude by then. He was doing what he wanted, he was going out whenever he wanted, and you can do that as long as you're playing well, but he stopped playing well. He lost his way and he couldn't get away with it any more. I think he just got out of hand and he went downhill very, very quickly. Alan was still trying to be jack the lad, the funny man, and people got a bit fed up with it.

For Steve McCall, the stark transformation was a major disappointment. 'Peter Shilton tried to get him on the straight and narrow,' he says. 'But he had problems with his digs, his food and all that sort of thing and he just couldn't seem to get that right off the pitch. His lifestyle and his attitude … he was drinking, getting in with the wrong people and it led him astray. Inevitably it eventually affected him on the pitch. In the early days he was absolutely magnificent but he just let it slip big time.'

Steve Castle tried to intervene, but inadvertently found his advice having an adverse affect on his young team-mate. 'I think Alan was a timebomb waiting to explode,' he says.

As an older person and skipper I tried to take him under my wing. During pre-season I talked to him about his weight and his drinking and stuff. I said to him, 'Rather than drinking beer, have the odd glass of wine and you'll keep the weight off.' But he ended up drinking whole bottles of wine and getting absolutely wasted on that instead. When I asked him what on earth he was doing, he said to me, 'You said wine would keep the weight off.' He always wanted to do the right thing, but he was just misled and had the wrong people around him.

Nicholls' parents admit their son had his problems, but suggest his meteoric rise and high-profile status in Plymouth had a major impact on his career. 'He was a bugger sometimes,' says his mum, Celia. 'But he was a twenty-year-old kid. He got a lot of hassle at Plymouth, not just with the club in the end but with the fans as well. He couldn't go anywhere, his life wasn't his own. It was hopeless. If he ever went out for a drink, people looking for trouble would always make a beeline for him. A lot of lads aren't angels at twenty, and he had to take on a lot in a really short space of time.'

Alan senior paid several visits to Plymouth, and couldn't believe the attention his son attracted from the locals. 'When I went down and stayed with him, I'd have to go out and get the breakfast stuff in the morning, because if he went you'd never see him,' he remembers. 'He would only go down to the corner shop but he'd be gone for two hours. Be it autographs, or talking about the game or whatever.'

Alan admits his son was an acquired taste. 'You either took to him or you didn't, but you had to get to know him first. Sometimes you could have wrung his bleeding neck, but at the end of the day you were just wasting your time talking to him because he'd just do his own thing. He was his own worst enemy, he really was.'

But even with his suspect reputation, Nicholls is still fondly remembered by most who crossed his path. 'He came in with one of the very first mobile phones I'd ever seen,' remembers Boardman. 'He didn't tell anyone he had it, and we're all looking around when it starts ringing. Next thing we know, he gets this big brick out of his pocket and all the lads just start falling about laughing. Mind you, if you were ever in a car with him you were taking your life into your own hands. He'd be lighting a ciggie, changing a tape on his stereo and talking on his phone all at the same time.'

'Alan had a side to him that a lot of people didn't give him credit for,' says Gordon Sparks. 'When I was editing the programme, I did a series called 'Away from Home Park', where the players talked about their hobbies. I asked Alan what he liked doing outside of football, and he said, "I love cooking." I thought he was taking the mick, but the photographer went to his house to do the picture and there he was in the kitchen doing his stuff.'

But it was perhaps his former manager at Cheltenham who came closest to unearthing the real Alan Nicholls. 'One summer the club took us all over to Crete,' recalls Lindsay Parsons. 'One night I walked back to the hotel with Nico and he was talking all the way back – it was just 100 per cent sense coming out of his mouth. He talked about the players, which ones he thought would make it and which ones wouldn't, and all the things he'd done wrong. I just couldn't believe what he was saying. I asked him why he did the things that made people turn against him, and he said he just didn't know, he didn't have a clue.'

After making twenty-six appearances in a less-than-successful second season at the club, Nicholls had a new manager to contend with by the summer of 1995.

Neil Warnock arrived with a big reputation and even bigger plans to revamp the squad he had inherited from the previous regime. With Nicholls struggling for fitness and form, not to mention the off-the-pitch misdemeanours that were still blighting his Home Park career, Warnock made up his mind almost from day one that the now 'former' England Under-21 international was surplus to requirements. 'I'd seen him play a few games and he'd played well,' remembers Warnock. 'But it probably just went to his head a little bit. So I called him in and told him he was better off getting another club. He'd had a few disciplinary problems before I came, and we felt it was the right time for him to move.'

Alan senior claims it was a fall-out between the pair rather than any footballing reasons that convinced Warnock to dispense with the twenty-one-year-old. 'What started it off with Warnock was that Alan didn't get on with him,' he says. 'So that was it, straight away really. Warnock wanted to bring his own lads in, his own keeper in, and of course, you'd rub Alan up like that.'

The final straw for the new Pilgrims boss came when Nicholls was involved in a high-profile drink-driving incident. 'He had a bump when he'd been drinking, he hit a taxi,' says Alan. 'There was a young girl in the taxi at the time as well, so that was the end for him at Plymouth.'

After seventy-eight appearances for the club, Nicholls was sacked the day after his twenty-second birthday on 24 August 1995, halfway through a two-year contract. 'The boy has got to come to his senses,' said Warnock at the time. 'His ability is not in question. From a personal point of view, I think he needs to get away from Plymouth and start again.'

It was chairman Dan McCauley who best summed up the errant goalkeeper's plight as he departed Home Park after two, often brilliant, but always troublesome years. 'He could have the world at his feet, but he hasn't even got his feet on the ground.'

Down and out without a club, Nicholls ran into the arms of his former mentor at Cheltenham. 'He phoned me up to say that he'd been released,' says Parsons.

I'd just gone to Gillingham with Tony Pulis, so I told him to come up and we'd have a look at him. The trouble was, Tony wasn't sure if Alan was big enough for a goalie, although for me he'd never let me down with crosses. We had Jim Stannard in goal at the time, he was a big keeper, and Alan looked small next to him. I think he was with us for the best part of three or four weeks, but he didn't get anywhere near the first team. One day Tony said to me, 'I'm going to tell Alan tomorrow that I'm letting him go.' So I see Tony a couple of days later and he says, 'Well, I let Nico go.' He said he pulled Alan out on the pitch, and told him he wasn't getting a contract. He was expecting a little bit of aggression from him, but he said Alan just cried. I wasn't surprised by that. He wasn't the big, tough lad everyone thought he was. Deep down he was a very sensitive lad.

A few days before Nicholls was released by Gillingham, a Stalybridge Celtic goalkeeper named Harvey Willetts had been sent off in a non-league match at Macclesfield, creating a vacancy that Nicholls would so fatefully fill. 'Shortly after we'd let him go, the Stalybridge manager phoned Tony saying he didn't have a keeper for a game that weekend. Tony put him on to me, because I knew the non-league scene from my time at Cheltenham, and I immediately thought of Alan. Their manager said it'd be brilliant if they could get him. I told him he was available, he was a good keeper and he wouldn't let them down.'

But Parsons had inadvertently double-booked the young keeper. 'Alan was actually still training with us on that Friday morning,' he continues.

So I said, 'Nico, I've had the Stalybridge manager on the phone, do you fancy playing for them tomorrow?' He said he did. So I told the Stalybridge manager Alan was up for it, and asked him who they were playing. As soon as he said Dover, I thought 'Oh God, no,' because I'd let Alan train with Peter Taylor at

Dover just the night before. So I went back out to see Alan and told him I'd dropped him in it. I said 'Get on the phone to Taylor, and tell him I've agreed to let you play for Stalybridge.' If I'd known they were playing Dover I would have come up with an excuse – I didn't have a clue on that one. So he called Peter Taylor from the office – and he told him he'd come back for training at Dover on Monday, but that he was playing against him the next day for Stalybridge. Taylor told him if he played for Stalybridge he'd never play for him. Ever.

Parsons recalls the last time he saw the player he had rescued from the scrapheap to such brilliant effect at Cheltenham. 'On that Friday morning, he drove off with Scott Lindsey – a lad who had been at Gillingham but was then at Dover. As they were about to drive off, I looked at the pair of them and I said, "Be careful you two, don't go doing anything stupid." And that was the last I saw of him.'

Scott Lindsey had been released by Gillingham shortly before Nicholls, and had become firm friends with the former Argyle keeper during their time at the Priestfield together. 'It was just after the season started that he turned up at Gills,' he says. 'He moved in with me and a mate and lived with us for a bit – so we became quite close in a short period of time.'

Nicholls had been told to report to the Tollgate Hotel in Gravesend to meet up with the Stalybridge party, who were staying locally in preparation for their Conference clash at Dover the following day. Lindsey remembers dropping his mate off at the hotel. 'I took Alan to the Tollgate on the Friday evening,' he says. 'I went into the bar and had a glass of Coke, and Alan went and met the Celtic manager and players, and I remember saying, "See you at the far post tomorrow."'

Pete Wragg was the Stalybridge manager who had made the desperate call for a keeper on the journey down from Manchester. 'We got to the hotel at about 10 p.m.,' he recalls. 'And when we got there it was full of Christmas partygoers, ladies and that, which is always dangerous from a manager's point of view. But we met up with Alan, and it was a case of him saying hello and trying to pick up a few names. I think he'd lost his way a bit, and that he was really excited to be playing for us, which was quite unusual considering he'd played for Peter Shilton and for England.'

Dave Pover, Celtic's long-serving physio, was called on to take a look at a minor injury Nicholls was carrying. 'When he met us at the hotel, I remember him saying he had a slight calf strain,' recalls Pover. 'So I treated him that evening. I had quite a lengthy conversation with him and I found him to be a very, very friendly lad. He was quite talkative, but I do recall the one thing that stood out with me was that he was a very, very strong-willed character.'

On the morning of Saturday 25 November 1995, Alan Nicholls arose from his hotel bed and prepared for his reintroduction into non-league football with Stalybridge Celtic. In a bizarre but retrospectively fitting gesture, Pete Wragg appointed him captain for the day over breakfast. After a relaxing morning, the team left the hotel for the short journey to Dover.

'I can remember giving him some advice before the game,' says Wragg. 'The slope was difficult at Dover so I gave him a few tips – kick top-side, be careful on crosses and so on. But he was fine, he didn't need any advice from me.'

Peter Taylor waited until half-time to remonstrate with Nicholls for his decision to play for Celtic that day. 'They had quite a large tunnel area at Dover,' remembers Dave Pover, 'and Peter Taylor was waiting for Alan. He gave him some stick about signing for us instead of them – I remember having a few harsh words with Taylor about that. It was out of order for him to do that at half time'

Nicholls performed admirably on his debut for the club, and pulled off a handful of fine saves to help Celtic to a 3–1 victory. 'After the game, I was the last person from Stalybridge to speak to him,' says Pover. 'I was always the last one on the bus making sure everybody got on before I did, but Alan wasn't travelling back with us. He was due to meet us again on the Tuesday because we were away at Hednesford. So we said cheerio and off he went.'

Nicholls was planning to travel back to his mum's house in Birmingham after the game, but Scott Lindsey invited him for a night out up north. 'My brother and my dad had come down for the game,' says Lindsey.

My dad used to come to every single game to watch me play, even though he lived in Scunthorpe. There was some problem with his car that weekend, I don't know whether it was in for a service or what, but he couldn't get down, so he'd spoken to my brother and asked him if he would take him down on his motorbike. They came down in the morning on the bike, parked it at my house and we went down to the game in my car. After the game, we were having a chat in the bar – and I said to Alan, 'Do you fancy coming up to Scunthorpe for the weekend? You don't have to be in training on Monday morning, I don't have to be in training till Tuesday night – let's go out on the piss.' He was well up for it.

Celia Nicholls remembers her son calling home to say there had been a change of plan. 'He called at about half past five that night,' she says. 'He was supposed to be coming home, but he phoned to tell me he was going to stay with Scott in Scunthorpe. "I'm not coming home," he said, and that was it. That was the last time I heard from him.'

The Lindseys and Alan left Dover at just before 6 p.m. for the journey north. Scott was driving – with his dad in the passenger seat and Alan in the back, while his brother Matt followed on his motorbike. 'We stopped at a garage just south of Peterborough for a break,' remembers Scott.

We were having a chat and I asked my brother if he was alright. He said, 'Yeah, though I'm a bit bored plodding along at 60mph behind you.' So I said, 'Well, we're halfway home, hour and a half and we'll be there.' Then Alan said, 'I'll get on the back with you if you like, Matt,' and my brother said, 'Yeah alright, I've got a spare helmet.' So they got kitted up and I turned round and said, 'We'll get cracking on and you can catch us up,' which is probably the worst thing I ever said in my life. My brother wasn't too great on directions, but I told him, 'A1 north and you can't go wrong. You'll come to a big roundabout, but you would have caught us up by then.' We drove out of the garage and that was the last we saw of them. Me and my dad were driving forever but there was no sign of them. So eventually we decided to turn back and look for them and that's when we came across the accident. We found ourselves from having a laugh in the garage with them, to three hours later identifying both bodies in a morgue. It was just unbelievable.

At just after 7.30 p.m., Matt lost control of his red and white Yamaha FZR1000 half a mile north of Norman's Cross roundabout on the A1 northbound carriageway. The investigating officer later concluded that the cause of the accident was a combination of Matt's unfamiliarity with the stretch of road, the night-time driving conditions and the damp road surface; he was not thought to have been travelling at excessive speed at the time of the accident. Witnesses reported the bike braking sharply before fishtailing out of control. Alan was killed instantly, while Matt died soon after at Peterborough District Hospital.

For Lindsay Parsons, the dreadful news came as a shock, but not a real surprise.

Tony phoned me on Sunday morning and he said, 'I've got some bad news. Your man has been killed.' I knew he meant Nico as soon as he said that. My first thought was that if he hadn't followed me up to Gillingham he wouldn't have been killed. But for me, it was no real surprise. One of his mates spoke at the funeral and said there was never a dull moment going out with Alan. Even going out for a pizza, there was always something liable to happen. I just feared that one day he'd been laid in a gutter somewhere. It was fate really.

Wragg received a call early on the Sunday morning from his chairman. 'I didn't know what to do. If it had been one of my own players, you know you've got to ring the family, you've got something to do – but I can remember not knowing what to do once the chairman told me. I didn't know who to speak to, I was just in shock, and I remember thinking that if I hadn't rang around for a goalkeeper, he wouldn't even have been on the bloody bike that day.'

Mark Patterson travelled up to Birmingham for the funeral with a procession of mourners from Plymouth. 'I went up with quite a lot of the local lads and a few of the Argyle squad from Alan's time,' he remembers.

We had a mini-bus full. We went to the chapel of rest and saw him, which was horrendous. I wasn't going to go in, but I was standing in the road outside and somehow the doors swung open, three doors all at the same time and I could see right through to everyone standing next to him. So I went in. We went off to a pub for a bit and then back to the house just before the procession, and it was just so cold – I can't describe how cold it was. It was almost as if the temperature had just fallen completely. It was a really, really strange atmosphere. It was the coldest day I can ever remember.

The first chance Argyle fans got to pay their respects to their fallen hero was in an FA Cup tie at Kingstonian on 3 December. The Pilgrims won the match 2–1, but the afternoon's most significant moment came shortly after kick-off, when a heart-felt chant began building in volume from the away terrace at Kingsmeadow. 'One Alan Nicholls, there's only one Alan Nicholls,' they sang – again and again and again. Never was the oft-heard refrain more appropriate, for there truly was only one Alan Nicholls. Of that, nobody who crossed his path was in any doubt.

Author's Note

St Paul's Parish Church in Blackheath, Birmingham, is a modest red-brick church set back from a bustling main road lined with newsagents, betting shops and fast-food joints. I visited on a sallow April afternoon when the sun was shining meekly and a jaunty breeze was toying with the padlock dangling from the church gates.

The graves immediately surrounding the church itself contain long-forgotten remains, marked by crumbling, mottled headstones etched with barely legible inscriptions. But a hundred yards or so away from the main lot, the stones are much newer, the ground still wet with tears.

Alan Nicholls is buried beneath a smart grey headstone engraved with the Three Lions of the England national team and an etching of him making a spectacular save in full Argyle kit. As I approached, I noticed a fox cub perched nonchalantly on the freshly-mown plot, and as I drew closer it trotted off towards the edge of the nearby undergrowth from where it sat eyeing me like a sentry.

After a few moments of respectful contemplation, I laid down my humble offering of green and white flowers, thanked Alan for the memories and reluctantly headed back down the path towards the church. As I entered the shadowy reverence of the main graveyard, I stole a final glance back towards the final resting place of an Argyle hero. The fox cub was still surveying me cautiously but, as I prepared to leave, it turned on its heels and with a defiant swish of its tail, disappeared into the undergrowth and was gone.

Chapter Eleven

THE UGLY DUCKLING

When Peter Shilton drove away from Home Park on the night of 18 May 1994, it should have been a one-way journey according to the small print of his encyclopaedic contract.

The grievous play-off defeat to Burnley meant that his Plymouth Argyle side would once again be kicking off the new season in the third tier of English football, a situation considered unacceptable under the terms of his employment at the club. Having agreed a three-year deal upon his appointment in 1992, the Argyle Board insisted on inserting a clause into the contract giving them the option to part company with the manager should promotion fail to materialise after two full seasons of the agreement.

The morning after the night before, Rick Cowdery spelt out Shilton's precarious situation in the *Western Morning News* following the play-off semi-final defeat. 'Despite a fine season in which Shilton took Argyle to third place in the Second Division playing some attractive football,' wrote Cowdery, 'Dan McCauley, the Plymouth chairman and major investor, is unhappy that the club remains in a worse position than when he took over.'

However, less than twenty-four hours after the Burnley debacle, Shilton – far from being given his P45 – had actually agreed a new contract and had been given a further two years' grace to find a way out of the Second Division. The highest paid manager outside the Premier League, however, was forced to relinquish that title when signing his new deal. 'I think he realised that he could not expect the same money that he had in the higher league,' said McCauley following the photo call. 'To be fair, he came in and he was completely different to what I expected – he was quite realistic. You shouldn't judge a man on promotion and relegation,' continued the chairman. 'It's a sweat over a whole season. I felt to break it up at this stage wasn't right.'

Shilton, however, was in no mood to project the same display of faith onto his players. 'I'm looking to change things around a fair bit,' he said. 'The process will involve more than just one or two players and positions being changed around. Although we didn't win promotion, we had a very good season. But I have always believed that you must aim to improve at the start of every year.'

It was widely accepted that Argyle's defence had been the ball and chain that had dragged them out of the automatic promotion race, and the numbers backed up the anecdotal evidence. Argyle may have outscored the rest of Britain during their promotion hunt, but they conceded fifty-six – a total that included the seventeen occasions when they shipped two or more goals in a single game.

Shilton didn't have to be a statistician to see that his side would continue to falter unless he could galvanise his rearguard. 'We are looking at several areas,' he said two days after the Burnley debacle. 'One area we are keen to strengthen is the defence.'

The smart money seemed to be on Bolton's Mark Winstanley – a twenty-six-year-old centre-back out of favour at Burnden Park with a £200,000 price tag on his head. Other rumours linked the Pilgrims with Birmingham City's Plymouth-born defender Richard Dryden, and Darren Bradshaw of Peterborough United. 'We are making enquiries all the time to see who is available and what terms they are asking to be persuaded to move,' Shilton said as the silly season began. 'You have to do a lot of groundwork first before making a decision on which player to go for.'

With the local press throwing different names into the hat on an almost daily basis, Shilton set about clearing the decks to give him the salary leverage he knew would be vital in attracting his primary targets to the club.

The headline departure of the close season was Adrian Burrows, who had been informed sometime previously that he would not be required to report for pre-season training in July '94. The thirty-five-year-old had been a stand-out performer in the final stages of the season, but would not be permitted to extend a ten-year sojourn at Home Park that began in 1984 when he was signed for £10,000 from Northampton Town. 'He has been a great servant of the club and he has come in this year and done a good job for us,' said Shilton, in announcing a decision he would live to regret. 'We must look to the future and a fresh challenge is what Adrian needs at this time of his career.'

Midfielder Darren Garner was also released, along with centre-back Matthew Smith – the free transfer signing from Derby the previous summer who failed to clock a single minute of playing time in his year at the club. Along with Burrows, two more popular figures – in the dressing room at least – were sent on their way in Shilton's spring slaughter.

Ray Newland had been reduced to turning out for the reserve team with schoolboy defenders in front of him, and his exit was considered a shoo-in. Alan Nicholls was the undisputed number one at the club, and Shilton was pursuing the services of veteran Martin Hodge as Nicholls' back-up. The manager had by then unofficially retired from playing to concentrate on his dugout duties, and had identified Rochdale's former Argyle keeper Hodge as a suitably experienced deputy for Nicholls.

For Newland, his Home Park exit was sweet relief tinged with sadness after a torrid second season at the club. 'For the last few weeks I had been a bit fed-up,' he remembers.

I don't think Peter treated me fairly or with respect. I was playing in the reserves, and my back four was a bunch of fifteen-year-old YTS lads. Shilton used to wind me up all the time – 'Have you kept a clean sheet yet, Ray? Have you kept a clean sheet?' And I remember in one training session he was again trying to belittle me and I just lost it. 'For fuck's sake gaffer, you go and play behind a back four of fifteen-year-olds and see if you can keep a clean sheet!' All the lads gave me a pat on the back later, but Shilton looked taken aback.

Newland believes Hodge – who had been visiting the club for monthly training sessions throughout the previous season – was behind Shilton's decision to cut him. 'Martin Hodge stitched me up like a kipper to be honest,' he says.

I remember the day Shilton told me I was going to be released. There were nine of us waiting outside his office, and the first four got contracts. Then Darren Garner went in and came out saying he hadn't got a contract. Then a couple of the other lads went in and also came out saying they were being released. I was the last one in, and because the first few had got contracts but the last few hadn't, I knew it wasn't good. So I went into his office, really cheesed off with him anyway, and he told me he wasn't going to give me a contract. I said, 'To be honest, Gaffer, the way you've treated me recently I think it'd be best if I go anyway.' He told me I was a good lad, and that he would put my name forward to Ray Clemence at Barnet. That was another mistake I made – I decided to go to Chester instead, and the keeper Clemence signed instead was Maik Taylor, and look where he ended up. So I shook Peter's hand and thanked him for the two years. I remember walking out and one of the office guys said, 'Sorry you've been let go Ray.' I said, 'How do you know that?' He says to me, 'Ray, Martin Hodge has got your position.' When Hodge came down for training, the lads used to say to me, 'Be careful Ray, he's going to take your position.' But I didn't believe them. I just thought he was a good lad. But in the end that's exactly what happened, he did take my position. So when that office bloke told me Martin Hodge had agreed to be a player/goalkeeping coach, I just thought, 'The lousy bastard.' If he'd been in the same room I think I would have swung for him!

Despite the circumstances of his departure, Newland left with fond memories of his two years in Devon. 'Plymouth Argyle were far and away my favourite club that I played for,' he says. 'I made a lot of friends down there, and if I'd had my way I never would have left. I know I didn't exactly set the world on fire down there, but there are lots of what ifs. If I hadn't got injured, if I hadn't agreed to let Shilton bring in Alan Nicholls, if Martin Hodge hadn't been around… I would have happily stayed there and waited for my chance. If Alan had been injured or lost form I would have gone in there and given a million per cent for Plymouth Argyle.'

Paul Boardman had been waiting outside Shilton's office with Newland, though he saw the end coming after finally accepting his body wasn't up to the rigours of professional football. 'After my debut against Bournemouth, I think I only played two or three more games, a couple of pre-season friendlies maybe, but that was it,' he says. 'I had more operations after my debut than games. It was so frustrating, because I really wanted to repay the faith that the management had shown in me, but I just couldn't get myself fit.'

Boardman and Newland were popular figures at the club, and were making light of their precarious situation right up to the end.

> Me and Ray were sat outside Peter Shilton's office waiting to hear if we'd been given new contracts, and I said to Ray, 'What are you going to say if Shilton offers you a new contract?' So Ray said to me, 'Well, what I'll say is "Thanks boss, it's great that I've been offered a new contract. I want to do well for you, and next season I'll come back fit and ready."' Then I asked him what he'd say if Shilton didn't offer him a contract, and he said, 'Oh, thanks boss, I wouldn't have fucking signed anyway.'

Boardman went on to enjoy a successful career as a comedian and presenter with Sky Sports – the former of which was a calling that perhaps should have been obvious to all from his early days at Home Park. 'My career at Plymouth didn't exactly get off to the best of starts,' he remembers.

> The first time I was named in the first-team squad, I turned up for the pre-match meal at the Moat House hotel wearing a tracksuit; no-one had told me it was club policy to wear a suit. I was horrified when I saw all the lads suited and booted, so I went into the kitchen and borrowed a suit off a waiter. It was three sizes too small, but I didn't want to be late for lunch so I just whacked it on without bothering to look in a mirror. I ran back down to reception looking like Charlie Chaplin and all the lads fell about laughing – even Shilton and McGovern. After lunch, Shilton led us out for a walk on the Hoe to get some fresh air, and it was only then that I caught a glimpse of myself in a window and realised how ridiculous I looked. I just thought, 'Shilton must think I'm a right joker, there's no chance of me playing today.' And I was right, I didn't even make the bench!

Despite his jocular nature, Boardman admits his flirtation with the professional game left an itch he could never quite scratch. 'I really wish I could have made my mark down there,' he says.

Nobody worked harder than me to become a pro footballer, and when I finally got there, I fell at the final hurdle. I do have something empty inside me when I think about my football career. I like to laugh about it, but there's something deep down in there that gnaws away at me. I just wish I'd had a fit and healthy body and a chance to really show what I could do. But it worked out okay for me. At the end-of-season dinner, they asked me to get up and say a few words on behalf of the team. I did twenty-odd minutes and from that I got a booking to do a comedy gig and that started my stand-up career. So out of the ashes of one career spawned the beginnings of another.

With Boardman released and Dwight Marshall departing for Luton, Shilton's pool of strikers consisted of three targetmen: Kevin Nugent, Richard Landon and Mickey Evans; as well as young centre-forward Marcus Crocker – whose handful of appearances for the first team up to that point hardly suggested he was capable of filling Marshall's boots.

The need for a new striker was arguably greater than that of a centre-back, but Shilton drew a blank in his summer search – with all of his targets deciding they had better offers elsewhere. Southend's Andy Ansah snubbed a move west for the second time, choosing Charlton instead, Nicky Forster opted for Brentford after leaving Gillingham, and Crewe's Tony Naylor was seduced by Port Vale's higher league status to leave Shilton empty-handed.

On the morning of Thursday 7 July, the manager entered a Home Park Board meeting to discuss his targets and to discover the size of the kitty he'd be able to pursue them with. When he emerged an epic seven hours later, he had been given the green light to go ahead and sign the player who would come to define his reign.

Port Vale's Peter Swan – whose tackle on Paul Dalton had gone some way to deciding Argyle's fate the previous season – was very much in the plans of a club preparing for life in the First Division, but had nonetheless requested to leave Vale Park for pastures new.

The former Leeds centre-back was being pursued by several clubs in his native North, and was considering several offers when he received a phone call out of the blue one evening from Peter Shilton. 'My contract at Port Vale was coming up at the end of the season,' he says. 'I'm the sort of player who likes to keep moving, I don't like to stay in one place too long, so I went to see John Rudge before the end of the season to ask for a move.'

Burnley, Notts County and Bradford City all made overtures to the twenty-seven-year-old, who was considering their offers when Shilton made his approach. 'I was on my way out the door one night to go out with my mates,' Swan continues.

> The missus ran out and said I had a phone call from Peter Shilton. Even though I obviously knew who he was, I didn't instantly connect him with Plymouth

Argyle. I asked my missus what club he was at and she said, 'Plymouth.' The first thing I thought was, 'We're not fucking going there!' She was pregnant with my first boy at the time so she didn't sound keen either. I went out anyway, with Shilton saying he would call back. So the next morning, before he calls, I've said to the missus, 'What I'll do is, I'll put £15-20k on top of what the other clubs are offering me and see what he says.' So Shilton calls again and I say to him, 'I've got a figure in my head, if you chuck an extra £20k on top of that, I'll be interested in coming.' So he said he'd get back to me. He called back ten minutes later and said they were still interested and wanted me to go down for talks. I got off the phone and said to the missus, 'Fucking hell, love, he's going to give us it.' She asked me what I was going to do, and I said, 'I've got to go down there, haven't I?' So I got hold of my dad and asked him if he fancied a mini holiday in Plymouth, and down we went.

With personal terms agreed, the only stumbling block to the deal going ahead was the size of the transfer fee. John Rudge was adamant that he wouldn't let his big defender go for a penny less than £375,000, and when Argyle drew the line at £125,000 less than that, Rudge boldly tested the water by suggested a player exchange deal involving Argyle skipper Steve Castle. Shilton refused to entertain the prospect of losing his goal-scoring skipper, and threatened to pull the plug on the deal. Vale blinked first and – with the player himself keen on the move – decided they had no option but to settle for £300,000.

Considering the way the deal eventually turned out, much has been made over the years of just whose decision it was to bring Swan to Home Park. All parties, however, are unequivocal in their agreement that Swan was the manager's choice. 'The person who wanted Peter Swan was Peter Shilton,' says director Ivor Jones. 'He felt from the season before that we needed a big, strong, experienced defender who could fill the hole he thought was in our defence. And it's true, that's what we needed. We already had a very good team, but he felt he would be the key player that would make all the difference.'

John McGovern agreed with his manager that a centre-back was what was required, but reveals that the pair differed on their preferred targets. 'I wanted to sign somebody else in that position,' he says. 'I'd done my homework on Mick Heathcote at Cambridge, and I said to Peter, "I think we should get this boy in," but he wanted to sign Swan, so he did. He's the manager, he makes the decisions, it was his choice.'

Heathcote did eventually sign for the Pilgrims with considerable success, but by then Shilton and McGovern were no longer around to enjoy it.

Chairman Dan McCauley shared his manager's belief that Swan would make all the difference to the side's fortunes. 'Shilton wanted someone in the middle of defence – and he came to us with two names: Swan and Winstanley at Bolton,' he says. 'He felt his defence was a bit suspect, and eventually Swan emerged as his number one target. I wanted Swan too, I thought he was the right man. He always played well against us.'

Indeed, it was his display against the Pilgrims in that 2–1 victory at Vale Park the previous February that some feel was the sole reason Swan was drafted in. 'He was signed on the basis of one good performance for Port Vale against us,' says Cowdery. 'He had a storming game up at Vale Park and made a couple of absolutely magnificent last-ditch tackles. He was a good footballer and he'd had a good career up to then.'

Shilton was keen to bring Swan to the club as soon as possible, but was forced to wait while the Board indulged in a spot of number-crunching. Says Jones, 'After a lot of to-ing and fro-ing that went on for a week or two, a phone call was finally made to Peter Shilton telling him that he could go ahead and do the deal.'

Peter Swan subsequently became the most expensive player in Plymouth Argyle's history when he signed for £300,000 on Wednesday 20 July 1994.

Shilton's major summer signing was unveiled amid a phalanx of journalists and photographers, much to his bemusement. 'They asked me if I minded signing my contract in front of all the press,' Swan recalls. 'I said it was no problem, so we went down to the stadium and I could not believe how many people had turned out for it. It was a big thing for that lot down there. To me it wasn't such a big thing, the fee wasn't in the millions or anything. I couldn't believe the attention it generated, it just amazed me.'

Swan duly signed his contract in front of the gathered pressmen, but not before he had noticed a discrepancy in the paperwork. 'Things went wrong from the start really,' he says.

> I was about to sign my contract, but rather than just going ahead and doing it, I checked it. The money that I asked for was supposed to be spread over two years, but they'd split it over three years. So I spotted this and told them they'd got my contract wrong. Dan McCauley told me to just sign it and we'd sort it out afterwards. My dad was with me, and I just said, 'Come on, Dad, we're going, I'm not signing.' So up we stood in the press conference and they all panicked and rushed out for a few minutes to sort it out.

Crisis averted, Swan put pen to paper and his manager was finally able to sing the praises of the player he viewed as a panacea for his side's perceived weaknesses from the season before. 'It is a big step in the right direction for Plymouth Argyle,' he said, in what was possibly the most erroneous statement in the history of the club. 'We are one of the few clubs in football at the moment looking to improve and spend a bit of money, and that is a credit to the club and its directors.'

But with Shilton sitting on a rather lofty perch after securing his number one transfer target, the manager received some news two days following the capture of Swan that would shatter his summer plans and set in motion a chain of events that would play a significant role in the unprecedented fall from grace that followed.

On Friday 22 July, captain Steve Castle shocked his manager and the club's fans by handing in a formal transfer request. 'I'd heard of interest from higher clubs, and my agent had advised me to go on the transfer list,' says Castle. 'Plymouth weren't forthcoming with a new offer – they didn't want to sell me, but they didn't seem to want to keep me either. I'd had me two years down there, and from an agent's point of view it was the right time to sell me. I'd just scored twenty-one goals, I was a commodity. So I went on the transfer list, in my opinion just to test the water more than anything.'

Shilton reacted to his skipper's request with as much good grace as he could muster, but made it clear his status at the club would immediately change. 'He took the captaincy away from me,' says Castle.

There was no argument between us, but he just said if I was on the transfer list I shouldn't be club captain. I explained to him that it really wasn't that much of an issue to me, I just said I wanted to see what was out there and he was reasonably understanding. But at the same time, he explained that he needed his club captain to be pledging himself to the club. But I was never given the chance to pledge myself to the club. There were people there on more money than me. I wasn't on great money, but they didn't offer me anything extra. There wasn't any malice behind my request, I wasn't desperate to leave or anything. If they'd offered me a new deal then I might have reassessed the situation, but they never came to me. From my perspective, Plymouth didn't really try that hard to keep hold of me. I was only on the list for a few weeks in the end anyway.

Peter Swan was subsequently awarded the captaincy, and he wore the armband for the first time in a 7–4 friendly win at Tiverton Town in mid-July. The big defender insists he was deserving of the honour, but admits Shilton could have handled it better. 'That was never going to help my cause,' he says. 'If I was the manager it would have been between me and Castle, but I probably would have done it differently. I did think I deserved it though, I never asked for it but I think I deserved it. I was a leader, a born leader. Steve Castle did fantastic for the club, scored a lot of goals for them and was a big part of the reason they'd had some success the season before. But I warranted it based on what I could do.'

If Swan thought he would inherit Castle's hero-like status among the club's fans along with his armband, he was resoundingly told otherwise when he made his first Home Park appearance in a friendly against Coventry City. 'When they announced my name all the fans booed,' he remembers. 'And I thought to myself, "What was that all about? Something's not right here." So that's when I started asking questions.'

Swan received the same emphatic answer from his various enquiries. 'Apparently it was all to do with that tackle I made on Dalton for Port Vale,' he says. 'That's what got the Plymouth fans on the wrong side of me straight away.

They kept showing that clip down there when I signed, and it didn't do me any favours to be honest.'

Ivor Jones suggests any initial ill-feeling wasn't all one-way traffic. 'What struck me when Peter came down was that he was a bona fide Northerner, and he really wanted to be in the North,' he says. 'He didn't want to be in the South, but he'd got a very good deal and Peter Shilton, as persuasive as he was, got him to come down. But in his heart, I don't think Peter Swan ever wanted to come, and so there were always going to be problems.'

Keith Hill lined up at left-back in the Coventry friendly, confirming his manager's admission earlier that summer that the former Blackburn defender was a mismatch for fellow centre-back Andy Comyn. 'I will be quite happy for Keith to stay with us because he's such a versatile player,' the manager had said. 'But I just don't see him as the ideal partner for Andy Comyn. They're too similar in style and I think both prefer to play off a central defender.'

For Hill, Swan's signing underlined his suspicions that the blame for the Burnley defeat had been laid squarely at his door. 'Swan's signing wasn't good from my point of view,' he reflects. 'I seemed to shoulder the brunt of the blame in respect of us losing to Burnley. I remember speaking to Peter Shilton afterwards and he seemed to find it very difficult to speak to me – as if I was to blame for the play-off defeat. But to bring in somebody like Peter Swan . . . I don't think he was a player that we needed. He was too much of a leader and we already had leaders in the squad.'

Swan insists his new team-mates made him feel like an outsider from the start. 'I felt atmosphere straight away,' he says. 'I asked to go out for a drink with the lads after the Coventry game, but they said they didn't really go out. So I've gone into a pub after the match and eight or nine of them were stood in the corner having a drink.'

Swan believes his high-profile arrival at the club turned his team-mates against him from the start. 'I'd gone down there after they'd just missed out on promotion thanks to that tackle of mine, so that might have been in their minds. I'd come for £300,000, I was supposed to be their big transformation that would get them out of the division by myself – but that's never going to happen.'

The apparently hostile atmosphere in the dressing room drove Swan into making a dramatic decision before the season had even begun. 'It went pear-shaped from day one,' he reflects. 'I knew I'd made the wrong decision as soon as I saw the group of players. I'd always been around a good bunch of lads, with me probably being the character of the team. I used to keep people together, take the piss out of people and vice versa – the leader off the field as well as on it. So when I went down there and saw what they were all like, I just thought, "Not for me." So I went and asked Shilts for a move before the season started.'

Shilton had seen two club captains request transfers within a matter of weeks, and his reaction was predictable. 'He nearly fell off his chair,' says Swan. 'He said, "Oh no, you're joking." "Nope, I've made the wrong decision," I told him.

We agreed to keep it to ourselves, he said, "Just give me time and I'll try and get you a move." I felt sorry for him, I knew what he'd brought me down there for, I knew how important my signing was to him. When I went out onto that field, I was thinking, "Those players aren't doing it for you, Gaffer, they're doing it against me." It backfired badly on Shilts.'

Argyle were to kick-off the 94/95 season at home to Brentford as the bookmakers' second favourites behind Birmingham City to win the league. With only one automatic promotion place available owing to the restructuring of the leagues, Argyle's task was even more arduous than the season before. Assistant boss John McGovern sounded a note of caution on the eve of the campaign. 'No two seasons follow the same pattern,' he said. 'Look at Leeds, who won the title two years ago and the following season could not win a single away match. We must look for more consistency if we are to go slightly better than last year.'

As for Shilton, he was pinning his hopes on a bright opening to the season. 'We must try and get a good start,' he said, before adding rather ominously, 'Last season has gone now and we are starting afresh. There is no given right to have another good year and we must take nothing for granted.'

Argyle were seriously hamstrung by injuries as they embarked on the new campaign. Want-away midfielder Steve Castle was out with an ankle injury (and later a mysterious and troublesome bout of jaundice that would see him miss five months of the season), while Player of the Year Steve McCall had a knee complaint and wouldn't play again that year. Paul Dalton would be absent for more than four months with a back injury, and Alan Nicholls and Dominic Naylor were also among the opening-day walking wounded. Throw in the departed Dwight Marshall and Adrian Burrows, and Argyle would be starting the season without seven of their most influential performers from the previous campaign.

However, even taking into account their patched-up opening-day XI, most Argyle fans were still expecting a continuation of the previous season's fine home form – which had seen them win sixteen of their twenty-three contests on home turf. And indeed, eighteen minutes into the visit of the Bees, it was business as usual.

Craig Skinner's ball into the box was cleared by a Brentford player straight into Peter Swan's leg, from where it flew into the net. The opening goal of Argyle's season was a fittingly comical way for the home side to get off the mark considering how the match would ultimately turn out. 'It went in off my right thigh,' says Swan. 'I had twenty quid on myself to score first and won 400-odd quid.'

But eighty minutes later, the traditional opening-day sun had disappeared behind foreboding grey clouds and Argyle's pre-season optimism had vanished with it.

Brentford answered Swan's fortuitous goal by scoring five rather more emphatic efforts of their own to leave Devon with a resounding 5–1 victory that shocked Home Park to its very core. One Argyle fan – in describing the ease with which the Brentford strikers broke through the Pilgrims' rearguard – suggested it had been like watching 'elephants chasing antelopes.'

The manager, however, was surprisingly pragmatic. 'We looked a bit lightweight in certain areas, but we can improve on that,' he said. 'We have lost three points and a bit of pride, but we also lost our opening game last year.'

Rick Cowdery was at the post-match press conference, and found Shilton's calm demeanour highly surprising. 'He came in and he said, "Well, things can only get better." But that's not what the fans want to hear after a 5–1 beating. You want a bit of contrition and a bit of anger. He must have been mortified, but what he said just sounded all wrong.'

As for the players, the defeat was a real slap in the face after the many highs of the previous season. 'You train all pre-season for the opening game,' says Craig Skinner. 'We were confident, but it was a horrible defeat, especially in the first game of the season when your expectations are so high. We came back down to Earth with a massive bump, and it did rather set the tone for the season.'

Striker Kevin Nugent believes the horrendous injury situation that never really eased had a major impact upon the team's fortunes, together with the disappointment of losing out in the play-offs. 'The players certainly had a hangover from missing out on promotion,' he says. 'There was definitely a carry-over of that to the following season, and it took us far too long to get over it. But we had far too many injuries as well, and when you're playing without three or four of your best players – it's going to take its toll. You're not going to be the force that you'd like to be.'

A month later, no amount of injuries or play-off hangovers could have explained away the worst start to a season in the history of the club. The stinging defeat to the Bees was followed by a 4–0 Coca-Cola Cup loss at Walsall, a second 5–1 thrashing at home to Bradford, 2–0 and 4–2 losses at Hull and Birmingham respectively, and another Home Park horror show – a 3–0 trouncing at the hands of Huddersfield Town.

A redundant 2–1 second-leg victory over Walsall and a 1–1 draw at Brighton were insignificant distractions in what amounted to a clear-cut sign that something was very rotten in the state of Home Park. With the Pilgrims entrenched in the bottom three by mid-September, without a win and having shipped twenty goals in their first seven games, supporters were wildly speculating over just how things had gone so badly wrong in the space of a few summer weeks.

'We had a very close knit squad the season before,' explains Keith Hill. 'But Peter Swan was the wrong signing at the wrong time. We already had the leaders within the squad, and we didn't need Swan to come in and undermine everything. And to make things worse, the captaincy was then taken away from Steve Castle and given to Swan – that was what split the squad.'

Swan himself agrees, but suggests Castle didn't make the captaincy transition any easier. 'Castle made it worse than how it should have been,' he says.

'Argyle are trying to keep the goals against tally down so they're playing
Smeaton's Tower between the sticks from now on.'

I remember coming out for the Walsall second leg, Castle's first game of the
season, and he was the last one out on the pitch. He was obviously trying to get
the fans on his side to help his cause. I just thought, 'If that's the way you want to
play the game, play it that way.' Some of the lads carried on calling him skipper
as well, which I thought was very petty. It didn't affect me one bit, I used to just
go in there and switch off really. It was a horrible scenario to be in, but by the
end I enjoyed being that person. They thought they were affecting me, but it just
made me a stronger person.

Swan scored his second goal for the club against the Saddlers, and suggests it
was his reaction to scoring that goal that drove a wedge permanently into the
growing gap between him and the rest of the squad. 'The ball came out to me
and I just smashed it in anger and it flew into the top corner,' he says.

I remember a couple of players trying to jump on me to celebrate, but I just
elbowed them off. I didn't want anything to do with them, I wanted to do it myself.
I just did my own salute in the middle of the pitch as if to say, 'Fuck you all' to
the fans. The other players started to get on my back from then on. But that's how
I wanted it to be: 'Come on, the more you can give me, the more I can handle.'
I used it to give me more fire in my belly to try and get myself out of there.

Swan also claims his team-mates discovered the details of his bumper contract, which he believes led to even greater resentment. 'One of the players' wives worked in the offices, so word got round about what money I was getting,' he says. 'They weren't happy with that. I was the big saviour who had come in on big money, and they were basically challenging me to go out there and prove it.'

It was then that Swan sent his wife back up North and decided to go it alone in Plymouth. 'I just thought, "Fuck it, I'll do this myself." So I sent my missus back home and I told her I'd handle the situation by myself.'

But Swan's team-mates insist it was a two-way street, claiming the big Yorkshireman took an instant dislike to certain members of the squad and set about trying to create divisions within the dressing room. 'The year before, everything was fine,' says Martin Barlow.

> Everyone got on well – if we had a party everyone would be invited. But it all changed when Swan arrived. He had this thing about Londoners. He just couldn't stand them. The Londoners would stick together and if you went and spoke to them, Swanny would get funny. But they hadn't done anything to him, so I couldn't understand it. He unsteadied the camp because he was trying to get people onside with him … it was really childish. I remember he once had a party and invited all the players except for the London lot. It was dividing the camp.

'He caused a clique in the club,' says Dominic Naylor.

> He was a big Northern bully really. He split a few of the lads. Dolly [Paul Dalton] didn't know which way to go, nor did Patto – he was quite friendly with Patto, and there was Martin Hodge as well who he was mates with. So it all went a bit tits-up. To be honest, I don't think it was anything to do with any of the lads who were there to start with, I think he just came in and wasn't the centre of attention, or wasn't the main man or whatever and I think that's what got his back up.

Castle believes that Shilton's decision to award Swan the captaincy was doomed to failure from the start. 'Unfortunately, the manager gave the captaincy to a player who wasn't committed to the football club from the first kick of the ball,' he says. 'Had he given it to an older, experienced lad, Steve McCall maybe, that might just have gelled us together as a unit. But I don't think Swan liked the area. I also don't think he liked how many Londoners were at the club and took an instant dislike to us. I think it was the cockiness of Londoners he just didn't like, and particularly myself. It was the biggest load of nonsense ever.'

If any public evidence was needed that the new arrival wasn't exactly inspiring his fellow players, it came when Swan was forced to miss a series of matches to be with his wife after the birth of their son. In his absence, his team-mates kept four successive clean sheets hot on the heels of that calamitous opening spell, winning ten points out of a possible twelve. Swan briefly returned to the side as the Pilgrims shipped two goals in a 2–2 draw with Wycombe, but was then out for five weeks with a broken cheekbone. Argyle's form was patchy at best during the captain's latest enforced absence, but his return in mid-December coincided with a wretched series of results that included one of the most crushing defeats in the club's history.

Keith Hill believes Shilton's faith in his record signing was misplaced, and as a result the dressing room turned against the manager at the worst possible time. 'Players aren't stupid,' he says.

> If you ignore them and their understanding of the game then you do so at your peril, because the players will lose belief in you as a manager and I'm afraid your head is well and truly in the noose then. As a manager, you've got to make big decisions and the players will respect you for that, there's no question about that – they'll play for you every day of the week as long as you're making the right decisions for the team. But as soon as you start making wrong decisions, then the players will hang you – no question. And I think that was the case with Shilton that season. It was glaringly obvious what should have been done, but it wasn't done.

The statistics overwhelmingly back up Hill's assertion that Swan adversely affected the balance of the side that season. The Yorkshireman made twenty-eight appearances in 94/95, in which fifty-nine goals were conceded and just one clean sheet recorded; but on the twenty-five occasions when he was absent, only twenty-six goals were let in and nine clean sheets were banked.

Swan, however, insists the whole team and the management was to blame for the frailties in defence. 'If you're organised and get everybody pissing in the same pots, you've got a half chance,' he says. 'But if you've got a team that's mismanaged, and the players don't know what their jobs are then you're going to struggle. I would try my nuts off, but the ball just kept coming back to the defenders. Mistakes would then happen and people would say, "It's fucking him again."'

With his cheekbone mended, Swan returned to the heart of Argyle's defence on 10 December at home to Brighton, and Argyle promptly lost 3–0 to a side without an away point for more than two months. But a week later, the case for the defence was blown apart when the Pilgrims were on the end of a humiliating 7–0 thrashing at Brentford – the team that had beaten them 5–1 at Home Park back in August. 'I remember it vividly,' says Wayne Burnett. 'We got hammered, we were all over the place, everything they hit went in. I was playing against some people that I knew, and it was frustrating and very embarrassing.'

Right-back Mark Patterson recalls a torrid afternoon. 'I remember being told before the game to make sure we kept it tight, but we were 2–0 down after eight minutes,' he says. 'I remember thinking, "Jesus, that's tight, isn't it?" We were an absolute joke that day. To lose 7–0, that just shouldn't happen.'

Striker Kevin Nugent was drafted into midfield at Griffin Park with injuries and suspensions still taking their toll on the Argyle squad. 'That game was just horrible,' he says.

> But my main memory of the day was having to go and meet the London branch of Argyle fans after the game. The support that I saw that day … they understood there were a lot of things going on, and the way they conducted themselves when we walked into the room was absolutely fantastic. I've never seen anything like it. There wasn't any criticism of the players at all. And Peter Shilton excelled himself professionally, he got on the microphone and spoke to the supporters, which was a very brave thing to do, a lot of managers would have shied away from that. He got a round of applause afterwards and the players spent a couple of hours there. That was something I didn't think was possible to happen after you'd just been beaten 7–0.

For Andy Comyn, the West London pummelling was the culmination of a season-long struggle trying to forge a partnership with Swan in the centre of defence. 'We just couldn't play together,' he says.

> We weren't a good match at all. He was very good coming onto the ball, but as soon as the ball went over his head he just didn't seem to want to run back, on his side or my side or anywhere. It made life very, very difficult because then you get caught in two minds. If a team was looking to play the ball over the top I just knew I'd be the one having to do the chasing back wherever it went, and that just unsettles you and you don't play your normal game. I spoke quite a lot with Peter Shilton about it. I gave my view that I seemed to be doing all the chasing and all the running, and that Swanny would just be waiting for the ball to come to him, and if it didn't he would just pretty much stand where he was. We talked at length but it never worked out.

Unsurprisingly, Swan lays the blame for their inability to blend squarely on Comyn. 'At Brentford, the goalkeeper would take a dead ball and keep kicking it to Andy Comyn, and he's saying to me, "Will you come over here? Do my heading for me, do my heading for me." And I'm thinking, "Fucking hellfire." I told him to do his job and I'd do mine, and the consequence was that we got beat 7–0. Yeah, I'll take part of the blame because it's a team game, but people have got to look in the mirror and some of them didn't want to be counted – whereas I would fight the cause for Shilts.'

The relationship between Swan and his team-mates reached rock-bottom shortly after the humbling by Brentford, when the players' Christmas party descended into an ugly brawl. 'Things obviously weren't going well for me at the time,' remembers Swan.

So Hodgey [Martin Hodge] said it would be best if I didn't go to the Christmas party. But on the morning of the do I thought, 'Well, I am captain, I should at least show my face.' It was in a hotel bar at the New Continental in town. I've gone in there and Kevin Nugent walks past. As he's gone past me, I've grabbed him to say, 'Do you want a drink?' But as I grabbed him the buttons popped off his cardigan. He grabs me straight away, so I say, 'What are you doing?', and he says, 'You just ripped my top.' I told him it was an accident, but he was just holding onto my shirt trying to rip it – so I've gone to push him away and he's come back at me so I've head-butted him. He's gone against the wall, and as he's come back at me, the rest of the lads have piled in to help him out. There were a couple of loose punches flying around, and the initial head-butt from myself, but it was handbags really.

Martin Barlow believes a physical confrontation was inevitable by that stage. 'It had been coming,' he says. 'It could have been any of the London lads really. A couple of punches were thrown but it was nothing really. Kev went for him, and I think Swanny was shocked. Kev was up for it, and Swanny was taken aback that he stood up to him.'

'It shows the type of team spirit we had at the time when that sort of thing happens,' adds Comyn. 'You just wouldn't think it would have been Kevin Nugent though, Swanny yes, but something must have happened to wind Kevin up because he wasn't that type of person.'

Several weeks later, Swan upped the stakes in his bid to earn a move away from Plymouth when he publicly revealed his desire to quit the club and leave a city he had grown to despise, and endeared himself to the club's fans forever by admitting he only signed in the first place for the money. 'I was sat in the Far Post Club having my lunch one day,' he remembers.

Natalie Cornah [a BBC Spotlight reporter] came over and asked what I was up to, so I told her I had an exclusive for her. 'Come round to my house tomorrow and I'll give you the story about how I don't want to stay here.' She was obviously bloody delighted. I had to do something to get away, and I thought the money thing would upset people and get me a move. So the story went out about how I'd only come to the club for the money, and I thought, 'Fucking hell, that's going to go down well.' But I'd lost the plot by that stage and I had to do something. My wife and son were miles away, so I used to just sit by myself all the time and do my own thing. I used to have dinner by myself, and have a glass of gin or two on my own. I was basically an alcoholic down there, every day, every afternoon. I'd just had enough.

Despite Swan's status as a pariah in the dressing room, it's perhaps surprising that his team-mates refused to place the blame for their fall from grace on his considerable shoulders. 'To be honest, that split wasn't helped by the number of defeats we were having,' says ousted skipper Steve Castle.

> I don't think splits happen when you've got a successful team. I've known divides at football clubs, whether it be North–South, black–white, whatever, but if you're winning games it's not an issue. And anyway, the bonding thing very rarely happens at clubs. We're all young men with opinions and egos – you have people that are having conflicts, verbal conflicts, physical conflicts … but the most important thing is the game on Saturday and that usually masks any issues. But unfortunately, when you're struggling it just aggravates the situation. And unfortunately for him, Swanny took the brunt of it. I had known him as a damn good centre half, and if we could have taken all those personalities out and put him in the team of the year previous with that solidity that we had, I think we'd have gone up – because he was a damn good player.

'He didn't fit in from day one,' says Steve McCall. 'I'm not sure he tried to fit in. Swanny was a tough character, but he had his camp and there were two camps working against each other and that's not conducive to a good season. What looked like a good signing turned into a bad one. Not through anything the lad did, just the way it didn't work for us. When you're struggling on the pitch, it becomes a bit fractious off the pitch and people start pointing fingers because they're looking for excuses.'

Mark Patterson was one of the few players at the club who Swan had any time for, and he felt a degree of sympathy with his fellow defender. 'I got to know Swanny quite well because he lived near me in Roborough,' says Patterson.

> A lot of people didn't like him, possibly because they didn't think we needed a centre-half, but a lot of stuff was levelled at Swanny's door that I think was unfair. When he came into the team there was a lot of injuries, and a lot of people said it was Peter Swan's fault that we had such a bad start, and I remember thinking, 'How can people blame one person for that?' Admittedly, Swanny didn't help himself either at times, some of the things he did and said. But it's a hard enough job moving away anyway, and when people are blaming you for everything that's gone on, it makes it even more difficult.

Craig Skinner lays the blame largely at the manager's door, insisting that the captaincy should never have been taken away from Castle in favour of the expensive new arrival. 'I don't necessarily think it was all about Swanny in terms of going from a play-off team to being relegated,' he says. 'I think it had something to do with it, but I think it was down to Peter Shilton's decisions as well, in terms of stripping Stevie Castle of the captaincy. Steve being as popular as he was, obviously it's going to have some sort of effect. You get someone new coming in and all of a sudden they're your new captain, it's not ideal. The whole dynamic of the club had been changed and there might have been the feeling that there was a bit of an end of an era.'

For Swan himself, his time in Plymouth began disastrously and slowly turned into a personal nightmare. In mid-October, just after he had smashed his cheekbone against Wycombe, Swan's diabetic dog died of an insulin overdose – an infamous incident that has become legend among the club's fans. 'I played on the Saturday against Wycombe and smashed my cheekbone in three places,' he says.

> So I go straight into hospital to have an operation. The dog was at the vet, and the missus is at home with the bairn – who was sick. I came out of hospital on the Sunday morning and apparently the dog was fine. Half-an-hour later my wife calls saying, 'Bad news, the dog has collapsed and died at home.' The vets were saying it had nothing to do with the insulin overdose they had given her – what a load of bollocks, dogs don't just drop dead like that without reason. It was bloody awful, and I got some nasty letters from the nice Plymouth fans about that.

Swan also claims his house was haunted. 'Things would go flying off the wall for no reason,' he says. 'You'd be in the kitchen and the television would just switch itself on. I was in the bath one afternoon and I heard a smash downstairs. I went down and my lovely Royal Doulton pot dog was in pieces all over the floor. It had just flown across the room. I couldn't believe it. I had to nip out for a pint to get over the shock.'

Following his public revelation that he had only signed for the cash, Swan turned from an expensive misfit in the eyes of the fans into public enemy number one. 'My missus got rammed off the road twice in the car with my name on the side,' he says. 'Tyres used to get slashed – we had four or five slashed tyres. People used to chuck stones at me as I was driving down the road as well. I could see why they were like that towards me, but the whole experience just made me a better person. It could have cracked some people.'

Swan's form improved as the side slid towards relegation, so much so that he ended up snatching a surprise third place in the club's Player of the Year stakes. 'That's how much things had changed for me, they could see that other people weren't performing. But I was doing it for myself in the end, I was self-employed.'

Unsurprisingly, Swan didn't shed any tears for his team-mates when Argyle's sad demise was confirmed come season's end. 'I had more pleasure out of seeing all them bastards get relegated than I got out of promotion the season before,' he says. 'That's how much it ate away at me. I just thought they got what they deserved. I'll hold my hands up and take some of the blame because I'm a team player. But the way certain players performed the season before but not the season after had nothing to do with me. I worked my nuts off that year. The fans might not have thought so, but out of that team, how many players got moves at the end of that season? I went for big money; where did they all go and what did they do?'

Swan eventually secured his ticket out of Plymouth when Neil Warnock arrived, moving – perhaps fittingly – to Burnley for £200,000 in August 1995. 'It was as obvious as day follows night that there was a huge split between the players,' says Warnock. 'Swan was training on his own most of the time, and he said that he did things on purpose because he desperately wanted a move, so he'd kick people in training and stuff like that. I remember saying to him, "It's obvious you're not training for me, I'll try and get you a move as soon as I can." I couldn't wait to get rid of him.'

Swan packed his bags and high-tailed it out of Plymouth on 4 August after fifty-four miserable weeks in the city. 'It wasn't the best of times at all to be honest,' he reflects, 'But it was probably the best thing that ever happened to me – it made me a lot better person. And I'm not blaming anybody else for it, it was my decision to go down there so I'll take the full blame for that.'

Is there a hint of regret that his time in Devon didn't work out differently? 'It is a nice place, when you look at it from a different perspective,' he says. 'I wish I could have settled there, it's a nice area. When I go back there now, I do wish it could have been different down there for me, my wife and kids. I may still have been down there now if circumstances had been different.'

CHAPTER TWELVE

THE LIGHTS GO OUT

There is a photograph of Peter Shilton and Dan McCauley that, on first glance, appears to suggest a relationship between manager and club chairman of the utmost harmony. Taken on the day after the play-off defeat to Burnley, the pair's hands are clasped in a firm handshake, both are bedecked in smart suits and are wearing smiles as wide as the River Tamar.

But on closer inspection, and with the benefit of hindsight, the portrait is a herring as red as the tie around McCauley's neck.

Having just agreed the manager's new two-year contract, the pair acted out a fairly convincing display of unity in front of the photographers; but both men are standing as stiff as boards, there is no eye contact and both have their left hand concealed in a pocket. A body language expert would have a field day. 'After the meeting,' writes Shilton in his autobiography, 'McCauley and I posed for photographers, smiling and apparently in unison, but I was thinking, "This isn't going to last."'

Shilton's fatalistic reaction to what should have been an auspicious development in his Home Park tenure was perhaps justified. The England legend and his garrulous chairman were polar opposites, and the frayed edges of their tempestuous relationship had long threatened to develop into an irrevocable tear.

The uneasy handshake outside Home Park on that warm spring day would prove to be the last semblance of pretence between the two, with the season that followed developing into a spiteful, farcical shambles that became undisputedly the worst in the club's entire history.

When Peter Shilton was appointed as Plymouth Argyle manager in March 1992, his new chairman was unequivocal that the right choice had been made. 'We have gone for a man with international experience,' said McCauley, 'one who is a model professional and we hope he can be our saviour. We think he will be.'

However, McCauley was instantly uneasy with the financial package he had handed his new manager, and the expensive summer recruitment program that followed relegation added further weight to a nagging feeling that he was being taken down a path he had no desire to tread.

Their squabbles at Cheltenham and Hereford in the summer of 1992 – when the chairman vehemently expressed his dissatisfaction at the new team's mediocre friendly results – set the tone for a fiery affiliation that was occasionally subdued but never fully extinguished.

Their first public fall-out came in November '92, with Shilton's big-ticket side floundering in a mid-table Second Division dogfight. After shelling out almost £800,000 on new players, McCauley could hold his tongue no longer and publicly revealed his dismay at what he saw as a 'deterioration in quality' in the manager's lavishly assembled side. Shilton was called before a special Board meeting to explain why his princes were being made to look like paupers – McCauley expected an immediate return to the newly named First Division and was in no mood to listen to his manager's excuses.

The chairman later insisted his comments had been 'blown out of all proportion,' but Shilton was not impressed. 'It seemed to me that there were a few things McCauley didn't understand about football clubs,' wrote Shilton in his autobiography, in reference to the chairman's mid-season outburst.

Publicly at least, the brief breakdown in relations appeared to be no more than an inconsequential blip, but behind the scenes the screw was already being turned and the manager was under no illusion as to the size of the task he had taken on.

In a letter dated 6 January 1993, McCauley let it be known that Shilton was to focus his 'undivided attention' on selling players to finance his costly summer spending spree that had brought in Steve Castle, Paul Dalton, Warren Joyce and Gary Poole. 'At a recent Board meeting, we specifically asked you to carry out the following before the end of December 1992,' went the chairman's letter. '1. Raise £300,000 in the transfer market, 2. Reduce the wage bill by £12,000 per month, 3. Reduce the playing staff to eighteen.'

The letter went on to emphasise that Shilton's squad rebuilding efforts had severely hamstrung the club's finances – with the balance sheet showing losses of up to £1.4 million. 'The Board adopted a high-risk policy of buying players prior to selling. And because the latter has not been carried out, the Board are in a strait-jacket with dire financial implications – and falling gates do not help the situation.'

If Shilton was in any doubt as to the club's parlous financial position, it was painstakingly spelt out to him when the home match against Huddersfield Town was washed out on Saturday 9 January. McCauley takes up the story. 'It was important from a financial point of view that we had a home game every fortnight at least,' he says.

It had been pouring down with torrential rain all week, so I went down to the ground on the Friday evening and spoke to Shilton and McGovern. I said, 'Look, you've got to make sure this game's on. Cover the pitch with a tarpaulin, do whatever you've got to do to make sure it's on.' I also told McGovern to make sure the tarpaulin stayed on even if he had to stay there all night. Well, he didn't stay all night and the wind lifted the tarpaulin off the pitch and it belted down with rain and the game didn't go on. I found out they'd also let the Football League know that the game might not go ahead. I had a go at both of them the next day, but Shilton just said, 'Ah, don't take any notice of him, he doesn't know what he's talking about,' and walked off while I was still talking.

McGovern had risked the chairman's wrath by disobeying his orders, but insists there was no chance of the game ever going ahead. 'He threatened to sack me for not getting the plastic cover on the pitch,' he says. But the wind was so fierce the ground staff told me there was no way we would be able to keep it down – never mind put it on in the first place. If you live in Plymouth for any length of time you know it does bloody rain down there, so I knew we were fighting a lost cause.'

McCauley wouldn't let the matter drop, and wrote to Shilton the following Monday to remind him of his responsibilities to ensuring the financial welfare of the club. 'I find it incomprehensible,' he wrote, 'that your department, knowing the financial situation within the club, sought to raise fears with the Football League over the game being in doubt without considering the implications. I instructed Mr McGovern to stay there all night, such was the importance. He cared to ignore such orders, which led to the cancellation.' McCauley was now in full flow, 'I do not take it kindly either when, as I was ranting and raving, you stated to Mr McGovern that "he doesn't have to listen to this," and you both walked away. Unfortunately you do have to listen.'

The chairman closed his missive by informing Shilton – who had recently borrowed defender Richard Dryden from Birmingham – that he was forbidden from bringing in any further loan signings until he had trimmed his squad: 'I can assure you that the Dryden loan, or any further ones, will not be extended or entertained until such time as our house in order.'

A month later, with Argyle's promotion voyage sailing dangerously close to the rocks, Shilton was once again in his chairman's bad books – this time for his lack of match-day mingling and for his dealings with the press. 'I am issuing a directive to you that after every home match you are to spend a minimum of fifteen minutes with the match sponsors, thirty minutes in the Vice Presidents' Lounge and thirty minutes in the Far Post Club,' wrote McCauley in a letter dated 4 February. 'Also, you must speak more openly to the press, and bury your differences with them [one assumes this referred to Shilton's strained relationship with the *Western Morning News*]. Unfortunately, because you have refrained from talking, they naturally only portray one side of any argument, which leaves you in an unenviable position.'

The lamentable Autoglass Trophy defeat at Torquay in early February dragged the feud between the pair kicking and screaming back into the spotlight. McCauley claimed he would sack the manager if only he could 'find the money' to pay off his contract. But Shilton, for his part, was a persuasive figure.

After being summoned to the Boardroom for the second time that season, the manager emerged with the full support of the chairman and his directors – with the tables turning to such an extent that McCauley even blamed himself for the unsavoury headlines. 'I'm the biggest troublemaker at the club,' he told the gathered media men outside Home Park – who had been expectantly awaiting a major announcement about the manager's future. 'I find I get all excited and have to say things, but I realise I shouldn't.'

Shilton was also in conciliatory mood, and publicly pledged to do his bit to protect the club's fiscal health. 'I realise the club's financial position,' he told the press. 'And also realise that I have to do some wheeling and dealing now. We've both got common goals to get the club to the top.'

In a surprising show of commitment to the supposed bold new era of peace at Home Park, McCauley vowed to gag himself in future and informed the press it would be a waste of time pursuing him for interviews from that point on. Director Ivor Jones was appointed as the club's unofficial spokesman, and suggests the breakdown in relations between McCauley and Shilton was largely due to the chairman's personality. 'Dan is an extremely volatile character and he found it very hard to control his emotions,' he says. 'Reporters were always around him because they knew they were going to get a controversial quote from him. But after that Board meeting, Dan said he needed to learn to keep his mouth shut. So he appointed me as a press spokesman and I was in that role for about six to nine months. And in fairness to Dan, during that time he didn't say a word – he backed me up 100 per cent.'

McCauley's imitation of a Trappist monk actually lasted just thirty-four days, when the 3–0 Easter Saturday defeat to Exeter City prompted his headline-making 'Stop their wages' rant.

Western Morning News reporter Alan English recalls the aftermath of the abysmal Devon derby defeat, and outlines a relationship between chairman and manager that had irrevocably disintegrated just thirteen months after Shilton's appointment. 'I went down to the Far Post Club after the press conferences,' English recalls.

> McCauley would occasionally call in there and talk to supporters, so I hung around in there for a couple of hours and sure enough, McCauley arrives at about 7 o'clock. You could see he'd already had a few G&Ts. He was stood at the bar and various supporters were coming up, having a go at Shilton. I collared him eventually; I always enjoyed talking to Dan, he was a straight-shooter and any journalist will appreciate that. He had held back from criticising the team and Shilton up to that point, but being humiliated in a local derby was always going to test his diplomacy and I couldn't see him biting his tongue over this one. I held back and let him shoot the breeze over another drink at the bar. Then I got the notebook out and he started coming out with it, about how the players and management team shouldn't be paid after their shambolic performance. Fans standing around him were all

nodding indignantly – people were seriously pissed off and maybe he was playing to the gallery a little, but you couldn't blame him. He had fronted up with a lot of money for some quality players, but they allowed Exeter to out-hustle them, there was just no spirit at that stage. I came out of the Far Post walking on air that night. Good old Dan – he had delivered big-time, and we had the 'Stop Their Wages' rant in the paper on the Monday. It was clear to me that his relationship with Shilton had completely broken down even at that early stage.

English and several fans also claim the chairman threw darts at a picture of his manager after his tirade at the bar, though McCauley himself denies this.

The root cause of the chairman's indignation was the club's financial position. With Shilton's misfits ensconced in mid-table, McCauley twice wrote to his manager, on 18 and 30 March, to demand that players be sold to plug a £300,000 shortfall in the club's finances that Barclays Bank were ready to call in. 'We are within a few days of our deadline [with the bank],' McCauley wrote in his 18 March letter. 'Your failure to raise [the £300,000] will be creating major concerns with the bank. I am sure the players will not welcome delays in payment and I can assure you that the bank will be more than displeased.'

Shilton had publicly expressed his displeasure that he was not able to make a bid to keep Tottenham Hotspur loanee Lee Hodges at the club on a permanent basis, for which he received a firm rebuke from his chairman. 'You should praise your Board,' wrote McCauley. 'After all, it was made abundantly clear prior to your job acceptance that no money was available. It is time now that you realised the money spending is over and you must make the most of what you have. Believe me, what this Board has given you is far in excess of any other manager in the history of the club, and it is time you realised and appreciated it. It is no good crying to the press when you don't get your own way.'

McCauley's indignation petered out along with an almost entirely forgettable 92/93 season, and an unlikely peace descended on Home Park as Shilton prepared for his second full campaign in charge at the club.

Minor scuffles over the sale of defender Jock Morrison and the appointment of a youth coach punctuated several months of harmony in PL2, and Shilton's promotion-chasing players were able to enjoy exclusive access to the spotlight.

With 93/94 unfolding so auspiciously, McCauley remained conspicuously silent in the shadows, his Irish ire reduced to barely glowing embers thanks to the calming effects of a winning team and rising attendances. But almost inevitably, the peace was not to last.

In early February 1994, with Argyle sitting pretty in the top two of the Second Division, the *Evening Herald*'s sports editor kicked off a story that was eventually to gain more ground than the team's promotion race. In an editorial on 8 February, Kevin Marriott urged the Argyle Board to demonstrate their ambition by offering new contracts to Shilton and John McGovern – who would effectively be able to walk out of Home Park through a loophole at the end of the season should promotion prove elusive. 'If the Argyle Board are serious about their ambitious and exciting long-term plans for the team,' wrote Marriott, 'then they have to secure the management team on longer contracts. The only risk the Argyle directors would be taking in securing Shilton and McGovern on longer contracts would be if they are intending to show them the door at some stage in the near future. But that's hardly likely, is it?'

Several weeks later, with the story refusing to go away, Ivor Jones was forced to allay snowballing rumours that the club's high-earning managerial duo was to be axed in the summer – but also gave a clear indication that the Board would be sitting on its hands until divisional status was confirmed in May. 'There is no reason for us to do anything at this stage, and we certainly have no intention of terminating the manager's contract,' said Jones. 'Nothing is up for consideration because no big decision is required of us at this moment.'

However, as the season entered the crucial home straight with Argyle among the front-runners for promotion, the contract controversy exploded onto the back pages of the national tabloids to leave the manager reeling just four games away from the finish line.

It was Shilton himself who inadvertently opened the can of worms when he publicly called on the Board to make him an offer. 'Nothing definite has been happening in regards to my contract,' he told the *Western Morning News*. 'Something needs to be sorted out.'

McCauley insisted the manager had been offered 'an excellent, first-class deal,' but upped the ante two days later when, despite expressing dismay that Shilton had taken his concerns to the local press, the chairman went national with his.

Under the headline 'Mr Greedy', McCauley told Brian Woolnough of the *Sun* that Shilton was seeking a pay rise despite his already 'fantastic' salary. 'Peter Shilton is one of the top earners in the country,' said McCauley. 'If George Graham is reported to earn £250,000 a year at Arsenal, our manager is not far behind that. We have offered him a new two-year deal but he wants more security. In that contract we told him that he would have to take a pay reduction if we were not promoted. If we go up then he would not be on the same money. He does not agree with that. He wants more.'

McCauley endeavoured to pre-empt any criticism by denouncing the *Sun* story as 'totally out of order', but Shilton was not amused and hit back against his chairman's accusations in the *Evening Herald*. 'I don't want any more money, I would be quite happy with the contract that I've already got,' he told the paper. 'But I don't think it's right to be offered a pay-cut either.'

With the contract storm battering Home Park, a clearly flustered Shilton watched his players succumb to an eye-watering 3–0 defeat at home to Cambridge and scrape a 1–1 draw at Brentford. Three more points in any combination from those two games would have ensured promotion at season's end and rendered the whole contract quarrel irrelevant.

As it was, the play-offs and Burnley intervened to make a mockery of the club's promotion ambitions, and the Home Park fates of both Shilton and McCauley were effectively signed and sealed.

A reasonably serene summer followed the play-off heartbreak, during which the new contract was finally agreed upon and the club's transfer record broken to secure the services of Peter Swan. But Home Park was soon to become the stage for a tragicomedy of epic proportions that made the club and its manager the laughing stock of English football.

Argyle's record-breaking start to the season – in which they conceded twenty-six goals in just eight games – could have been placed squarely on Peter Swan's unwelcome shoulders, but a casualty list that put the Charge of the Light Brigade to shame hardly helped matters. Key figures Steve McCall, Paul Dalton, Steve Castle, Alan Nicholls, Mark Patterson, Andy Comyn and Wayne Burnett all suffered ailments that denied the manager of their services for lengthy periods. 'There's a lot of politics involved with injuries,' says physio Paul Sumner. 'If a player's not playing well it can manifest itself in an injury. Politically, they don't want to play that match because they want to be ready for another match, or if they're not playing well they'll blame it on a sore foot or something. In the play-off season I was twiddling my thumbs, but the season after the place was swamped with players.'

With almost all of his key men missing in action at various stages of the season, Shilton was forced to paper over the chasms with a flurry of sub-par youngsters and loanees. Chris Twiddy, Simon Dawe, Ian Payne, Jamie Morgan, Marcus Crocker, Danny O'Hagan and Paul Wotton were all thrust into the mixer before their time – with only Wotton going on to enjoy a career in the professional game.

Shilton's return from the loan market was similarly fruitless. Graham Shaw from Stoke, Millwall's Phil Barber and Darren Bradshaw from Peterborough all donned a green and black shirt – though none with any distinction.

By mid-September, Argyle were third from bottom with a meagre return of five points from a possible twenty-four, but things were about to get worse. Much worse. On 12 September, John McGovern shocked the club to its core by resigning to leave Shilton without an assistant and the club's supporters banging their already throbbing heads against the wall.

The forty-four-year-old's astonishing departure was initially shrouded in mystery, but McCauley was only too happy to wade in and reveal the unsavoury circumstances surrounding McGovern's exit. 'John McGovern's resignation is all to do with money,' said the chairman – by way of explaining that his number two had quit after lending his number one a sum of money that hadn't been repaid (£7,500 plus interest). 'I don't think John will leave it as it stands and, therefore, it is in Shilton's interests to try to resolve the problem.'

McGovern refuses to elaborate on the details, but contends that the situation between himself and Shilton was a major factor in the team's awful start to the season. 'I obviously had personal problems with the manager and I think it showed in some of the results,' he says. 'Although to be honest, I wasn't that bothered at the time, my involvement wasn't 100 per cent anyway. I told the chairman I didn't want the circumstances of my resignation made public, but he went and revealed all in one of the Plymouth papers the next day. He was losing me and he didn't want that to happen I suppose. I genuinely thought there was a possibility we could have achieved something at Plymouth, but once the personal issue slices that in half, the thing's finished.'

For Ian Bowyer, the dissolution of relations between his two former Nottingham Forest team-mates was a complete bolt out of the blue. 'I didn't see it coming, I have to say,' he reflects. 'I didn't get wind that things weren't great between them until John came up to me one day and said, "Look, Ian, I'm leaving," and basically that was it. He explained to me what had happened and he was gone, just like that.'

But Bowyer reveals that McGovern wasn't the only member of Argyle's backroom staff who had acquiesced to a cry for help from the manager. 'I did understand why John was leaving, because in a minor way it involved myself as well,' he says. 'I actually lent Peter some money as well. But that was while I was at Plymouth, it wasn't as though I'd lent him the money five years before and he hadn't paid me back. Saying that, I could understand why John left, being a very principled person.'

Bowyer believes McGovern finally cracked when he discovered the extent of Shilton's financial problems. 'I think that when John found out I'd lent Peter money as well, he got a little bit annoyed that possibly Peter was going to stiff the two of us. So I don't know more than that, but that was the crux of the matter between Peter and John.'

McGovern was a popular presence at Home Park, and his departure was keenly felt. 'John leaving was, I would say, the final nail in the coffin,' says Ivor Jones. 'The atmosphere around the place just went from bad to worse at that point.' Paul Dalton describes it as a 'kick in the teeth', while Keith Hill feels the club's number two had become an increasingly distant figure. 'John was a very passionate man,' he says. 'But his relationship with Peter had obviously changed and he clearly found it very difficult to work alongside him – he looked like a man who'd lost the will to compete. I don't think he felt as though he had much opportunity to change things and obviously that affected his role.'

Mark Patterson believes McGovern's exit was a watershed moment for the Shilton era. 'The story had cracked open just around the club about Peter owing some money to John,' he says. 'Obviously if somebody owes you that kind of money you're going to be a bit pissed off. And when he went it was a shame because John was good for us, I think him leaving was the beginning of the end for everybody. Things started to fall apart then.'

Although the team's fortunes on the pitch could hardly have got any worse at that point, McGovern's exit sparked an unlikely mini revival. The assistant manager's final game in the dugout was the 3–0 home defeat to Huddersfield on 10 September, after which Shilton led his team to four wins in the next seven games.

However, any flickering hopes that a play-off phoenix might be snatched from the flames of an increasingly torrid season were snuffed out when the dispute between manager and chairman took a sensational and terminal turn for the worse on Saturday 1 October 1994.

Under the lurid headline 'Shilton begged £100,000 off me', McCauley delivered a catastrophic blow to the England legend's credibility by laying out the full extent of his cash-flow issues. 'He says he hasn't got financial problems … but he must have come to me seven times for money advances,' McCauley told the *Sun* reporter Ben Bacon.

Rather more worryingly for the club's horrified fans, the Argyle chairman also spelt out the virulent personal relationship he shared with his manager. 'As a person, I don't like him,' he said. 'I've had lots of rows with him … I don't get any hassles from anyone else apart from Peter Shilton. I've got one big hassle and it's him. He's harder to get on with than anyone I've known.'

Reflecting on his infamous dalliance with the tabloid press, McCauley is adamant that it was the newspaper reporter – and not himself – who instigated the damaging interview. 'I'd just come back from America when they [the *Sun*] came onto me,' he says. 'It wasn't reported exactly as I said it though, which is normal. They never do, do they?'

As McCauley's can of worms was on its way to the printing press, the Argyle party was preparing for a crucial visit to Brisbane Road to take on fellow strugglers Leyton Orient. 'We were staying just outside of London,' says Ivor Jones. 'Dan was making cryptic comments like, "Wait till the sun comes up tomorrow," things like that. When I saw the paper the next morning I was just devastated. I always had respect for both Dan and Peter, but you knew at that point that it was all going to end.'

Shilton had been warned to expect the interview the day before it went to press, and he immediately informed his increasingly exasperated players. 'We went up to London for the Orient game,' says Keith Hill, 'and the manager pulled everybody together the night before. He said, "There's going to be some revelations in the *Sun* tomorrow. I've just been informed by my agent." We just couldn't believe it, and the next day it was all over the news.'

Shilton was the talk of football for all the wrong reasons as he took his side to Brisbane Road on that autumn Saturday, but somehow managed to mastermind a 2–0 victory. 'I don't know how he did it,' says Mark Patterson. 'How must you feel when your chairman goes to a national newspaper about you? Just incredible that was. Peter had got himself into a situation with his finances and he had to accept that, but it still can't make you feel too clever when your chairman's spreading stuff like that around.'

Despite the three points, Hill believes Shilton was never the same again. 'We turned up to Orient and we won 2–0, sometimes stuff like that can galvanise

'With all these arguments about money, we decided we could save some money by running the central heating off the situation...'

players,' he says. 'But from a personal point of view it can't be healthy for the manager. The job involves a lot of pressure, and if you've got personal problems as well then obviously it's going to affect your ability. But I think exposing him like that was disrespectful – he was the best England goalie to play for the country and deserved more respect than the chairman showed him.'

McCauley says he apologised to Shilton at Brisbane Road, telling him the interview had been 'completely misinterpreted.' But Rick Cowdery believes the chairman was taken aback by the newspaper's treatment of his seemingly innocuous telephone chat with Ben Bacon. 'Dan could be quite eloquent if you got him at the right time,' says Cowdery. 'He would just go off on one, and I think that's just what happened. I don't think it was planned. I can't think that Dan would have thought in all his wildest dreams that he would have had three pages in the *Sun* – I don't think he saw that coming at all. But once that kind of stuff is out in the open, you can't put it back in the bottle – the genie's out.'

McCauley insists he had been driven to desperation by Shilton's constant requests for financial assistance. 'He wore me out. He used to harass me all the time,' he says. 'He would get on the phone and ear-bash me for money, money, money, money. He'd already taken the signing-on fee from his contract, but he was looking at the next year – that's the sort of thing he was up to. He could see the pot of gold there but he couldn't get to it. When you're desperate, I suppose you're going to try all avenues open to you.'

Shilton, however, claims he was simply 'negotiating an advance on payments contractually due to me,' and insists he had offered to pay interest on the advance of PR payments.

The Argyle boss's dire financial straits had already been raked over by the national press several months earlier, when the *Daily Mirror* revealed the Argyle boss was facing legal action over a £25,000 debt on one of his properties in Leicestershire. But after McCauley's day in the sun, England's most capped player became fair game.

A week after the chairman's interview, it was Shilton's gambling problem that made tabloid headlines when Malcolm MacDonald revealed all to the *Mirror* under the predictably coarse headline, 'Born Loser'. 'Peter Shilton is losing the most important match of his life – against the demon called gambling,' said the former England striker in an interview laced with tabloid hyperbole.

McCauley suggests Shilton kept his habit well hidden from his chairman, and insists he only accepted that there was fire behind the unpalatable smoke circulating around Home Park when he was finally presented with hard evidence. 'Everybody thought he gambled, except me,' he says. 'I was the only one who didn't believe it, I gave him the benefit of the doubt when everyone else was saying he had a problem. But one day someone at the club rang me and said, 'Look, he's always ringing these expensive 0891 numbers, why don't you phone them?' So I did, and they were clearly race information lines. The phone bill ran into thousands. So it was only then that I realised he had a problem, and I gave up on him at that point.'

There were indications, however, that Shilton's habit had already begun to have an impact on his role at the club. 'I remember we were playing Huddersfield away, and we stayed in a hotel overnight,' says McCauley. 'We came out at lunchtime to go to the ground, but the manager was missing. The coach was due to leave at 12.30, so I asked where he was – and someone said he was watching the 12.30 race on the telly.'

One of Shilton's players had rather more direct exposure to his manager's covert pastime. 'Peter told me he wanted to see me in his office after training one day,' says Mark Patterson.

His door was ajar when I got there, so I looked in to see if he was in there and I saw him reading about the horse racing in *Sporting Life*. I banged on the door and told him it was Mark, and he said, 'One second,' and I saw him put the paper on the floor and get out a pad, then he said, 'Come in, Mark, I'm just thinking about tomorrow's team.' I didn't say anything because it was nothing to do with me, but it did seem strange that he had just called me across for a chat and there he was reading a betting newspaper about the racing.

Ignoring the gambling revelations, Shilton attempted to maintain a dignified silence following his chairman's astonishing attack in the *Sun*, but let his guard down long enough to express his exasperation at the situation. 'I am shocked and fed-up with Mr McCauley's public attacks in the press,' he said. 'It needs to be sorted out.'

In what would become a familiar pattern in the coming weeks, McCauley hit back in the following day's papers, saying, 'He says he's fed-up, well, I'm fed-up with fighting for Plymouth Argyle, trying to keep football at the top of the agenda.'

The pair came face-to-face for the first time since the *Sun* article when Shilton attended the Board's monthly meeting, four days after it was published. Unsurprisingly, the warring pair found a new hot potato to play catch with. Shilton demanded his chairman issue a public apology for one of his more innocuous tabloid missives – that in which McCauley claimed his manager only worked eight hours a week. The chairman, however, refused point blank, and the public slanging match gained fresh ground with the club's fans coming down firmly on the side of their manager.

Rumours surfaced of an anti-McCauley protest planned for the visit of Wycombe on 15 October, prompting the chairman to threaten to pull the plug on his controlling interest. 'If that's what the majority of supporters want, then I will not stand in their way,' he said, before warning ominously, 'I will take the money and run. I could stop spending for a change and start recouping.'

Support for the chairman came from an unlikely source, when Shilton himself urged the fans not to get involved in off-field issues – a stance that finally prompted the chairman to make amends for his 'eight hour' slur. In a letter dated 13 October 1994, McCauley informed Shilton that he had acquiesced to his demands for a public withdrawal of his remark. 'I unreservedly apologise should the comment be considered offensive in any way,' he wrote. '[I would also] advise you that an apology was made earlier in the week to both Westcountry Television and BBC Radio which may not have been broadcast.'

With a ceasefire of sorts declared between chairman and manager, McCauley directed his ire elsewhere – this time towards the *Evening Herald*, whose press facilities he withdrew citing the paper's 'very political and very biased' coverage. 'I think Dan saw me as a bit of a Shilton mouthpiece,' says the *Herald*'s then Argyle reporter Graham Hambly. 'I went and sat in the Lyndhurst Stand in disguise, and we did make a little bit of a feature of it in the *Herald*. We weren't trying to conceal the fact that I was there, I came in, wore this hat and sat in with the fans. I wasn't allowed into press conferences, so I used to ring Shilton and get his thoughts that way. He had checked something within his contract and he wasn't prevented from doing it.'

By late October, Argyle's post-McGovern run of good form had seen them climb to the relatively heady heights of seventeenth. But with heavy-hitters Dalton, Castle and McCall still missing, bodies were thin on the ground and Shilton was forced to draft in his fourth loan signing of the season.

Mick Quinn was by then winding down a colourful but prolific career in Premier League Coventry City's reserves, and was persuaded by Shilton that a guaranteed first-team place fighting Second Division fires was a better assignment than scrapping in the Sky Blue stiffs. 'It was Shilts who talked me into going down there,' Quinn reflects. 'I turned him down three times, but he called me again one night and caught me off guard. I'd just come in from the pub and was in a drunken stupor, so I agreed to go down. I thought it'd be better than playing in the stiffs at Coventry. There's nothing like first-team competitive football, so I thought: go on then, I'll have a month down there.'

The famously portly centre-forward made a big impact on his Argyle debut, pulling the strings in a morale-boosting 4–1 win over Wrexham – with the gate boosted by an extra 3,000 fans keen to see if the Mighty Quinn could turn Argyle's season around. The former Newcastle and Portsmouth striker failed to get on the scoresheet, but was influential in all four goals and was evidently ecstatic at putting the ball in the net in the eighty-third minute until it was ruled out for offside.

However, the Quinn Effect quickly wore off as Argyle slumped to successive defeats to York and Brighton without scoring. Despite a fee of £125,000 being agreed with Coventry before the loan period began, Quinn quickly realised that Home Park was not the kind of place he fancied seeing more of.

We won my first game 4–1 and I thought, 'Aye, aye, this could take off here.' But the next two games were poor, we lost both of them without scoring. On top of that, it was pretty obvious that the club was in turmoil, with Shilts and the chairman at loggerheads. There was something in the local paper every night about the two of them – Shilts having a go at the chairman, the chairman having a go at Shilts, and it just seemed that the whole battle between them seeped down to the lads and it just wasn't really a harmonious club. There was a move agreed but I wasn't going to stay there in a million years.

Quinn also asserts that he was driven away by the manager's persistent requests for horse racing tips. 'Football and gambling go together, it's part of life at a lot of clubs,' says Quinn, a player who himself loved a frequent flutter. 'The thing with Shilts was that it was every single day. As soon as I walked into the dressing room he would be asking me for tips, that was the surprising aspect of it. But then when I found out how much trouble he was in financially, it became pretty obvious that he had a real problem. I laughed and joked about it, but it's a serious issue, like drug addiction or alcohol addiction. I think he had it bad at the time.'

The extent of Shilton's financial problems were publicly revealed midway through Quinn's loan period, when horse trainer Martin Pipe filed a bankruptcy petition against the Argyle manager over debts of more than £3,000. 'It's probably my fault,' said Shilton, who had by then sold his three racehorses. 'I have sort of kept it on the shelf and probably should have sorted it out before now, but I let it ride,' he added, not apologising for the pun.

McCauley couldn't resist a few strokes of the whip, telling the *Western Morning News* that the manager had a clause in his contract that would enable the club to terminate his employment should he be made bankrupt. 'Unfortunately, we are not in a position to be able to lend him any money,' said the chairman, adding that £70,000 had already been loaned or advanced to the manager in the past two and a half years.

Shilton settled his debt in advance of the bankruptcy hearing, but he was dealt another crushing blow when John McGovern finally broke his silence in an interview with the *Sunday Mirror* the day after Argyle were trounced 3–0 at home to Brighton on 10 December.

The former assistant manager revealed that he had raised a £7,500 loan with his own bank to help Shilton overcome his cash-flow difficulties in July 1993, and the sum had spiralled to £9,000 with interest charges when it was not repaid within the agreed six-month period. McGovern claimed the full amount was still outstanding twelve months later – leading to his eventual resignation.

The latest revelation garnered a degree of sympathy for the manager from an unlikely source. 'Is all the publicity affecting the manager's ability to concentrate on the team?' said McCauley. 'Peter Shilton has to live with all this, but he seems to be able to tough it out. I'd give him credit for that.'

Shilton's players disagree over the impact the manager's personal situation had on his performance. 'Any issues there may have been with the chairman, we didn't see any evidence of that,' says Kevin Nugent. 'We didn't know a lot about it until it came out in the papers. It shows the integrity of the man – we didn't see any effects from the press stuff. He handled himself impeccably throughout the whole situation.' Steve McCall agrees. 'It came to light more in the papers than it ever did in the changing rooms,' he says. 'Peter Shilton was so professional. When he opened that changing room door and said, "Come on, lads," he was still the same Peter Shilton that had been there twelve months earlier. You wouldn't have known that he had any problems off the field.'

Martin Barlow, however, remembers it differently. 'With all the fall outs, Shilton just lost it really,' he reflects.

> He was like a different person to the season before. All his problems just got him down. I always remember one day he pulled me and Wayne Burnett into his office and asked us which side he thought he should play that weekend. He had two teams scribbled down on bits of paper, so me and Wayne picked the one that would suit us. I'd gone from thinking that I was never going to play for the

club again when he first arrived, to becoming a regular the next season and then Shilton asking me what team I thought he should play. But when things like that happen, you know something's not right. It was a shame what was happening to him. He should have been sitting pretty after the career he had, but the financial stuff had taken over his life.

However, far from taking over his life, Shilton's escalating financial problems were about to completely engulf him.

Accounting giants KPMG had been invited by the Inland Revenue to carry out a routine audit of the club's PAYE records in November 1994. Waiting for them was the kind of financial black hole that accountants' dreams are made of: evidence of an unpaid tax bill of some £50,000.

The contract negotiations that preceded Shilton's appointment in March 1992 had been carried out amid an intoxicating haze of excitement, and almost inevitably the Board let their guard down with the clock ticking on their attempts to secure their illustrious candidate's signature.

At the eleventh hour, Shilton's lawyer requested that the signing-on fee of £125,000 be paid to his client in gross, insisting the £50,000 income tax requirement would be dealt with upon receipt. However, the Inland Revenue still hadn't seen their share almost three years later – and they wanted their money. 'The negotiations were very intense on that Sunday we met in Exeter,' remembers Ivor Jones. 'The Board wanted to do the deal, Shilton and his people wanted to do the deal, but then Peter decided he wanted to be paid in a certain way. It was a last-minute decision, it had reached the point where we were almost ready to do the press conference on the Monday when this matter came up.'

Jones insists the arrangement was all above board from the club's point of view. 'It all seemed straightforward at the time, absolutely straightforward,' he says. 'Certainly in my experience of dealing with tax, it seemed like a pretty logical and normal transaction. It didn't seem as though anything underhand was happening or would happen. But then the Inland Revenue came in a couple of years later and discovered this money. We didn't know that the tax hadn't been paid, we thought it had been accounted for some time previously as Peter's people had said they would. So that was a real bolt out of the blue for us.'

The Inland Revenue informed Argyle in writing of the missing £50,000 on 15 November 1994, and demanded payment within thirty days. The Board forwarded the notice on to Shilton's solicitor, but on 13 December – two days before the deadline – they summoned their manager to an emergency Board meeting when it became clear Her Majesty's tax collectors were not going to be appeased in time.

Shilton was informed he would be given a further seven days to settle the tax liability, but he reacted angrily when the Board broached the rather less pressing matter of the team's on-pitch fortunes. A target of eight points from the next four matches was put to the manager, who argued that such a measure would merely heap even more pressure on him to deliver results.

With Argyle just a single point above the relegation zone and facing encounters against high-flying Brentford, Swansea and Crewe, as well as a trip to relegation rivals Bournemouth, Shilton's defensive reaction was to be expected. 'I don't think setting targets is an answer to anything, it's a very negative thing to do,' he told the gathered media with barely disguised fury. 'It's about time that I had a bit of help at the club in what has been a very difficult start to the season.'

The manager's greatest ally on the Board, Ivor Jones, was fully behind the chairman's decision to put pressure on Shilton to improve results, but angered McCauley by later going back on his assessment and suggesting the manager should actually be given more time. 'I formed the clear impression that Ivor was as frustrated as the rest of the Board by the manager's belligerent attitude at our meeting,' McCauley said. 'He said then that he didn't think that the differences could be resolved and I don't know why he is backtracking now.'

However, Jones believed Shilton would turn the team's form around, and was adamant that the manager's financial indiscretions should be excluded from any decision on his future at the club. 'I always felt that there were two sides to it,' reflects Jones.

> There was the footballing side, in which I was 100 per cent behind Shilton, and then there was the financial side. I accepted on the basis of the tax bill that there was a problem, but I would always defend Peter on the footballing side. I would stand by him and argue that you couldn't dismiss him on footballing grounds. Even though things weren't going that great on the pitch, I always felt he would put it right. But with the Inland Revenue bill, that was really the point at which Dan had probably had enough and wanted a change. He took a different view to me and we got into conflict.

McCauley's long-serving accountant, Sean Swales, elaborates on Jones' recollection of the Boardroom in-fighting. 'There was some disagreement on the Board over what grounds Shilton should be suspended,' he says. 'I think Dan fell out with one or two directors over it. The whole dispute was whether to remove him on footballing matters or financial matters. Dan was the controlling shareholder, and he pretty much decided that ultimately it would be over non-footballing matters.'

Halfway through the four-match mini-season his Board had enforced upon him, Shilton was clinging on to his Home Park future by the very tips of his famous fingers. The black comedy that was the 7–0 evisceration at Brentford was swiftly followed by a 3–0 reverse at Swansea, but the chairman was past caring about results – he had 50,000 other reasons to want to sack his manager.

The initial seven-day deadline for Shilton to fulfil his tax requirements had passed by some two weeks, but had been replaced by a rather more perilous written ultimatum to come up with the money by 4 January 1995 or face dismissal. 'I'm not denying liability for the money the Inland Revenue are claiming,' said Shilton, who took it upon himself to reveal the Board's latest D-Day. 'I'm just asking for a reasonable opportunity to come up with a payment proposal. I feel I am being unfairly stampeded into a corner at a time when I should be getting support and backing from the chairman.'

However the desperate appeal fell on deaf ears.

Peter Shilton's final match as manager of Plymouth Argyle came at home to Crewe on 2 January 1995. Wearing a dark blue tracksuit and with heavy bags under his eyes, Shilton watched as Mickey Evans headed home an injury-time winner to secure an unlikely 3–2 victory – only the Pilgrims' sixth from twenty-two league games.

However, if the manager thought the three points would be accepted by the Board as a part payment for his tax debt – or would at least ease the pressure – he was sorely mistaken.

Despite signs of a revival on the pitch, and with more than twenty-four hours remaining for Shilton to come up with the £50,000, McCauley yet again moved the goalposts and revealed that the manager's position at the club had become untenable – regardless of the on-pitch and financial deadlines. 'It doesn't really matter whether the money is paid before the deadline or not,' said the chairman the day after the Crewe victory. 'The relationship between myself and Mr Shilton is at such a low ebb that it appears it really is in the club's best interests to change the manager. All we are doing is playing Russian Roulette and waiting for the right bullet to come round.'

Later that night, on Tuesday 3 January 1995, McCauley pulled the trigger one more time and Shilton's luck finally ran out. 'We have suspended Mr Shilton short-term while we get further advice from our solicitors,' said McCauley, in announcing the Board's decision to a scrum of reporters outside Home Park. Aware that an unfair dismissal claim could result in a substantial compensation pay-out, the Board had opted to proceed with caution – consulting a specialist in employment law who had made them aware of the expensive consequences a contract termination could have entailed.

The 'short-term' part of McCauley's announcement was elaborated upon as being 'one to two weeks,' but few expected Shilton to return to Home Park for any reason other than to clear out the contents of his office. The manager himself reacted with genuine bemusement to the development, saying, 'I've asked the chairman to confirm to me what terms of my contract give him the right to suspend me.'

The national media were also befuddled by the complex developments from sleepy Devon, as illustrated by the *Guardian*'s reaction to Shilton's apparent demise. 'The former England goalkeeper has been cast into soccer limbo by a rare Board decision – the Football League "could not recall" a precedent – after the saga descended through an afternoon of drama into muddle and a morass of legal complication.'

Schadenfreude was surprisingly thin on the ground, even from a tabloid press that had gleefully fanned the flames of a raging Home Park fire just weeks earlier. 'It was awful, humiliating and painful,' went an editorial in the *Star*. 'When he left Plymouth's Home Park ground, Shilton had just discovered that time, even for legends, does eventually run out. As 1995 begins to take shape, Shilton is deeply, shamefully in the mire, and the man who loves to gamble may be about to lose the biggest punt of his life.'

The Board moved quickly to replace the outgoing manager – at least temporarily – when they promoted veteran midfielder Steve McCall to the post of caretaker while Shilton's office chair was still warm. The thirty-four-year-old had yet to make an appearance for the first team that season, but was lobbed into the lion's den by McCauley and his directors and admits he was shocked at the extent of the dressing-room disharmony. 'The problems started on my very first day in the job,' he says. 'Peter Swan came to see me and told me that Peter Shilton had promised him a move, and then one of our best-paid players came in and told me he had financial worries. This was all on my first day, and I was thinking, "Is this what management is all about?" It was unbelievable. I'd been in the dressing room with these players and I hadn't an inkling what was going on.'

Almost a week after Shilton's suspension was announced, his solicitors revealed their client had terminated his employment with the club, but were adamant he had not resigned. 'They [Argyle] have broken his contract and therefore he has terminated his employment in response to their breach of contract,' said Mike Morrison, a specialist in football contracts.

Shilton also issued a writ seeking damages for breach of contract, and refused point blank to appear at a Home Park disciplinary hearing to answer allegations of obtaining cash from the club by issuing cheques that later bounced – among other undisclosed matters.

In the end, the writ failed to stick, though the Board did have to satisfy the Inland Revenue bill – which they did thanks to an injection from McCauley's Rotolok company. 'I think wherever Peter had gone, a very similar thing would have happened,' reflects Ivor Jones. 'Peter has since admitted what his problem was at the time, and wherever he'd gone that problem would have been there. And as for his relationship with Dan McCauley, it was obvious that was going to happen when you look back. They were two people who were used to success and having control over their success, so their personalities competed and there was a clash there.'

Fellow director Dennis Angilley was dismayed to see the back of the manager he had a hand in appointing. 'Ivor and I were so, so disappointed to see Peter go,' he says. 'I remember after he left, Ivor said something that has stayed with me to this day. He said, "When Peter walked out, it was like someone had switched the lights out in this place." And he was so right.'

Ian Bowyer, who had left his role with the youth team to assist Shilton with first-team matters following John McGovern's exit, laments how far the off-field rows were allowed to overshadow the club's efforts to stave off relegation. 'There are lots of football clubs where the manager and chairman will have disagreements in private, but at Plymouth it was almost like a soap opera,' he says. 'On Monday the chairman would say this, on Tuesday Peter would say that – I'd never seen anything like it before or since. The whole affair was very sad, and I don't think anybody wins when the laundry is washed out in the public domain. The big, big losers were obviously Plymouth as a club and the supporters, because they became a laughing stock in the football world.'

But nobody at Home Park was laughing, least of all the man who arrived in Plymouth as a national legend on a wave of exaltation, but departed an utterly broken figure with his reputation in tatters. Peter Shilton's spell as Pilgrim-in-chief lasted 1,038 days and took in 156 matches with a win ratio of 39.7 per cent. But the statistics tell barely half the story. Rarely can a managerial tenure – at any club, in any country – have unravelled from riches to rags in so spectacular a manner.

From the moment Shilton walked through the Home Park gates carrying giant helpings of hubris and ambition in his considerable hands, the footballing fates were already conspiring to ensure he was destined to leave unfulfilled in the opposite direction. Lady Luck undoubtedly dealt the legendary goalkeeper a spiteful hand: a querulous chairman with a thirst for confrontation; a spate of bizarre and untimely injuries to key players; a collective failing in a potentially career-altering play-off game; a record signing seemingly intent on sinking a listing ship.

The outrageous script threw a barrage of slings and arrows at its central character, but Shilton himself was a busy player in the piece. From the moment he banked his lavish signing-on fee to assuage a dire personal financial situation at the expense of the taxman, his fate was sealed.

A debilitating gambling habit and an ill-advised personal loan from his assistant manager, John McGovern, would deliver further hammer blows to his managerial career prospects; blows that would eventually prove terminal.

Despite the abject dénouement, Jones refuses to accept that Shilton's spell at Home Park tarnished his reputation in football. 'No matter what happened, Peter Shilton will always be a legend,' he says. 'In twenty, thirty, forty, fifty years from now, when we're all dead and gone, Peter Shilton will still be remembered as a footballing legend. Nothing will ever change that.'

EPILOGUE

With Peter Shilton locked in a legal battle with the Plymouth Argyle Board, rookie manager Steve McCall embarked on a desperate battle to save the plummeting Pilgrims from relegation. Despite his own return from injury coinciding with the welcome comebacks of Steve Castle and Paul Dalton just days after Shilton's exit, results continued to prove elusive. Several senior players admitted they found McCall's transition from team-mate to manager difficult, and only three wins in fifteen matches suggested McCall himself found the step up equally taxing.

The Argyle Board attempted to bring in former Argyle boss Dave Smith to assist with first-team affairs, but McCall sensed dressing-room resistance to the idea and stepped down from his position when given an ultimatum by Dan McCauley and his directors.

Russell Osman, who had been helping his former Ipswich team-mate with coaching duties, replaced McCall as manager on an unpaid consultancy basis, and immediately guided the team to a three-match unbeaten run. But despite losing just three of their nine matches under Osman, the Pilgrims finished in twenty-first position and were relegated to the fourth tier of English football for the first time in their history.

Neil Warnock was appointed Argyle manager in June 1995, and within weeks all but one of Peter Shilton's signings remained at Home Park.

Plymouth Argyle finally made it back into the second tier of English football twelve years after Peter Shilton's appointment as manager.

MARTIN BARLOW made more than 350 appearances for the Pilgrims before being released by Paul Sturrock in 2001. He had a brief spell with Exeter City before returning to Plymouth where he now lives a stone's throw away from Home Park.

WAYNE BURNETT earned a place in Neil Warnock's new-look side, but left in late 1995 to join Bolton Wanderers. He also played for Huddersfield and Grimsby Town before managing a handful of non-league clubs. He is currently assistant manager at Dagenham & Redbridge.

ADRIAN BURROWS drifted into non-league football with north Devon side Elmore FC. He now lives in Exeter where he works as a driving instructor.

STEVE CASTLE left Argyle after relegation in 1995 to sign for Birmingham City. After two years at St Andrew's he moved to Peterborough United, where he averaged a goal every four games over three seasons. He is currently in his second spell as manager of St Albans City.

ANDY COMYN recovered from a serious back injury to sign for West Bromwich Albion in 1996, but quit the professional game after just a few months at The Hawthorns and now works as a commercial director in Birmingham.

PAUL DALTON moved on to Huddersfield Town in 1995, where he spent five years before winding down his career with Carlisle United. He now works as a coach for Middlesbrough's youth academy.

KEITH HILL stayed at Home Park until the summer of 1996, when he left to join Rochdale. After five years at Spotland, he had spells at Cheltenham and Morecambe before returning to Rochdale in 2006 to take over as manager.

RICHARD LANDON left for Stockport County in 1995, before moving back into non-league football with Altrincham. He returned to Edgeley Park in 2004 and went on to become the club's kitman.

DWIGHT MARSHALL spent three seasons at Luton before returning to Home Park, where he scored twelve goals in 98/99 to book-end his Argyle career by leading the scoring charts in his first and last seasons at the club. He now works in a north London college.

STEVE MCCALL left Argyle in 1996 to become Kevin Hodges' assistant at Torquay United. He returned to Home Park in 1998 when Hodges was appointed manager, but the pair lasted just two years. He is now Ipswich Town's chief scout.

JOHN MCGOVERN had spells as assistant manager at Rotherham United and Hull City, before a short-lived period as manager of Woking. He now works as a summariser for BBC Radio Nottingham.

DOMINIC NAYLOR joined Gillingham following relegation in 1995, and also had a spell at Leyton Orient before seeing out his career in non-league football.

RAY NEWLAND made just 10 appearances for Chester City before returning to Devon with Torquay United. He spent one season at Plainmoor before moving into non-league football. He now runs a goalkeeping coaching company called Just 4 Keepers.

ALAN NICHOLLS had a player of the year trophy named after him at Stalybridge Celtic, which is still presented to this day. In August of 2009 he would have been thirty-six years old.

KEVIN NUGENT left Home Park in the summer of 1995 to sign for Bristol City. He went on to have spells at Cardiff, Leyton Orient and Swansea City and is now assistant manager back at Brisbane Road.

MARK PATTERSON was one of the few players who survived Neil Warnock's cull, and went on to win promotion at Wembley before moving to Gillingham where he is now in charge of the club's youth set-up.

CRAIG SKINNER joined Wrexham in 1995 before moving on to York City. He currently works for League Football Education, helping to promote the education of apprentice footballers.

DAN MCCAULEY endured arguably the most torrid reign of any Argyle chairman in the club's history. Including Kemp and Shilton, he sacked five managers in eight seasons as the club slumped to its lowest ever finish in the Football League in 1999. McCauley eventually sold his controlling interest to Paul Stapleton's consortium in 2001.

PETER SHILTON went on to hit the 1,000 league appearances mark with Leyton Orient, before retiring from the game in 1997. He was linked with a return to management with Port Vale in 2007, but these days his involvement in football is limited to after-dinner speaking and the occasional national media interview.

Information correct as of July 2009.

An original Robby Bullen – March 2009.